I0727711

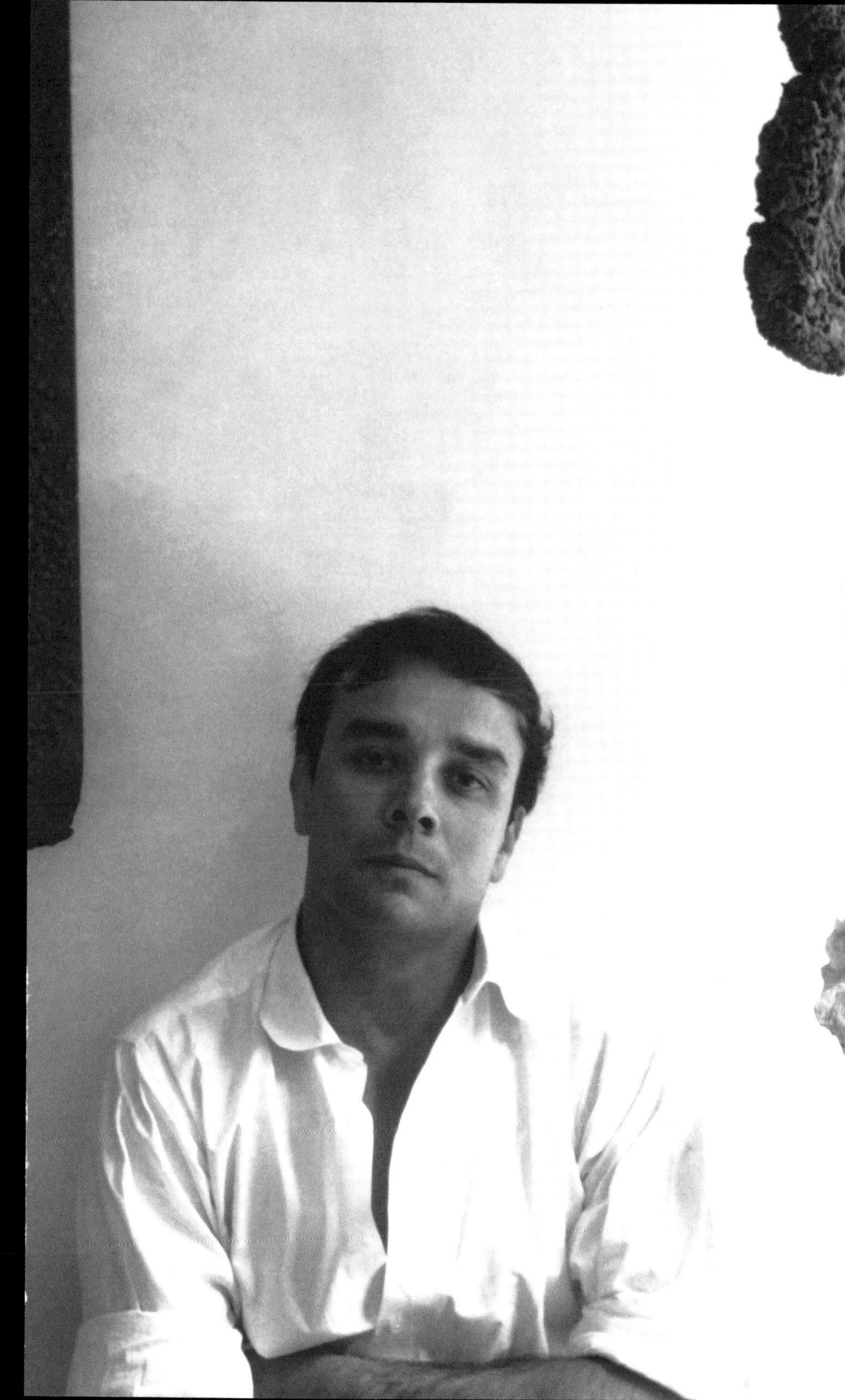

Yves the Provocateur

Yves Klein and Twentieth-Century Art

Thomas McEvilley

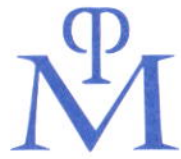

DOCUMENTEXT

McPherson & Company

2010

Published by McPherson & Company, Publishers, Post Office Box 1126,
Kingston, New York 12402, with assistance from the Literature Program
of the New York State Council on the Arts, a state agency.
Typeset in Apollo with Bernhard Modern titling.
Designed by Bruce R. McPherson.
Manufactured in the United States of America.
FIRST EDITION
1 3 5 7 9 10 8 6 4 2   2010   2011   2012   2013

Library of Congress Cataloging-in-Publication Data

McEvilley, Thomas, 1939-
 Yves the provocateur : Yves Klein and twentieth-century art / Thomas
McEvilley. — 1st ed.
    p. cm.
 "Documentext."
 ISBN 978-0-929701-91-2
 1. Klein, Yves, 1928-1962—Criticism and interpretation. 2. Klein, Yves,
1928-1962—Influence. 3. Art, Modern—20th century. I. Klein, Yves,
1928-1962. II. Title. III. Title: Yves Klein and twentieth-century art.
 N6853.K5M38 2010
 709.2—dc22

                                          2009051320

PHOTOGRAPHIC CREDITS AND ACKNOWLEDGMENTS APPEAR ON PAGE 272,
WHICH CONSTITUTES A CONTINUATION OF THIS COPYRIGHT PAGE.

TABLE OF CONTENTS

Foreword

by Rotraut Klein-Moquay

O N THE OCCASION OF THIS NEW PUBLICATION OF THE WRITINGS OF
Thomas McEvilley, I again salute him.

Yves Klein's adventure started in the late 1940's with his first experiences influenced by his family circle, as both his mother and father
were painters. Coming of age in a Europe torn by the monstrosities of
the Second World War deeply influenced his destiny: everything needed
to be rebuilt and nothing could resemble the past. This enlightenment
prompted him to develop a new approach early on—no longer could art
satisfy itself as a realistic representation; neither could it be an abstract
composition of shape and color, as l'Ecole de Paris had claimed after
breaking away from their figurative inheritance. A city that was trying
to reconstruct its future, looking for a new path, failed to notice that the
world of painting had already fled to brighter horizons.

Yves, with his vitality, his force of persuasion and magnetism, quickly
conquered the European art scene (Milan, Paris, Düsseldorf, London).
His trip to Japan, from 1952 to 1954, as well as to Spain, sparked his
realization of the global culture, making him a citizen of the world. For
him, Art had more to do with a philosophy, a spirituality, a transcendence, than with a juxtaposition of objects. The message is clear: the
immaterial, through the means of the color blue, invades space; it is the
magnified presence of art without artifice.

His life and his death were the purest example of an oeuvre without
concession, which calls upon and gives hope in the human being.

The numerous testimonies and interpretations, which succeed one another, are the very proof of this. "Long live the immaterial"—Yves Klein.

Author's Preface

YVES KLEIN DIED IN 1962 AT AGE 34. HIS CAREER AS AN artist had lasted only seven years but in some ways had been quite distinguished. In 1958, for example, there was so much talk about his upcoming exhibition of an empty gallery, *Le Vide*, at Iris Clert's, that three thousand enthusiasts showed up, including Albert Camus, who wrote in the guestbook, "With the void, full powers." At once the exhibition became an icon of anti-art. Three years later, during his only visit to the United States, Klein exhibited at the two most prominent and prestigious avant-garde galleries, Leo Castelli in New York and Virginia Dwan in Los Angeles. One would think his career very successful; but if one looked closer, there were problems.

Le Vide was a sensationalistic event in which some of Klein's judo students admitted a swelling throng in small groups to keep the emptiness pure. The exhibition was widely received as a neo-Dada gesture, though in Klein's mind it was a serious metaphysical demonstration. He became regarded increasingly as a comedian and showman—not really an artist. This reputation preceded him to New York, where newspaper headlines greeted him as "Little Boy Blue," "A Dali, junior grade," and asked, "Have you ever been all blue?" His shows of identical blue monochromes were treated as hoaxes. By the time of his return to Paris he was more of a mockery than he had been after *Le Vide*. By the time of his death a year or so later Klein was regarded as an exhibitionist whose fifteen minutes were over and who was better forgotten.

In 1977 I was an assistant professor in the Department of Art and Art History at Rice University in Houston, Texas, though I also practised the field of classical philology in which I had taken my Ph.D. The art department, and indeed my position, were both involved in the project of the collectors and patrons Jean and Dominique deMenil. Off to the rear of the Rice campus a large metal building housed the Rice Museum, which had lately been founded by Jean and Dominique and which would be the predecessor of the Menil Collection. There Dominique put on a series of distinguished shows that featured strong areas of the collection, a memorable Magritte show, for example, a stunning Ed Kienholz show, and others.

Jean deMenil had died in 1971 and Dominique, adjusting to widowhood, adopted the policy of inviting certain individuals for a series of one-on-one dinners at her home in River Oaks. I was one of those individuals. One evening in 1977 Dominique and I had a pleasant dinner and conversation, in which as always we went over certain points of mutual interest. This may have been the memorable occasion when she asked me if she should build her museum underground, to protect the artworks in case of war. In any case, this was the occasion when I mentioned that I had been reading Edward Lucie-Smith's *Late Modern Art* [or was it *Art Since 1945*?] and had been charmed by his coverage of the work of the French artist Yves Klein in the years following World War II. After dinner she was seeing me out and we stood chatting in the vestibule of the house. Dominique said, speaking, it seemed, impulsively, "I want to do a show with you. You write the catalogue, I'll make the show. Who do you want to do?" She was proposing a show at the Rice Museum, which at the time was more or less her personal exhibition space. As I gazed at her I noticed that she was standing in front of the arresting Klein work *Anthropometry: People Begin to Fly*, and I said, "Why not Yves? Let's do Yves." As a French person who already had some Klein works in her collection, she agreed immediately. I, who had never written art history or art criticism, started researching the catalogue, mostly with materials found in the Rice library.

I spent a couple of weeks that summer at the deMenil house

in Paris, from which I travelled daily to the archives of the Centre Pompidou where Klein's books and papers had landed, at the same time conducting a series of interviews with people who had known him. The highlights were conversations with Yves' best friends from childhood days in Nice, Claude Pascal and Arman, and with his widow Rotraut Klein, who was more than gracious—I would have to say that we became friends in a lasting way. For two more years I would return to Paris in the summers and continue my researches into Yves' life and his mysterious personality.

Back in Houston I started writing a series of texts for the exhibition. This turned out to be my initiation into art criticism, curation, and the functioning of the art world in general. I first wrote the essay "Yves Klein and Rosicrucianism," which derived from my training as a philologist. I argued that Klein's writings—although they were typically treated as amusing hoaxes—made perfect sense if read in conjunction with the book *Rosicrucian Cosmo-conception* by Max Heindel, the German founder of the group called the Rosicrucian Society (to which Klein belonged), whose headquarters were in Oceanside, California. I discovered that Klein's writings were a brilliant and only slightly disguised parody of these writings when analyzed in the context of art history. As time passed, with more trips to Paris, more interviews and more research in the Yves Klein Archive at the Centre Pompidou, I went on to the longer biographical profile, "Yves Klein, Conquistador of the Void." At about this time Dominique was engaged in the building of her museum, to be called The Menil Collection. She had signed on Renzo Piano as architect, and was searching for a person to become the founding director. One day she told me, "I think I have found the right person," and it was the well-known curator and museum director Walter Hopps. Before long Walter was living in Dominique's guest house and joining enthusiastically in the planning and preliminary work for the show, "Yves Klein (1928-1962): A Retrospective." He and I worked on the pictures together late into the nights. Walter participated as well in the design of the catalogue and would, when the time came, become deeply engrossed in the installation of the works. He never interfered, however, with my self-expression as the writer. I produced my third piece for the catalogue, an expanded chronology, which would include ambient political and scientific events relevant to Klein's ambitions and plans and dreams. The catalogue began emerging into the light, and in time the works began arriving and piling up in their cartons in the loading area of the Museum.

Meanwhile, as our plans advanced, the scale of the exhibition grew almost out of control. First Pontus Hulten, director of the Centre Pompidou in Paris, asked Dominique for the show, and then Tom Messer, director of the Guggenheim Museum in New York, did the same. It would no longer be a small show in a university gallery, but a major exhibition at major museums. It was hardly noticed when the Museum of Contemporary Art in Chicago also signed on for the show. Increasingly my life became wrapped up in the show and Dominique's world. Pierre Restany came to Houston and stayed at my house; Walter Hopps signed on as director of the Menil Collection, which was being built a few doors from my house; Jean Tinguely was often around. I lived across the street from the Rothko Chapel, which I usually visited every day or so. In the evenings I would often be at Dominique's working with whoever was in town and connected with the Klein show. Rotraut and her new husband Daniel Moquay passed through my house, as did Restany, Arman, and others of the constant Parisian interchange—curators at the Beaubourg, consultants with whom I was working, old friends of Yves', and so on. Ingrid Sischy, then editor of *Artforum*, asked for an article on Yves for the issue which would coincide with the Guggenheim opening; for that I wrote the article "Yves Klein: Messenger of the Age of Space."

At last the time of the openings came around—first at Rice, then the Chicago MOCA, next the Guggenheim, finally the Beaubourg. At the Guggenheim I filled in as hands-on curator when Walter couldn't show up, conceiving and installing the huge floor-installation of IKB pigment. (I wrote a booklet for it, *The Impregnation of the Guggenheim Museum*, in which Rotraut, Arman, Claude, and I signed my text as representatives of the International Klein Bureau.) Half of Paris, it seemed, was in New York, and soon after, half of New York seemed to be in Paris when the Beaubourg opening swung round.

My catalogue came out first in English and then French editions, and immediately touched a nerve. Ted Castle, writing in the British *Art Monthly*, stated rather grandiosely it was simply the best art catalogue he had ever seen. Grace Gluck in the *New York Times* happily called my catalogue writings "brilliant," and Kay Larsen in *New York Magazine* declared my biographical essay "Yves Klein: Conquistador of the Void," "the best life of an artist in living memory." Werner Spies, writing in the *Frankfurther Allgemeine Zeitung,* described my essay "Yves Klein and Rosicrucianiam" as the key to Klein's works. From that time until this I have been continually occupied with writing about art and artists.

Soon after the Beaubourg opening a German publisher contacted me and asked for permission to publish my Klein writings as a book. I signed a contract but the book never appeared. Years passed. Meanwhile, interest in Klein steadily grew; one year Harold Szeeman asked me for an essay for the catalogue of his Klein show at the Jean Tinguely Museum in Basle, and it appears here as "Living a Contradiction." As Dominique and I had originally hoped, our attentions seemed to have reclaimed Yves Klein from increasing obscurity.

Now, on the occasion of the latest international Klein retrospective, I have the pleasure of welcoming a collection of these writings into print. My thanks to Bruce McPherson for designing and publishing this volume, and to Rotraut Klein-Moquay for generously providing many pictures as well as a few prefatory words of her own. To Dominique, Walter, Claude, Pierre, Arman, and other friends I met along the way to the Klein show, and who have since passed away, my farewell.

Pages 14-15: *Anthropométries de l'époque bleue,* performance at Galerie Internationale d'Art Contemporain, Paris, March 9, 1960.

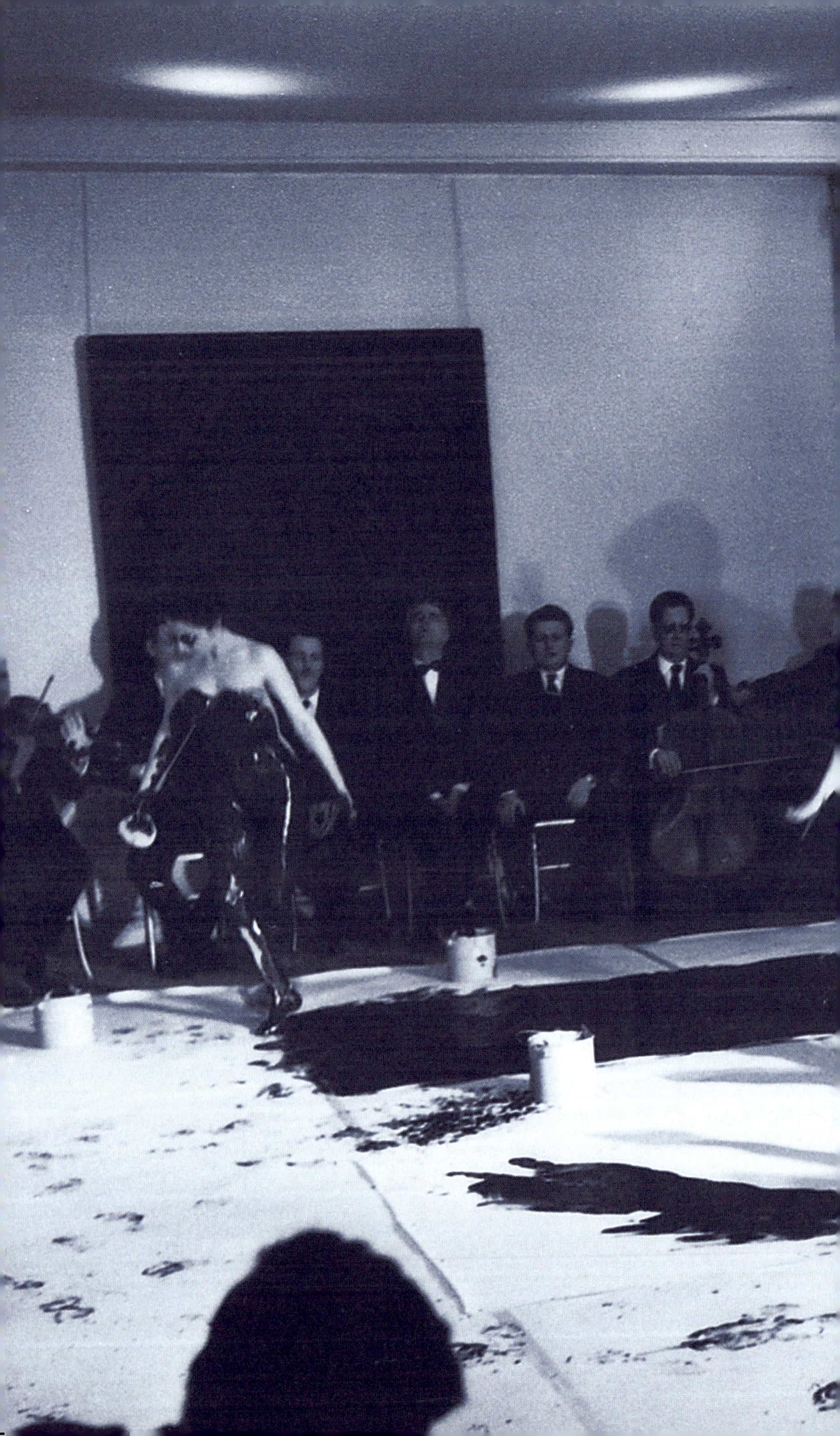

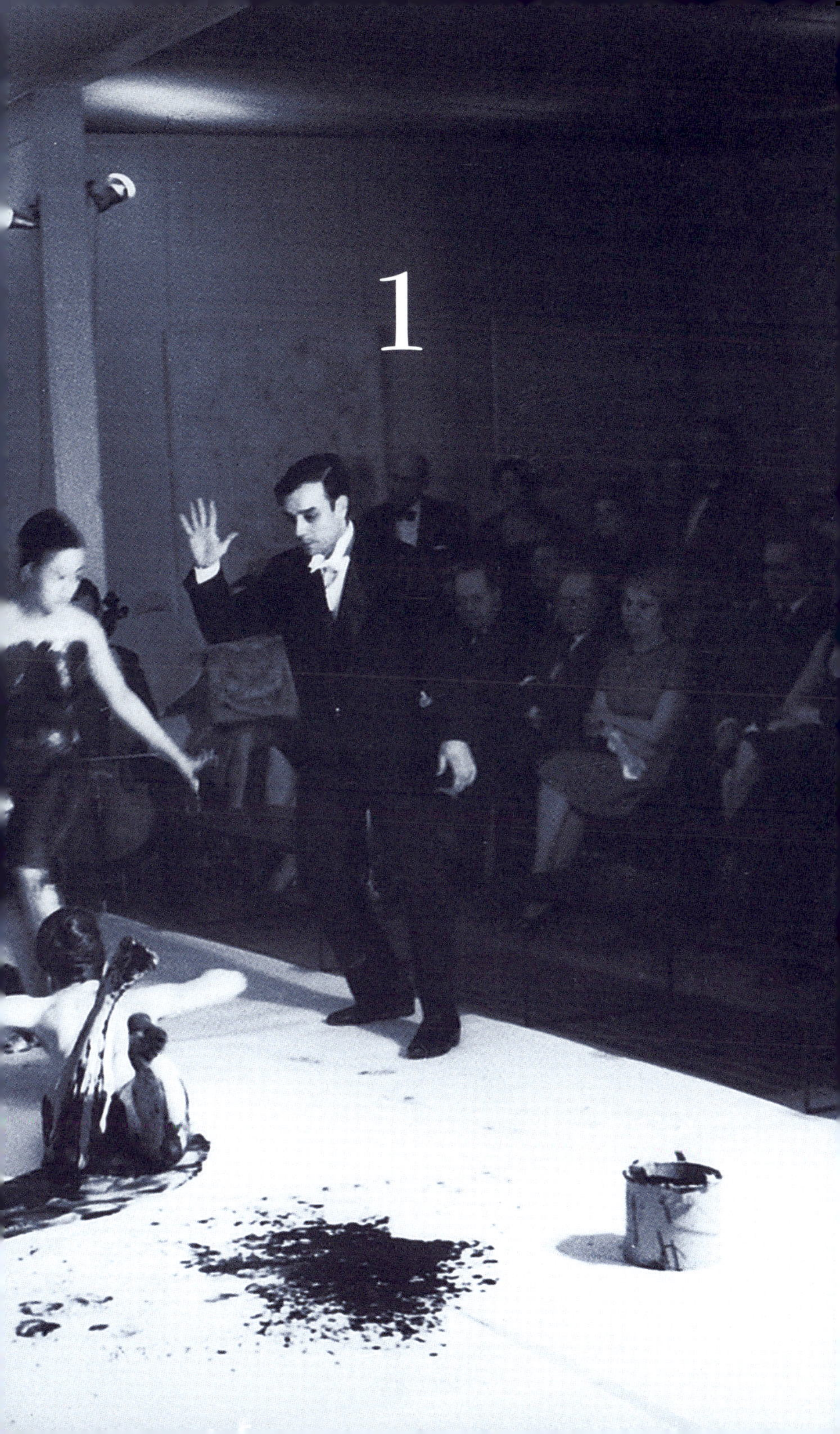
1

Living a Contradiction

MORE POINTEDLY THAN MOST OF US, YVES KLEIN EMBODIED a contradiction. Again more than most, he embodied his moment of history in an unusually sensitive and raw way. To put it simply: Klein felt that he was supposed to proceed historically to the task of visually intimating ahistoricality. Or, to put it more personally: he felt that he was an ahistorical or archetypal figure who had to present himself to others, and somehow to account for himself, within history. In his own mind, and in the estimate of many who attended on his brief (seven years long) career, he was a World Historical or trans-historical figure in the Hegelian sense, meaning that though he acted within history, his actions carried an archetypal force that transcended their historical moment; yet at the same time, so preposterous was this ambition, and so aware was he of its absurdity, that he contrived to carry the weight of history with the Chaplinesque whimsy of the clown.

Klein's oeuvre attempts in a self-conscious way to comprehend the conflicting requirements of this contradictory role. On the one hand, a Modernist artist, committed to the transcendental idealism of a Hegel or a Schelling, was to deal only with the beyond. Schelling had said that when a great artist paints a picture it is as if he has pulled aside the curtain before the Platonic realm of Ideas. Klein strove to live up to this idea though he had to balance it with Dada slapstick like Alphonse and Gaston bumping at the curtained doorway. On the other hand, a post-Modernist artist, who no longer believes in the transcendent beyond, is expected to place his work within the minutiae of history with all possible precision. Those are the opposed mandates of Modernism, with its transcendental ambitions, and post-Modernism with its desire to put history back on its feet (as Marx had said of Hegel) or demystify it.

Klein felt both Modernism and post-Modernism (or in terms of his private point of view, Rosicrucianism[1] and Dada) as personal responsibilities. In line with his special sensitivity to both, he was torn in regard to such questions as historical influence or artistic lineage. At times he felt that the ahistorical or trans-historical dimension of his work rendered questions of influence on it peripheral or paradoxical; at other times, that the petty entanglements of historical connections were a humbling self-parody that offered, at least, basic sanity.[2]

This complicated feeling manifested itself in his attitude toward two artists whom he was reluctant to discuss—or whom he went out of his way to dismiss: Kasimir Malevich and Marcel Duchamp. The complication arose from the fact that much of his own achievement paralleled works and attitudes that those two artists had expressed in the early years of the century. Sensitive to questions of priority, obsessed with the Modernist idea of the artist as innovator, and at the same time willing to play the fool, Klein argued that by a proper understanding of time he in fact preceded Malevich. The point he was trying to make (he was never merely thoughtless, always trying to make a specific point) was that his work's trans-historicality rendered it, as it were, omnipresent in time. Through such an argument he took refuge from the historical dimension in the trans-historical. At other times he performed the opposite diversion.

Being French, Duchamp was a closer threat. Repeatedly Klein fended off the seemingly plausible idea that he was a Dada, or Neo-Dada—a designation that did not do justice to his sense of spiritual mission. When the spirit of Malevich threatened to take him over, Klein acted like a Dada; when Duchamp approached, he was swept up in the defense of Malevich's desert of pure form (which he interpreted in Rosicrucian terms.)

But there was something deeper involved than a denial of

influences or forerunners. Klein knew that his practice was contradictory, and defended the contradiction as the greater truth. He felt that neither a Malevichean occultism nor a Duchampian Dadaism could comprehend either the duality or the unity of his position. The special nature of this position involved a quintessentially late Modernist feeling—the conviction of uniqueness, the anointed feeling of being World Historical. It seemed clear to him that he was the one person necessary to the world at his particular moment, and thus he was not available for mere art historical comparisons; he was above all that. In this sense his intense historicality functioned to forestall questions of influence, as at other moments his feeling of trans-historicality did.

In a sense that Klein tended not to address, Malevich and Duchamp together can offer a parallel to what his contradictory dual selves enacted as if in an immaculate conception. One way of placing Klein in the art historical map of his century, in other words, would transpire by figuring the intersection of the trajectories of Malevich and Duchamp, and trying to imagine what kind of mind could occupy that torn, self-annihilating juncture which offered all the comfort of a head-on car crash. Those two artists, after all, represent the most strongly opposed tendencies of twentieth century art, and each would probably have regarded the other as a kind of enemy in terms of their visions of the role of art in the world.[3]

The History

NINETEEN-THIRTEEN—THE YEAR BEFORE THE BEGINNING OF World War I—can serve as a symbolic date for the articulation of these two opposing paths. This was the year of Malevich's *Black Square*, of Duchamp's first incorporation of chance (the *Three Standard Stoppages*) and of his first Readymade (*Bicycle Wheel*). With the *Black Square* and the writings accompanying it Malevich set going the central stream of Modernist abstraction—the tradition of the abstract sublime with its obsessive desire to intuit the beyond and to embody something of that intuition in visual terms. With the *Stoppages* and *Wheel*, Duchamp set in motion the opposite forces, a demystifying emphasis on everyday life.

This conflict was based on a tradition—found both in Hegel and in a variety of occult systems, including Theosophy, Anthroposophy and Rosicrucianism—that the present age of material complications and difficulties is about to give way to an age of pure spirit.[4] In Hegel's view, this event would be the end of history, meaning that there would be no further need for change in the world: he did not define it much beyond that. The occult prophets—Helena Blavatsky, Rudolf Steiner, Max Heindel, and others—were more forthcoming with details. The age of gross matter, they felt, would soon yield to an age of levitation, out-of-the-body travel, telepathic communication, four dimensional seeing, and so on—an age of a kind of etherealized superhumanity not subject to the present limitations of the body and its needs. Humanity would somehow have attained again the primal state of the soul in the *Egyptian Book of the Dead*, when it is a star and has a body of light, and feeds on light.

A point that is usually neglected in the enthusiasm generated by this idea is that both the Hegelian and the occultist models, enraptured as they were by the idea of entering into Spirit, assumed without regret the end of the material world—the destruction of the mountains, forests, and oceans; the earth, the moon, and the sun; bird, beast, and bug; the map of the stars and the procession of the seasons; the alternation of night and day, and so on. The blackness of Malevich's *Black Square*, or the blankness of Klein's blue deep, was an only slightly hidden apocalyptic prophecy, an obscure yet unequivocal announcement of a universal fire.[5]

Abstract art, especially that of the sublime, was deeply involved in this end-of-the-world spirituality. At some level it understood itself as a visual sign, or portent, that the age of the body was nearly at its end and the age of spirit was imminent. Abstraction showed the things of everyday losing their outlines and being gathered up, or melted down, into a universal sameness, in preparation for the dawning of the age of pure spirit. It was a prefiguring and imagining in physical terms, a prophecy or revelation, of what the post-physical realm of pure spirit would be like. Malevich described it as a quest in which, as one struggled up a mountain that continually faded away, the world of objects dwindled until one reached a "desert beyond form."

This reductivist art was so deeply committed to the way of the sublime, to the reality of a beyond, to the desert beyond form, that it denigrated the present world of everyday reality and even called prophetically for its destruction.

Confusion

REPRESENTATION OF ANY KIND BEARS TROUBLING PARALLELS to magic. In the broad category of ritual practice that has been called "sympathetic magic," the establishing of a representation of what is desired is regarded as a way to make what is really desired appear. If something like what is desired comes along, then what is desired might not be far behind. In terms of visuality, if something that looks like what is desired comes along, then what is desired may be next to appear. In this way the pictorial representation of things has sometimes been confused with the impending presence of the things themselves. Representation becomes metaphysicalized as a form of ontogeny. In a related way, the history of art as expressed in western cultures (and maybe others too) has involved a theory of conquest through representation. On this view, to represent something visually is to gain a kind of cognitive control over it, in a sense to readjust a metaphysical hierarchy in one's favor. In terms of western art history, this process of mastery by representation was supposed to proceed step by step through the universe. When art seemed to have mastered the representation of the physical world in the 19th century realisms, it turned its attention to the level of reality that is beyond-the-world, to the sublime as a universal abstraction that devours all particulars. In the ongoing confusion of representation and presence, the transition to abstraction was felt as a spiritual annulment of the world of form and the official setting of human sights on a beyond. All this happened in a rough flow from about 1860-1950. The world of form had been called into being, or somehow substantiated in being, by the long advance of representational art, and now the stage was set for visual domination of the world in a mode beyond specific form—the reality of the abstract and the sublime.

The Intersection

DUCHAMP'S CLASSIC STATEMENT OF AESTHETIC THEORY, ENUN-ciated in his works of 1913 and after, was the opposite of Malevich's. Whereas Malevich pursued the thread of transcendental art up to the heights of the mountain of nonobjectivity, casting aside the world of everyday life like a bagatelle, Duchamp pointed to the aesthetic presence in the midst of everyday life, as if it could not be found anywhere else, as if there were no other option. Whereas Malevich, in his Suprematist years, presented pictures without any representation of recognizable things, Duchamp presented recognizable things without any pictorial representation—everyday objects in their frank self-declaring presences. Whereas Malevich renounced representation as too realistic, Duchamp renounced it as too illusionistic. Whereas art for Malevich was the most serious metaphysical project, for Duchamp it was a means of mocking solemn and metaphysical ambitions. One expressed the constructive impulse, the other the deconstructive. One was metaphysics, the other dialectic. One fetishized oneness and sameness, the other multiplicity and difference.

From these polar sources, or primary articulations, the principal threads of meaning in 20th century art derived. One might, for the sake of convenient communication, characterize them as the sublime and the ridiculous: transcendent abstraction and deconstructing parody, Action Painting and Pop, Neo-Expressionism and Simulationism. In general, twentieth century artists can be classified as emphasizing one or the other of these spiritualities. Many—perhaps most—are moved by elements of both. Yet it may be that Klein more than anyone else actually epitomized both these tendencies, expressing intense clarity and commitment on both sides—while yet maintaining a credibility in terms of art historical criteria.

The Aftermath

AT THE SAME TIME THAT KLEIN'S OEUVRE SYNTHESIZED THE main currents of earlier twentieth century art history, it also presaged the era to come with uncanny thoroughness. In his works between 1955 and 1962 he stated virtually all the themes which would develop as the avant-garde of the 1960s and '70s. Monochrome painting, anti-painting, the shift of emphasis toward sculpture and installation, the dematerialization of art, the rejection of illusionism, the incorporation of found objects and new media, body art, land art, Conceptual Art, Performance Art—all these aspects of the emerging avant-garde were coherently unified in a single body of work within Klein's seven year period of production. In the generation after his death—especially in Europe but also, significantly, in America—the traces of his presence have been everywhere. His footsteps resonate both in the survival of metaphysical painting and in the parody of it. The combined intensity and variety of his brief career had built such a momentum that his early death left that momentum free to be harnessed by others.

Painting and Anti-Painting

KLEIN DIED AS A PARODIC WARRIOR ABOUT PAINTING, CHAMP-ioning now one side, now another, highlighting both. Soon after his death the wars of the successors began. The two contradictory strains in Klein's oeuvre separated out, and each endured. To this day some painters are producing mystical monochromes, and to this day others are using the one-color plane as a conceptual critique of expressionist painterly practice. These two strains of legacy spread through Europe immediately upon Klein's death. In Italy, Piero Manzoni and Lucio Fontana took up the momentum and carried it—or were carried by it—in opposite directions. Fontana's slashed monochromes restated Klein's metaphysical-futurist program with the formal addition of the slit opening into infinity; Manzoni's Achromes were repartee-like responses to Klein's metaphysicalism, attempting to rebut it with a strong materialistic statement—from gold to excrement. In Germany the artists of the ZERO Group—Heinz Mack, Otto Piene, B. Aubertin—began their affirmation of the void as fierce partisans of Klein's metaphysical monochromism, then gradually developed in other, more kinetic and conceptual directions. Fluxus arose in time from this stream, carrying on the legacy of Klein's crypto-dadaism rather than of his metaphysicalism.

In America, the metaphysical monochrome arose in the 1950s and came to something like dominance in the 1960s in the near-monochromne works of Mark Rothko, Barnett Newman, Ad Reinhardt, and others. These events began contemporaneously with Klein's career; they were not spawned by it but by the same post-War end-of-the-world spirituality from which Klein's oeuvre arose. To the New York School as to Klein the monochrome seemed an important statement of the end of physical painting and the simultaneous end of an historical era, or of history itself. Physical painting was to consummate itself, drawing its long identity-shifting shape-changing dance toward the close; in the monochrome form would dive into the ocean of color and disappear.

In America the overflowing intensity of this post-War monochromism drained off into the spiritual deflation of Minimal and Color Field painting. In 1959 Frank Stella exhibited his first series of black paintings, and Robert Irwin made his first near-monochrome "line paintings." Jasper Johns monochromed the American flag, and Robert Rauschenberg monochromed newsprint. Through the sixties the momentum picked up. In 1961 Dan Flavin began making monochromatic works involving electrical light fixtures. In 1961 Brice Marden began exhibiting beeswax-encaustic monochromes. In 1967 Robert Ryman's first one-man exhibition in New York City showed the Standard series—thirteen all-white paintings on steel. Though it cannot be said that these American developments arose out of Klein's influence, they nevertheless attained meaning in an international milieu in which the aura of his work and his attitudes were both formative and pervasive. In this sense these American works were in fact dependent on Klein as well as on their recent American forebears; it cannot be said that they could have realized their full art historical importance without his statements, both visual and verbal, being in the record already. In keeping with his dialectic of incorporated contradiction, Klein was as much an anti-painter as a painter. His creation of imaginary paintings in the booklet *Yves Peintures*, his use of the monochrome as a demystifying device to reduce the idea of the easel painting to absurdity through caricaturing its self-absorbed intensity, his rejection of the tradition of touch in favor of first the roller and later the "living brush," his reduction of the art of the figure to absurdity in the Imprints, his symbolic destruction of the easel painting in the Fire Paintings, his creation of paintings through random methods in the Cosmogonies, his exhibition and sale of "invisible paintings"—all these were parts of the anti-painting project, which he worked out in great detail and with great precision within a few years. In the ensuing era of Conceptual Art, artistic oeuvres came to be based on different nuances of this project. This was one of the sequences through which an artist could lay claim to a conceptual signature. Starting in 1966 Daniel Buren made identical "paintings" of stretched red fabric that drew out the parodic element in Klein's monochromes. In the following year, restating Klein's idea of the immaterial, or of absence over presence, Buren and others hung their paintings in an inaccessible room in a Paris museum and distributed a leaflet describing them. Historically this piece refers to the fact that, a few years earlier, in the same museum, Klein had performed his act of removing paintings from a gallery. Throughout the 1960s and 1970s the ramifications of this work proliferated. One element that had to be absorbed was its conflation of the painting tradition with Performance Art and Conceptual Art. This quickly became a new tradition. In the next few years Mel Ramsden exhibited a black painting with a plaque beside it saying, in effect, that the black painting the viewer saw was not really a painting but a concealment of one which was hidden beneath the black surface; Jannis Kounellis exhibited a stretched canvas with a black curtain hung in front of it; Gerhard Richter made sets of identical Gray Paintings, echoing the identical blue monochromes of Klein's 1957 show in Milan. Such gestures are perhaps the most characteristic imprint of Klein's influence on the tradition he so longed to enter. But there are other strong candidates.

Creation by Designation

DUCHAMP DESIGNATED STOREBOUGHT ITEMS AS HIS ARTWORKS through signing them. The signature—the act of designation—replaced what had traditionally been called the act of creation. Klein was the first, decades after, to take up vigorously the challenging implications of this technique. His fantasized signing of the sky made it his artwork in 1947. In his *Theatre of the Void*, 1961, he designated the entire world his theatre and every person in it both an actor and spectator for one day. After patenting the IKB (International Klein Blue) formula he designated previously existing things as his works through color. The Athena Nike was thus brought into his portfolio, as was the entire world when Klein dipped a globe in his blue.

Creation by designation was the principal means of Conceptual Art in its early period, and also one of its primal themes and stylistic differentia. The elaboration of his or her new methods of designation was an early conceptual artist's signature. These developments tended to merge with Klein's performance ethic, expressed in his famous remark that an artist only has to make one work, himself or herself, constantly. Designation rather than creation merged with the emphasis on life rather than art. Manzoni, for example, developed his so-called *base per scultura vivente* in response to Klein's designations by blueness—a sculpture base on which a person would stand and become a work of art. Manzoni's "Certificates of Authenticity," which would declare a specific human being to be a work of art, were based on Klein's printed receipt forms for Zones of Immaterial Sensibility. Klein's designation of the whole world as his artwork in the blue globe elicited Manzoni's *Socle du monde*, an upside-down sculpture base on which the entire earth was understood to stand, wrestling the world, as it were, from Klein's portfolio into his.

Ben Vautier, inheritor of the School of Nice, made the continuation of this line of theoretical gesture his speciality. In 1962 he designated Klein's death as his (Ben's) artwork and a year later signed Manzoni's death, too. Also in 1962 Ben put himself on display as a "living moving sculpture"—an act soon echoed in a variety of works by Gilbert and George, James Lee Byars, and others. Along with the style of designation, the presentation of the artist's person or everyday life as his or her artwork became one of the principal themes of the era dominated by Conceptual and Performance Art. The conceptual strain in Klein's work was isolated and made explicit in Ben's simple designation of the entire world as his artwork.

The Dematerialization of Art

FOR KLEIN, REAL ART WAS THE MANIPULATION OF SPIRIT THROUGH sheer will; the highest art didn't involve matter at all. Despite the theosophical tinge of these feelings, they were one of the formative influences on Conceptual Art with its denigration of the physical object. Klein's void or dematerialized works were landmarks in the formation of the 60s-and-70s' ambience of permissiveness in which Conceptual Art exerted its brief hegemony. The most important piece in this regard was *Le Vide*, 1958, in which the Iris Clert Gallery was exhibited apparently empty but allegedly filled with non-sensual aesthetic presences; the *Immaterial Room*, 1961, was a more intensely atmospheric void where light defined space in obvious, transcendently gleaming, geometrical volumes. As an unpacking of the implications of this work, in 1968 Robert Irwin and James Turrell began exhibiting their atmospheric empty spaces which, by blurring geometric distinctions in a lucid haze of light, attempted to concretize the idea of fullness/emptiness; these were in some ways, such as their use of hidden lighting and scrim screens, more sensually elaborated than Klein's *Le Vide*, or even than the *Immaterial Room*, but still were in the tradition established by those works.

In another direction, primarily in Europe, *Le Vide* led to a series of conceptual works in connection with the Duchampian tradition of designation. There was a very rational sequencing here. Duchamp had put everyday objects in an art context and called them art. Klein reasoned that if placing things in an art context makes them art, it is then the context rather than the thing that contains the art essence; he proceeded to exhibit the gallery by itself. Buren, then, reasoned in turn that if it is the gallery that is the art object he will decorate the gallery—beginning with the awning over the sidewalk in front. Throughout the early conceptualist period the project of exhibiting emptiness was one of the areas, like that of designation, where an artist could establish a signature style. In 1967 Claes Oldenburg installed an "invisible sculpture" behind the Metropolitan Museum of Art in New York City, digging a grave-sized hole, then filling it up again. In 1968 Ron Cooper showed what he called volumes of atmosphere; Robert

Barry exhibited invisible electronic waves. James Lee Byars presented *The Ghost of James Lee Byars*—an apparently empty room that, like Klein's *Le Vide*, supposedly held an invisible entity that could be sensed by an occult dynamic on the viewer's part. The same year, Takis, a former colleague of Klein's in Paris, exhibited apparently empty rooms filled with magnetic fields; Tom Marioni arranged an exhibition called Invisible Painting and Sculpture for the Richmond Art Center, and Exhibition, Number 7, organized by Lucy lippard in a New York gallery, was an apparently empty room containing various invisible works such as a magnetic field installed by Barry, air currents by Hans Haacke, existing shadows by Robert Huot, and other works. In 1969 Barry presented his *Telepathic Piece*, in which the artist stood in front of an audience and telepathically communicated to them the physical appearance of his artwork, which the audience never directly saw; in the following year he exhibited a closed gallery in Los Angeles. In 1973 Eric Orr's *Zero-Mass Space* was a large empty paper room with a minimal light level. These and many related works took Klein's seminal gesture in *Le Vide* into new areas of meaning, some suggesting metaphysical parallel worlds, others socially satirizing the function of the gallery.

Self-Endangerment

IN 1960 KLEIN PUBLISHED THE FAMOUS PHOTOGRAPH OF THE *Saut dans le vide* (*Leap into the Void*), in connection with which he had actually made self-endangering leaps on at least two occasions.[6] Others of his stylized public acts also involved the threat of his death or the promise of his self-sacrifice, as in *La tombe–ci-gît l'espace* [*The Tomb: Here Lies Space*]. Along with his ritualism the self-endangerment pieces exerted a seminal force in the Performance Art of the next generation. The Leap was actually repeated by a number of artists, among them the American Paul McCarthy and the Taiwanese Tehching Hsieh. More broadly, there is a genre of work in which the artist's own body, or a surrogate of it, is offered up as a kind of cosmic sacrifice. Yves Klein, Joseph Beuys, the Viennese Aktionists, Carolee Schneemann, Marina and UIay, Terry Fox, McCarthy, and countless other performance artists have been deeply influenced by this model. Indeed, 1960s Performance Art could be divided into two historical streams, one derived inspirationally from Klein and the other from the American Happening as hatched in the Cageian enclave of Black Mountain College in the 1950s. The Kleinian thread features intense emphasis on the idea that the artwork should not be separable from the artist's person, the principle to which the self-endangerment works are a demonstration of commitment.

New Media

THE 1960S AND 1970S WERE CHARACTERIZED BY A CONTINUAL search for new media and materials to replace the inherited ones that were being cast aside as relics of a Modernism that was passing. A key issue was the shift of emphasis from painting to sculpture, and especially the attempt to find areas in between those two media. In America the early "combines" of Rauschenberg pointed the way and in Europe Klein's practice, from 1957 on, of exhibiting his paintings a few inches in front of the wall, as objects in real space rather than as illusionary windows to a beyond. This was one of the first gestures toward seeing the painting as a real object occupying its own space and significant for what it was rather than for what it represented. A few years later, in the first articulations of the California space-light tradition that would have so much in common with Klein's gestures, Robert Irwin and Doug Wheeler began exhibiting their paintings away from the wall. Richard Jackson, Immants Tillers and others have since used stretched painted canvases as sculptural objects.

Klein's Sponge Reliefs were similarly neither exactly paintings nor exactly sculptures; they combined elements of both by affixing real world objects to the canvas, as in Europe, Manzoni was to do in his Achromes and, in America, Rauschenberg had begun in his "combines," with Jim Dine and others soon to follow. Even more so, Klein's body casts pushed at the limits between sculpture and life, or representation and presence. Here too he was pioneering a sculptural mode that would be carried out in the work of others, especially the Americans Ed Kienholz, Duane Hanson, John Ahearn and others. Klein's bodycasts are close to actual presence, and his "Imprints" serve the same theoretical end, confuting the distinction between presence and representation.

Klein's revery on alchemy led to other shifts of emphasis in the choice of art materials. He is the father, for example, of the use of fire as an art material. Fire, as he conceived it, is not only an alchemic force of reduction and transformation, but also an apt material for an encapsulation of the late Modernist inferno or apocalypse, the fire of history's consummation burning up all the masterpieces and books and scores and distilling them into a final pure smoky essence floating momentarily by the eye before loss of consciousness. Many works by Jannis Kounellis, Eric Orr, and others have extended this theme.

Klein's projects such as the reclimatization of France, the architecture of the air, the rearrangement of the earth's topography, and so on, are to an extent the forerunners of Land Art or Earthworks. James Turrell's *Roden Crater*, Walter DeMaria's *Lightning Field*, Robert Smithson's *Spiral Jetty*, and other works in their tradition participate in the utopian ambition of art and architecture to museify the environment as a transformative impetus for both society and the individual.

The Artist's Role

AFTER AN ERA IN WHICH THE ARTIST WAS TO FOCUS, LIKE A specialized research scientist, on a limited area of formal investigation, Klein gave a sense of breadth back to the artistic project. The multiplicity of his oeuvre, and the inclusive breadth of his conception of it, left a mark on succeeding generations. Sculptor, painter, photographer, performance artist, conceptual artist, body artist, land artist—his career was the first of a polymorphous type that became typical for a later generation. Artists such as Beuys, Kounellis, Dennis Oppenheim and others who have pursued the idea that the artist's career should be Leonardian, were following in Klein's footsteps or in areas opened up by him; although in some cases the consciously received influence was slight, the atmosphere in which the work transpired had already been enlarged and prepared. But Klein's expanded conception of the artist's role went farther than that, extending it grandiosely into the public sphere along the lines of the Romantic conception of the poet or artist as, in Percy Shelley's phrase, the "unacknowledged legislator of mankind." Klein wished to act out this role openly. His "Architecture of the Air" was an attempt, along Corbusian lines, to inject the artist into questions of utopian social engineering. He proposed a new form for the French government to lead ultimately to a new world government, and a new educational system called the World Center of Sensibility. These acts lie behind Beuys's Free International University and German Students' Party, and other gestures toward the aestheticization of public institutions. Beuys's calls for the unification of science, art and religion closely parallel Klein's way of thinking (Klein's Heindelian Rosicrucianism shared roots with Beuys's Steinerian Anthroposophy), as did his crownings of himself. Like Klein, Beuys displayed outrageous reactionariness along with his groundbreaking innovations. Both acted out the easy shift from "unacknowledged legislator" to "prince of an imaginary kingdom," as Disraeli called the dandy.

After an era when a deep confusion existed between the role of the artist and that of the illustrator, Klein was the first major artist who never learned how to draw. In a renunciation of the preciousness of the formalist cult of touch, he made his paintings with rollers. Newman had remarked that he could phone out specifications for a painting and have it come out right--but he didn't do it. Klein more or less did, in the first clear articulation of the principle that Lawrence Wiener would make famous a few years later, that the artist may make the piece himself, the piece may be fabricated by others, or the piece need not be made at all. Klein characteristically farmed out the mechanical and technical parts of his works to specialists, as would become the standard means for the next generation of artists. John Baldessari in the late 1960s was completing a Kleinian sequence when he had his paintings made by a commercial signpainter in a mockery of the sacredness of the artist's concentration and self-expressiveness. Collaboration, along with other forms of the decentering of the self, has become one of the signature traits of post-Modernism. Klein was a pioneer in this area, too. The New Realists group was formed under his influence, and his relationship with Tinguely repeatedly veered into the area of outright collaboration. In 1960,

Klein founded the International Klein Bureau, empowering the other members—Mirouze, Restany, Pascal and Arman—to make IKB monochromes and sign them with his name.[7] End-of-Modernism works like Sol leWitt's drawings to be executed by others and signed by him extended this gesture. There is hardly a later artist who cannot find something to admire and emulate in Klein's career. The opening of the retrospective at the Guggenheim Museum in 1982 was accompanied by a panel on which I sat with Arman, Julian Schnabel, Joseph Kosuth and Olivier Mosset. All these artists felt they had incorporated something of Klein's essence into their very different practices.

Reapproaching the Intersection

KLEIN'S SELF-PROMOTION AMOUNTED TO A CLAIM THAT HE was a World Historical Individual, an essentially Modernist type of self-image; yet his world-historical role was to announce the end of the Modernist age, the advent of the age of pure spirituality —that is, to draw the cloak shut over the world of historical form and of the World Historical Individual. His title *Dépassement de la problematique de l'art*, 1959, is a plain-spoken declaration of the end of Modernism. In 1960, in a meeting at "La Coupole," he founded A.D.A.M.—Association pour le Dépassement de l'Art Modern [Association for the Bypassing of Modern Art]. In his belief that there was such a thing as the necessary next step of art history Klein was a classical Modernist, while in his continual self-parodying sense of himself as a participant in the existential absurd he was a post-Modernist. Through his work both threads run—on the one hand the metaphysical monochrome and the solemn approaches to the void, on the other the performative parodies of solemnity, the deconstructive irony, the antics of the clown. In this sense Klein may be regarded as a phenomenon of the very end of Modernism. His obeisances to the mystical and metaphysical ambitions of art were strictly Modernist in a tradition going back to the Romantic ideology of Schelling and the Schlegels. Yet he could not quite perform these obeisances straight-facedly, but had to incorporate a counterview or ironic reversal, and in this his work is essentially post-Modernist. Perhaps this is how the duality of Klein should be perceived: that he straddled the Modernist/post-Modernist impasse with a special clarity and intensity. He practiced the one ideology as wholeheartedly as the other, embodying at once the historical moment, its conflicting forces, and the opposing realities of their claims. His Passion Play was in a sense the death of Modernism enacted in his body with post-Modernism coming to birth in it at the same time. In this sense he was stating the truth when he remarked, after the exhibition *Le Vide* in 1958, "In my modest person four thousand years of civilization have found their exhaustive culmination."

YVES KLEIN PRÉSENTE :
LE DIMANCHE 27 NOVEMBRE 1960

NUMÉRO UNIQUE

FESTIVAL D'ART D'AVANT-GARDE
NOVEMBRE - DÉCEMBRE 1960

La Révolution bleue continue

Le journal d'un seul jour

SEANCE DE 0 HEURE A 24 HEURES

Dimanche

27 NOVEMBRE

0,35 NF (35 fr.)   Algérie : 0,30 NF (30 fr.) - Tunisie : 27 mil.
Maroc : 33 f'm. - Italie : 50 lires - Espagne : 3 pes. 5

THÉÂTRE DU VIDE

LE théâtre se cherche depuis toujours ; il se cherche depuis le début perdu.

Le grand théâtre, c'est l'Eden en fait ; l'important est d'établir une bonne fois nos positions statiques, chacun d'une manière individuelle et non plus personnelle dans l'univers. Depuis longtemps déjà j'annonce partout que je suis le peintre... Je n'en connais pas d'autre aujourd'hui ! Je tiens à dire aussi : « Je suis l'acteur, je suis le compositeur, l'architecte, le sculpteur. » Je tiens à dire : « Je suis. » L'on m'objectera sans doute que cela a déjà été hurlé de toutes sortes de manières variées ; c'est certainement juste. Par conséquent, je répète peut-être cela, mais conscient, bien conscient, d'avoir atteint le droit de le dire : et voilà que, pour moi comme pour tous, il n'y a plus rien à faire ; le théâtre officiel, aujourd'hui, c'est « être » et je « suis » bien effectivement tout ce que l'on veut bien que je « sois » et même tout ce que l'on ne veut pas que je « sois » ! J'atteindrai même à ne plus « être » du tout un jour !... Mais, que l'on ne s'y trompe pas : il ne s'agit pas de moi quand je dis je, moi, mon, etc.

C'est parce que l'esprit dans lequel je vis est un esprit d'émerveillement, stabilisé et continu, un esprit classique, que je n'ai aucun caractère d'avant-garde, de cette avant-garde qui, elle, vieillit si vite, de génération en génération.

Mon art n'appartiendra pas à l'époque, pas plus que l'art de tous les grands classiques n'a appartenu aux époques où ils ont vécu, parce que je cherche avant tout, comme eux, à créer dans mes réalisations cette « transparence », ce « vide » incommensurable dans lequel vit l'esprit permanent et absolu délivré de toutes dimensions !

Non, je ne me laisse pas prendre à mon propre jeu en parlant aujourd'hui d'un théâtre du vide avec un tel avant-propos orgueilleux, égocentrique et même vaniteux sans doute en apparence : mon théâtre prendra une valeur universelle dans la mesure même où mes compagnons connaîtront mieux ma pensée que moi-même je ne la connais, car s'ils sont des milliers, ils la refléteront des milliers de fois alors que moi je suis seul.

★

Je me rends très bien compte que je me présente, tout seul, en écrivant ces lignes avec ce qui semblerait une sorte de complexe du plus fort. Je signale à ceux qui seraient assez aveugles et maladroits pour me donner l'avantage d'attaquer mon exagération du moi qu'il est bien facile de m'entraîner à la défaite : mais à cette sorte de défaite que sont les veilles des grandes victoires définitives pour ceux qui entrent dans le grand jeu et savent s'exposer.

J'ai lutté contre ma vocation de « peintre », en partant au Japon pour y vivre l'aventure Judo et Arts martiaux anciens de même j'ai lutté contre ma vocation « d'homme de théâtre » ; mais précisément, le Judo par la pratique physique et spirituelle des Katas s'est constitué malgré moi, ma formation dans cette discipline de l'art qu'est le théâtre, d'une manière imprévisible, mais tout aussi profitable et profonde, sinon peut-être plus encore, que n'importe quelle autre. En présentant ce qui suit, j'obéis à une nécessité profonde, j'agis en réaliste plein de gros bon sens. J'aime Molière et Shakespeare parce que, dans leur œuvre, se trouve cette transparence du vide qui me fascine.

Pour moi « théâtre » n'est pas...

ACTUALITÉ

DANS le cadre des représentations théâtrales du Festival d'Art d'Avant-Garde de novembre-décembre 1960, j'ai décidé de Présenter une ultime forme de théâtre collectif qu'est un dimanche pour tout le monde.

Je n'ai pas voulu me limiter à une matinée ou à une soirée.

En présentant le dimanche 27 novembre 1960, de 0 heure à 24 heures, je présente donc une journée de fête, un véritable spectacle du vide, au point culminant de mes théories. Cependant, n'importe quel autre jour de la semaine aurait pu être aussi utilisé.

Je souhaite qu'en ce jour la joie et le merveilleux règnent, que personne n'ait le trac et que tous, acteurs-spectateurs, conscients comme inconscients aussi de cette gigantesque manifestation, passent une bonne journée.

Que chacun aille dedans comme dehors, circule, bouge, remue ou reste tranquille.

Tout ce que je publie aujourd'hui dans ce journal est antérieur à la Présentation de ce jour historique pour le théâtre.

Le théâtre doit être ou doit tout au moins tenter de devenir rapidement le plaisir d'être, de vivre, de passer de merveilleux moments, et de comprendre chaque jour mieux le bel aujourd'hui.

Tout ce que je publie dans ce journal ont été mes étapes jusqu'à ce jour glorieux de réalisme et de vérité ; le théâtre des opérations de cette conception du théâtre que je propose n'est pas seulement la ville, Paris, mais aussi la campagne, le désert, la montagne, le ciel même, et tout l'univers même, pourquoi pas ?

Je sais que tout va fonctionner très bien inévitablement pour tous, spectateurs, acteurs, machinistes, directeurs et autres.

Je tiens à remercier ici M. Jacques Polieri, directeur du Festival d'Art d'Avant-Garde, pour son enthousiasme en me proposant de présenter cette manifestation « le dimanche 27 novembre ».

Yves KLEIN.

...du tout synonyme de « Représentation » ou de « Spectacle ».

D'importants chercheurs qui, eux, ont été d'avant-garde, comme Taïroff, par exemple, voulaient théâtraliser le théâtre.

Evreinoff rêvais du monodrame, de la théâtralité de la vie quotidienne, pensée - geste - parole.

Stanislavsky, réaliste extrémiste, aurait souhaité la mort effective et définitive de l'acteur qui doit jouer sa mort en scène. Le précurseur Dada Vakhtangof enferma le public dans une salle de théâtre pendant deux heures dans le seul but cynique de les enfermer tout simplement. Cet événement faisait partie, d'ailleurs...

★

Ce que je désire : Plus de rythme, surtout plus jamais de rythme !

Et puis mon œuvre n'est pas une « recherche », c'est mon sillage. Elle est la matière même de la vitesse statique vertigineuse, à laquelle je me propulse sur place dans l'immatériel ! Attention encore, je tiens à bien préciser que je ne dis pas, en parlant de mon œuvre : « C'est bien plus beau parce que c'est inutile » ! Non, je dis : « C'est ainsi ce sera ainsi, et personne ne pourra jamais rien faire pour que ce ne soit pas ainsi » ! Pour quoi ? Parce que, précisément c'est « classique » !

★

...Ainsi, très vite, on en arrive au théâtre sans acteur, sans décor, sans scène, sans spectateur... plus rien que le créateur seul qui n'est vu par personne, excepté la présence de personne et le théâtre-spectacle commence !

L'auteur vit sa création : il

● SUITE EN PAGE 2

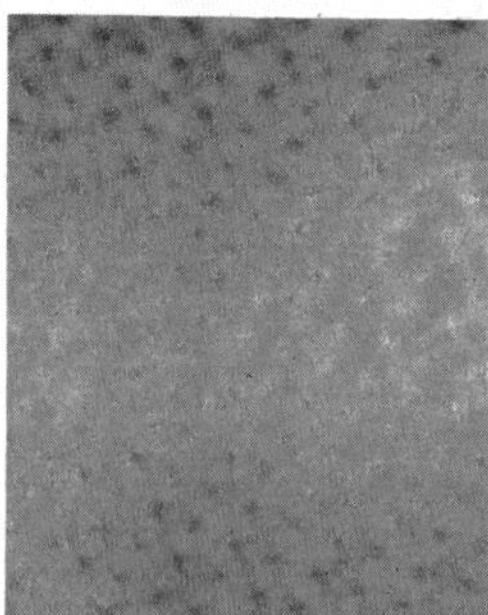

L'ESPACE, LUI-MEME.

leurs, de son « théâtre de la révolte » et s'intitulait « La Soirée insolite ».

Le Tchécoslovaque Burian créa un théâtre synthétique ; les personnages de sa pièce, « Roméo et Juliette », étaient des machines fantastiques et infernales qui évoluaient sur la scène pendant que les acteurs en coulisse disaient le texte. Amphithéâtroff montait des piécettes laconiques de dix minutes, coupées de discussions ; les discussions faisaient partie évidemment du programme. Ce qui l'amènera à déclarer souvent à son public, qui lui commandait d'avance ses représentations, qu'il était prêt à supporter les tomates, les œufs pourris, mais, en autre manière, les pavés.

Les photographes, dans « Les Mariés de la Tour Eiffel », de Jean Cocteau, sont aussi de très beaux phénomènes.

★

Il serait trop long de citer ici toutes les tentatives qui ont été faites pour sortir de la convention, de l'optique apprise de l'académisme, dans le domaine du spectacle de la représentation théâtrale depuis le début du siècle. Je crois que presque tout a été fait, jusqu'à Jacques Polieri dans sa mise en scène de la pièce de Tardieu ces temps derniers, qui fait entendre des voix sur la scène où trois panneaux-écrans sont là pour tout décor et toute présence ! (Son idée d'ailleurs est de faire vivre et parler les décors.)

Bravo ! — Quel bonheur que tout cela ait existé, mais attention : j'avertis bien le lecteur mon œuvre théâtrale n'a rien absolument rien à voir avec l'une quelconque de ces directions ou recherches sauf, peut-être, avec celles d'Antonin Artaut, qui sentait venir ce que je propose aujourd'hui ici. Cependant Artaut, malgré bien d'autres « Grands » du vrai théâtre, se perdait dans cette fausse conception artificielle et intellectuelle du Verbe qui en a dérouté tant et longtemps. Pour ma part, je ne sais qu'une chose, c'est qu'au commencement était le Verbe, et le Verbe était Dieu » ; deux fois « être » pour deux fois « Verbe » plus « Dieu », en tout cinq points qui, si on les médite un peu, disent bien ce qu'ils veulent dire : le « Verbe » dans cette aforme n'est pas « Parole » articulée ni même désarticulée.

UN HOMME DANS L'ESPACE !

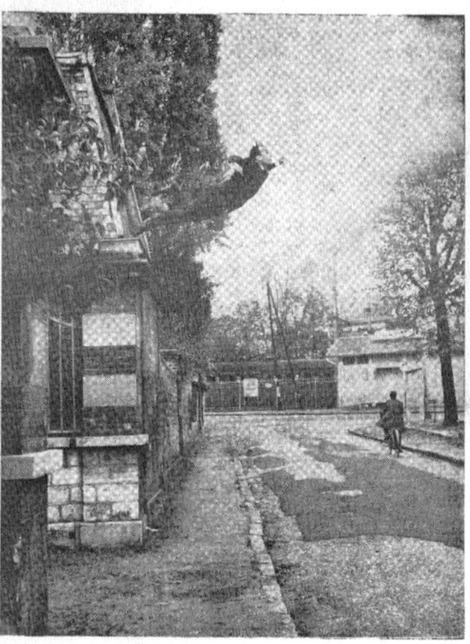

(Photo Shunk-Kender)

Le peintre de l'espace se jette dans le vide !

Le monochrome qui est aussi champion de Judo, ceinture noire 4e dan, s'entraîne régulièrement à la lévitation dynamique ! (avec ou sans filet, au risque de sa vie).

Il prétend être en mesure d'aller rejoindre bientôt dans l'espace son œuvre préférée : une sculpture aérostatique composée de Mille et un Ballons bleus qui, en 1957, s'enfuit de son exposition dans le ciel de Saint-Germain-des-Prés pour ne plus jamais revenir !

Libérer la sculpture du socle a été longtemps sa préoccupation. « Aujourd'hui le peintre de l'espace doit aller effectivement dans l'espace pour peindre, mais il doit y aller sans trucs, ni supercheries, ni non plus en avion, ni en parachute ou en fusée ; il doit y aller par lui-même, avec une force individuelle autonome, en un mot, il doit être capable de léviter. »

Yves :

« Je suis le peintre de l'espace. Je ne suis pas un peintre abstrait, mais au contraire un figuratif, et un réaliste. Soyons honnêtes, pour peindre l'espace, je me dois de me rendre sur place, dans cet espace même »

Sensibilité pure

Une petite salle.

Les spectateurs, après avoir dûment payé chacun leur entrée, assez chère... pénètrent dans la salle et prennent place.

Le rideau est baissé. La salle illuminée.

Dès que la salle est pleine, un homme se présente sur la scène, devant le rideau toujours baissé et déclare :

« Mesdames, Messieurs en raison des circonstances, ce soir nous allons être contraints de vous enchaîner chacun à vos sièges (et, de plus, vous bâillonner) pour la durée de la représentation.

» Cette mesure de sécurité est nécessaire, afin de vous protéger contre vous-même, en présence de ce spectacle particulièrement dangereux, d'un point de vue affectif pur !

» Nous exprimons d'avance nos regrets aux personnes qui ne pourraient supporter d'être ainsi enchaînées et bâillonnées avant le lever du rideau et nous les prions aimablement de bien vouloir quitter la salle pour se faire rembourser à la sortie. Aucune personne non enchaînée solidement à son siège ne sera tolérée dans la salle pendant le spectacle. Merci »

...Aussitôt un groupe d'enchaîneurs-bâillonneurs pénètrent dans la salle et, systématiquement, rang après rang, passent rapidement tous les spectateurs.

● SUITE EN PAGE 2

Yves Klein: Messenger of the Age of Space

If you come back someday
You who dream also
Of this marvellous void
Of this absolute love
I know that together
Without a word to one another
We will hurl ourselves
Into the reality of this void
Which awaits our love
As I wait for you each day.
Come with me into the void!

—YVES KLEIN[1]

THE MOST FAMOUS IMAGE OF YVES KLEIN—THE STARTLING photograph of the artist, dressed in business suit and necktie, leaping into flight from a second-floor ledge on a quiet Paris street—is usually seen out of context. Yet with Klein, context is everything. Originally part of a literary document, the photograph contributed to an intricate mingling of visual and verbal signifiers in Klein's most characteristic style. Klein's imitation newspaper, *Dimanche 27 Novembre: Le journal d'un seul jour (Sunday November 27th: the Newspaper of a Single Day)*, his contribution to the Paris Festival d'Art d'Avant-garde in 1960, headlined the phrase:

"Théâtre du vide" *(Theater of the Void).* Beside the headline was the remarkable photograph, captioned underneath: "Le peintre de l'espace se jette dans le vide!" *(The painter of space launches himself into the void!)* Characteristically two-edged, Klein's point was not merely self-advertisement, but provocation; it included an invitation to the readers to effect a Leap, or an analogue of the Leap, themselves. The poem excerpted above was found on the second page.

Klein's own fate in the United States has been the same: he has been assimilated out of context. Klein, who is widely regarded in Europe as the most important French artist since the Second World War, has remained, in the North American consciousness, primarily a showman and a clown. When he arrived in New York in April 1961, on his only visit to this country, the New York School was arrayed against the fading hegemony of the School of Paris,[2] and Klein, with his fanciful personae and self-ordained titles—Champion of Color, Proprietor of Color, Painter of Space— looked like Paris come slumming again. New York artists virtually boycotted his show of monochrome paintings in "International Klein Blue" (his own patented formula of blue) at Leo Castelli's gallery. The art press, which did not bother to investigate the wider context of his work, found him easy prey. *Art News* called him "the latest sugar-Dada to jet in from the Parisian common market," and "the George M. Koan of French Neo-Dada." *Time* called his works "tricks" and his reputation in Europe "a fad." "Have you ever been all blue?" inquired the New York *Herald Tribune.*[3] Six years later, John Canaday, reviewing the Jewish Museum show of his works for *The New York Times,* called him "a vaudevillian," "full panoplied in cap and bells," whose work is "only stuntmanship." "I Got the Yves Klein Blues," the headline on this story read. In reference to the same exhibition, the *World-Journal-Tribune* called him, "a Dali-junior grade."[4]

When, after two months in New York, Klein moved on to Los Angeles for a show of his works at the Virginia Dwan Gallery, he found a somewhat friendlier reception. To this day in Los Angeles Klein is regarded as in some sense a "California" artist: particularly for his use of space and silence as primary materials, for his works in natural phenomena such as fire and water, for his use of his own body as the locus of the art event, for his reckless mixing of artistic codes and roles, and for his deliberate ridicule of his own serious works. But not even in Los Angeles was the labyrinth of Klein's gestures, his poses, his mutually cancelling intentionalities, perceived as a coherent whole. His show was regarded as a one-liner, and so were the fragments of his broader career that floated across from Europe, usually inaccurately. There was little sense of his work overall, either its varied sensual appeal or its deep-structure and swift intellectual interplay; his reputation solidified around a series of Neo-Dada art jokes.

Klein had leapt past the American consciousness too quickly, and never had a chance to set it right. A year after his visit to America, he died of a heart attack at the age of 34. In the seven years before his death he produced over a thousand art objects in various media, as well as many prophetic works of nonstatic art, and numerous writings. His oeuvre has a maze-like coherence, with circular corridors and cul-de-sacs deliberately built into it. While rooted in Late Modernism, its principal thrust was anti-Modernist. It includes objects and events in all media, interpenetrated, mutually referenced, and carefully layered into a semantic stack.

It was Jean Tinguely who called Klein "Messenger of the Age of Space," meaning that he had come from the future to announce a new age. In art historical terms he might be renamed the Messenger of the Age of Anti-Art, who showed it forth in his own body to herald its dawning.

Klein was a dedicated craftsman (as well as a despiser of craft as an end in itself), and his works, even when conceptually anti-art, have a vivid and arresting sensual presence, a directness that, as Susan Sontag said in another context, "frees us from the itch to interpret."[5] But in this case it was the artist himself who was never freed from the itch to interpret. He overlaid on his physical works a set of semantic dictions and contradictions, in the forms of essays, gestures, symbolic events, and photographs, which interacted with the physical works on many levels. His project was an aggression against the fundamental premises of art as known.

Klein personally detested all existing art vocabularies and felt that, if only they could be terminated, far more powerful and elegant ones might be found. He saw himself at the turning point of two epochs—the "Messenger" of the incoming age, as Tinguely put it.[6] His ambition was to terminate the existing forms of art by revealing their inner contradictions and breaking down their boundaries; at the same time, he set out to discover, or at least to proclaim, the way toward the new ones. The complexity of such a project was not lost on Klein, who once dedicated an all-blue painting in an Italian miracle-cult shrine with the prayer: "May the Impossible arrive and establish its Kingdom *quickly*."[7]

In a sense, what happened to Klein's reputation in New York was an appropriate consequence of his challenging and enigmatic style. Though he is known in this country primarily for his blue monochrome paintings, his career as a whole can be described best as a sustained seven-year-long performance, and Joseph Kosuth says rightly that he fits into Conceptual Art "somewhere."[8] This indeterminate placement would have pleased the Painter of Space, who specialized in turning up "there" as soon as one had placed him "here." He was an escape artist among critics, the escape system symbolized by the famous Leap—an image of primary hermeneutical value for his career—through which he sought (among other things) to escape from all closed categories.

The New York School's descent into the underworld of mono-chromy, where the issues of Hell are worked out, portrays a voluntary confinement in a closed room: "Newman closed the door, Rothko pulled down the shade, and Reinhardt turned out the lights."[9] But if Yves the Monochrome (as he called himself) is added to the formula, it acquires a paradoxical dimension of both self-destruction and escape, both the ending of one age and the beginning of another: "Newman closed the door, Rothko pulled down the shade, Reinhardt turned out the lights, and Klein jumped out the window."

> *Lines, bars of a psychological prison...are our chains... They are*
> *our heredity, our education, our framework, our vices, our aspi-*
> *rations, our qualities, our wiles... Color, on the other hand, is free;*
> *it is instantly dissolved in space... And that is why, in my work,*
> *I refuse more and more emphatically the illusion of personality,*
> *the transient psychology of the linear, the formal, the structural.*
> *Evidently the subject I am traveling toward is space, pure Spirit...*
> *By saturating myself with the eternal limitless sensitivity of space,*
> *I return to Eden....* —YVES KLEIN[10]

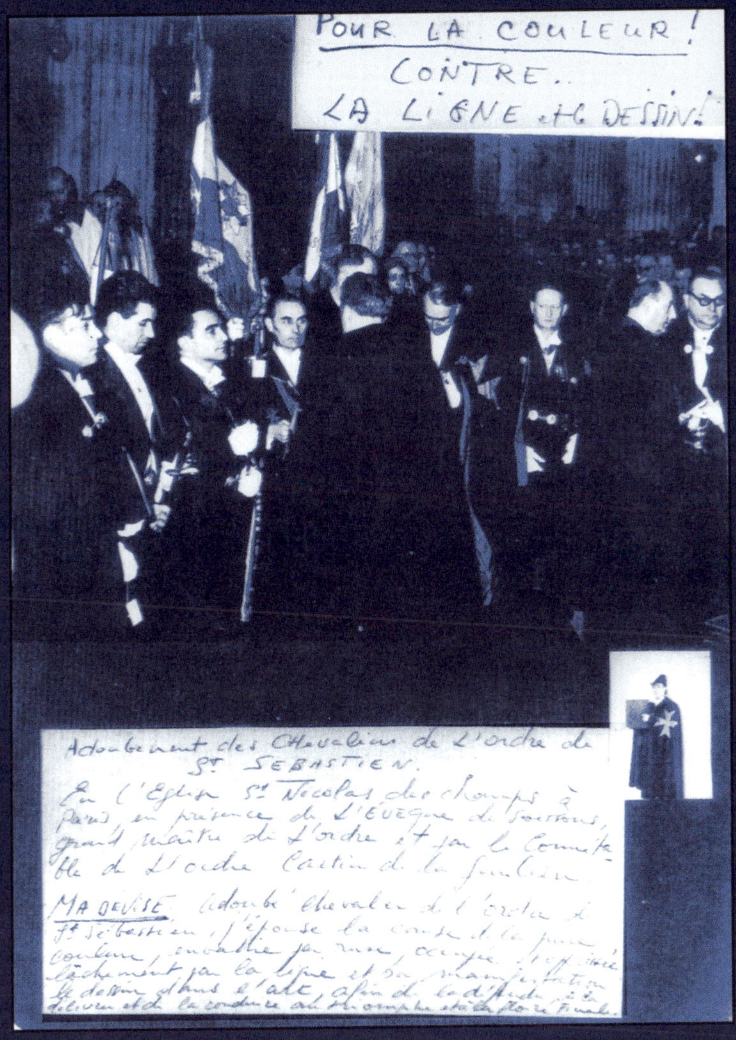

Yves Klein's Induction into the Knights of Saint Sebastian. *Inset:* Klein's declaration of himself as Champion of Color; Klein holding an IKB monochrome in the Saint Sebastian regalia. The text of the declaration reads: *Having been made a knight of the Order of Saint Sebastian, I espouse the cause of Pure Color, which has been invaded and occupied guilefully by the cowardly line and its manifestation, drawing in art. I will defend color, and I will deliver it, and I will lead it to final triumph.*

KLEIN'S WORK, LIKE BOTTICELLI'S,[11] INVOLVES A FULLY AR-
ticulated allegorical content arising from a traditional body of
metaphysics that the artist systematically translated into plastic
terms. This (bottom) level of the semantic stack was based on
the Rosicrucianism of Max Heindel, which Klein had studied
and practiced during six formative years of membership in the
Rosicrucian Society (see footnote page 80). Klein's commitment
to Rosicrucianism was probably strong during his adolescence,
but by the early to middle 1950s it had come to function as a
somewhat sardonic persona. His membership lapsed, never to
be renewed, but meanwhile certain Rosicrucian ideas had entered—again somewhat sardonically—his artwork.

In Heindel's version of theosophical cosmology, Spirit (or Life)
is identical with Space. It is represented by color (which, as Klein
wrote, is "free," because "it is instantly dissolved in space"), but
especially by the color blue; it is infinite expansiveness with no
internal divisions to affront its wholeness. Space/Spirit/Life permeates and contains all transient forms, thereby negating their
apparent differences and boundaries. Human evolution, according
to Heindel, is approaching the end of the age of form and solid
matter, and soon will reimmerse itself in an age of Space/Spirit/
Life that will restore the condition of Eden. This transition will involve the erasure of all boundaries, both outer (political, national,
occupational) and inner ("our heredity…education…framework…
vices…aspirations…qualities…wiles"). Accordingly the Age of
Space/Spirit will be a return from the entanglements of lines to
the openness of color, and especially of the Edenic/spiritual color:
Blue. Klein took on the role of Champion of Color.

When Klein, in his first major shows, exhibited identical blue
monochromes in Milan and Paris in 1957 under the title *L'epoca
blu* (The Blue Age, or Period), Pierre Restany wrote that the moment of confronting one of these all-blue paintings was a "moment
of truth."[12] The systematic Rosicrucianism of the works was one
aspect of this "moment": the viewer, in confronting an International Klein Blue monochrome, is staring into the depths of infinite
Space/Spirit itself, gazing, as it were, into the coming age of Eden.
But this "moment of truth" that Klein offered was more than the
confrontation with the Allness-of-Blue: it required, as his later

works make clear, the realization of higher levels of contradiction that rise out of the infinite when it is understood dialectically. (The All is made up *only* of contradiction—like Anaximander's *Apeiron* or the *Avatamsaka Sutra's* "Net of Indra.")

This dialectical critique was acted out on another semantic level as a critique of art theory. Before this new age can arrive—which Klein hoped to see in his own time—cultural codes must annihilate one another through their semantic and ethical contradictions, dissolving into the wholeness of Space. Klein's deliberate semiological inversions, subversions, and self-refutations are techniques to demonstrate this self-erasure as a meta-hermeneutics of the Leap. (In Zen meditation, which Klein had practiced both in France and in Japan, the Leap into the Void represents the moment of going beyond all codes and interpretations, into the void where, as the Buddhist Prajnaparamita texts say, "one stands firmly because one stands upon nothing.")[13] The Blue Age exhibitions focused his project of destructuring on the premises of painting.

[Monochromism is] a sort of modern day alchemy practiced by painters, born of the tension of experiencing...a bath in space vaster than infinity... It is the only physical way of painting which permits access to the spiritual absolute.... My monochrome paintings are landscapes of freedom...—YVES KLEIN[14]

KLEIN WAS AMONG THE FIRST TO FEEL UP AGAINST THE WALL about up-against-the-wall art. His monochromes, though powerful and alive within themselves, were attempts to destroy "the painting" as known and to pursue its sculptural and environmental transformations. (In this sense, as well, they foreshadow much work of the '60s and after.) Klein never accepted the basic premises that a painting, whether illusionistic, geometric, or tachist, was (1) a more or less passive two-dimensional plane that waits for you to approach it, and (2) a field for personal expression by the artist. He wanted his paintings to come off the wall and invade the viewer's sensibility in the most violent way—and at the same time to eliminate the driving force of personality from the event.

It is remarkable that Klein's monochromes, which at first glance seem to be among the simplest paintings ever made, are among the most complex. Deceptively austere at first, their physical presence grows strangely rich. The delicately varied surfaces and textures of one unvaried and vibrating blue (or gold, yellow, red, pink, white, black, green) elicit a subtle range of what Donald Judd called "an unmitigated, pure, but very sensuous beauty."[15]

But as this first moment of immersion in Klein's blueness fades into memory, the strong sensory impression convolutes into a question mark. Several of the qualities of these paintings are unusual: (1) they are hung on visible vertical supports some distance away from the wall, like sculptures; (2) their corners are rounded to stress their sculptural presence; (3) they are identical, like stamps, prints, or machine-made objects; (4) they are rollered, to remove any quality of personal touch. They seem to seek a zero degree of what was generally recognized as painting. On this level they are anti-paintings, functioning as critical forces as well as sensory immersions and prophetic allegories.

Besides alluding to Rosicrucian prophecy, the exhibition title ("The Blue Period") was a parody of art critical categories. Further, the paintings themselves were designed to confute category distinctions, and successive conceptual overlays (in Klein's writings) sought to remove them from the reach of all such terms as Minimal or Color Field. First was the Rosicrucian overlay. These paintings are Blue as Spirit-that-holds-all-things-dissolved-in-itself. And Blue Spirit does not just lie there. It invites you into it (invites you to *Leap)*, and even more it contains you already. It comes off the wall instantaneously, permeating the surroundings with its atmosphere, and "impregnates" you with itself as a new, undifferentiated sensibility.

But, next, the paintings are removed from conceptual allegory or claims of ensorcellment by their return, ironically, to direct representation: they are neither more nor less than portraits of the cloudless sky as seen through Klein's studio window. With this image, the abstract, the figurative, the minimal, and the allegorical are conflated into a single hugeness that opens in all directions behind, above, below, beside, and in front of the picture plane.

Through this series of interpretive devices provided by the artist himself, the paintings become environments; more than limited environments, they are the engulfing space in which the earth itself resides. No longer passive on the wall, they invite you, as does a window, to look—or even to Leap—into the question mark of the dark and featureless sky. The "moment of truth," then, is an existential confrontation rife with questions of courage and identity. ("Come with me into the void!")

In short, these paintings take a stand upon nothingness. ("International Klein Blue" was later rechristened "International Klein Nothingness.") Exhibiting them, Klein asserted a role (the painter's) that his controlled interpretation at once denied. "My works are only the ashes of my art," he said, in a famous one liner whose reverberations can still be felt in European art.[16]

Seen in this way (as the artist directed us to see them), the blue paintings are an ethical imperative: it is not the window that is important, but the Leap through it. Not the abyss, but the entering of the abyss. Not the eros of Space/Spirit/Life, but the impregnation by it.

> *[Artists who] wish to save their personality at any cost will kill*
> *their spiritual selves and lose their LIFE. [Art] should be like an*
> *open channel for penetration by impregnation in the sensibilty of the*
> *immaterial space of LIFE itself...*—YVES KLEIN[17]

THE CIRCULARITY WITH WHICH KLEIN LEADS US THROUGH various possible interpretations of his work, each of them cancelling one or more of the others, is itself part of the work, giving it cognitive shape. Each series of pieces leads through conceptual circuitry to others, a system closing itself in full circle on one level of the semantic stack only to reopen on another. A recurring focus of the project was Klein's critique of the artist. On one semantic level all Klein's works are attempts to purify the art object of the "entanglements of lines" that are the artist's personality. The monochromes began it; but the hand on the paint roller was still too close to a signature. Other series seek to distance the artist even farther from his art.

The sponge works of 1957 and afterward are explicit mockeries of technique. "Painting is a mode of existence," Klein insisted; art

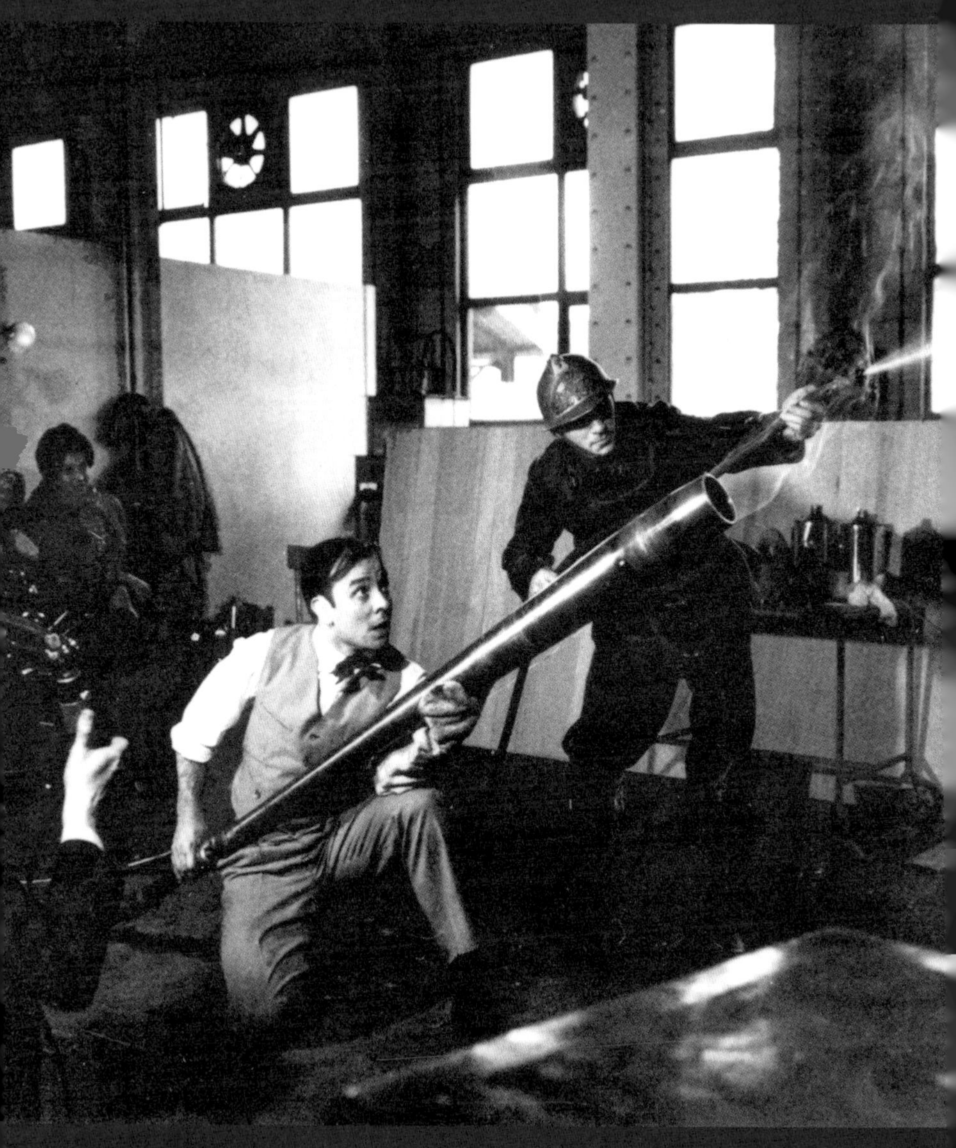

Yves Klein producing a fire painting, July 19, 1961,
Centre d'essai de Gaz de France, La Plaine Saint-Denis.

should be made as effortlessly as the sponge absorbs its color, and viewed with the same lack of resistance as the boundaries of the self are invaded by new sensibility. As Klein had identified his blue monochromes as "portraits" of the sky, similarly he regarded his "Sponge Sculptures" as "portraits" of the viewers of those paintings, who, whether they realized it or not, had been "impregnated" by Life/Space/Spirit vibrating off the rippled surfaces.

In other works the elimination of direct involvement of the artist was pursued on the analogy of alchemy, in which the magician is seen only as the helper of Nature. The "four elements" must be invited to express themselves directly, with a minimum of interference from the artist. Strapping a canvas to the roof of his car, Klein drove from Paris to Nice and back in the rain, capturing on the prepared surface "the mark of the rain, of the stirring of the atmosphere." At the Haus Lange in Krefeld he exhibited a "Fire Fountain" and "Fire Wall," which have echoes in much later art based on the manipulation of natural phenomena out-of-doors. In the Gaz de France building, with a helmeted fireman on hand, Klein "painted" with a flamethrower, later adding color selectively to some of the partly dematerialized canvases. In these "Fire Paintings" (of which well over a hundred were made) the satire of the artist's "signature" or "touch" was pressed to the limit and fused with the alchemical theme of the pursuit of the natural elements in their pure state. In their rich tattered surfaces one glimpses what Friedrich Nietzsche called, in reference to Wagner's work, the "voluptuousness of hell."

Klein's classic works of this type were the "Anthropometries of the Blue Age," first presented to the public in an evening performance before a seated audience in 1960. The artist, in formal dress and white gloves, directed the event without touching the materials. At his gesture, a string ensemble began playing his "Monotone-Silence Symphony" (a single D-major triad in second inversion to be played for 20 minutes, then followed by an equal period of silence). As he gestured again, naked girls appeared carrying pails of International Klein Blue paint. With his gestural guidance they applied the paint to their bodies (becoming "living brushes") and pressed themselves against huge sheets of paper. When the performance was over, the "Anthropometries"

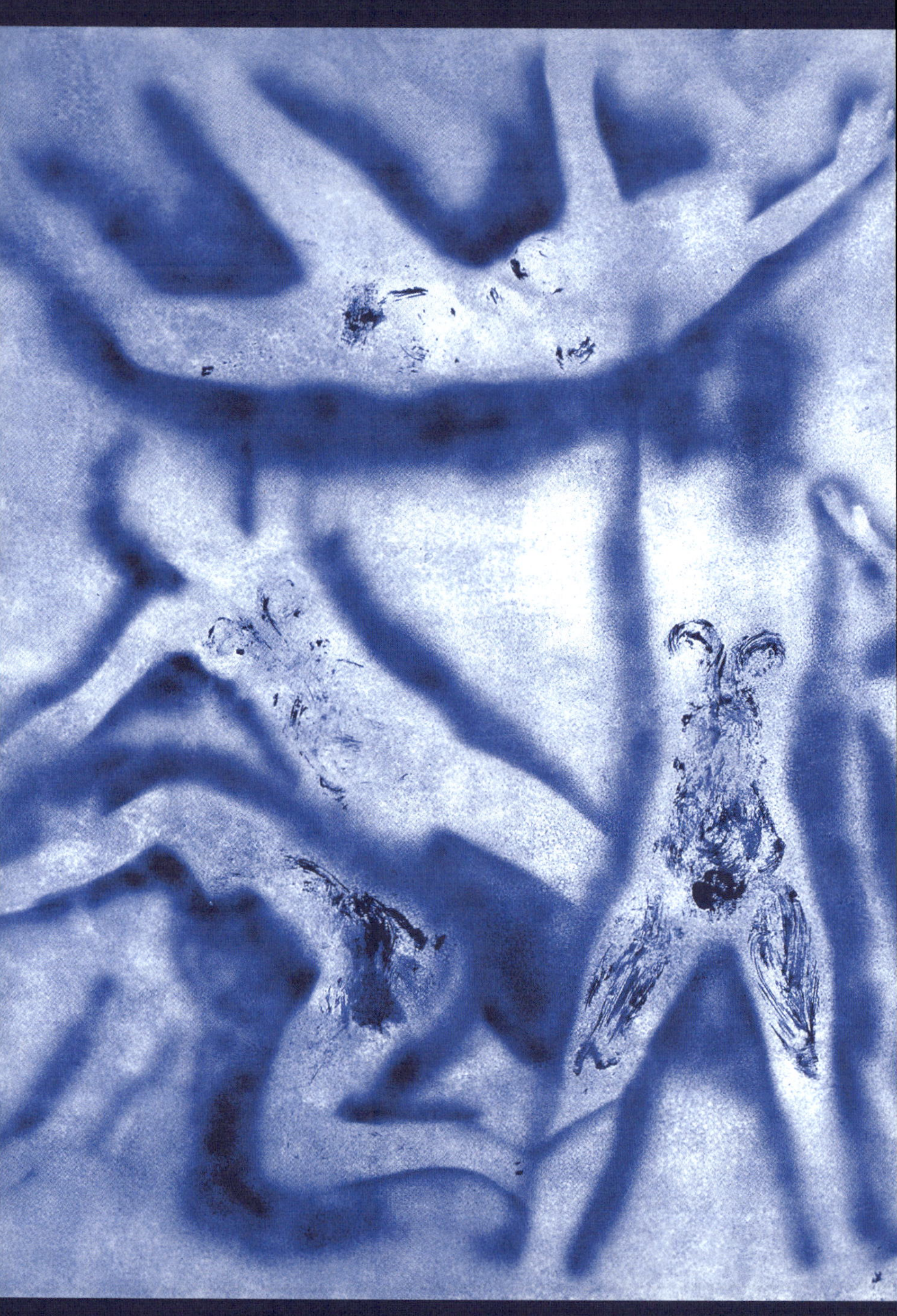

People Begin to Fly, 1961, anthropometry, 98½ x 157½".

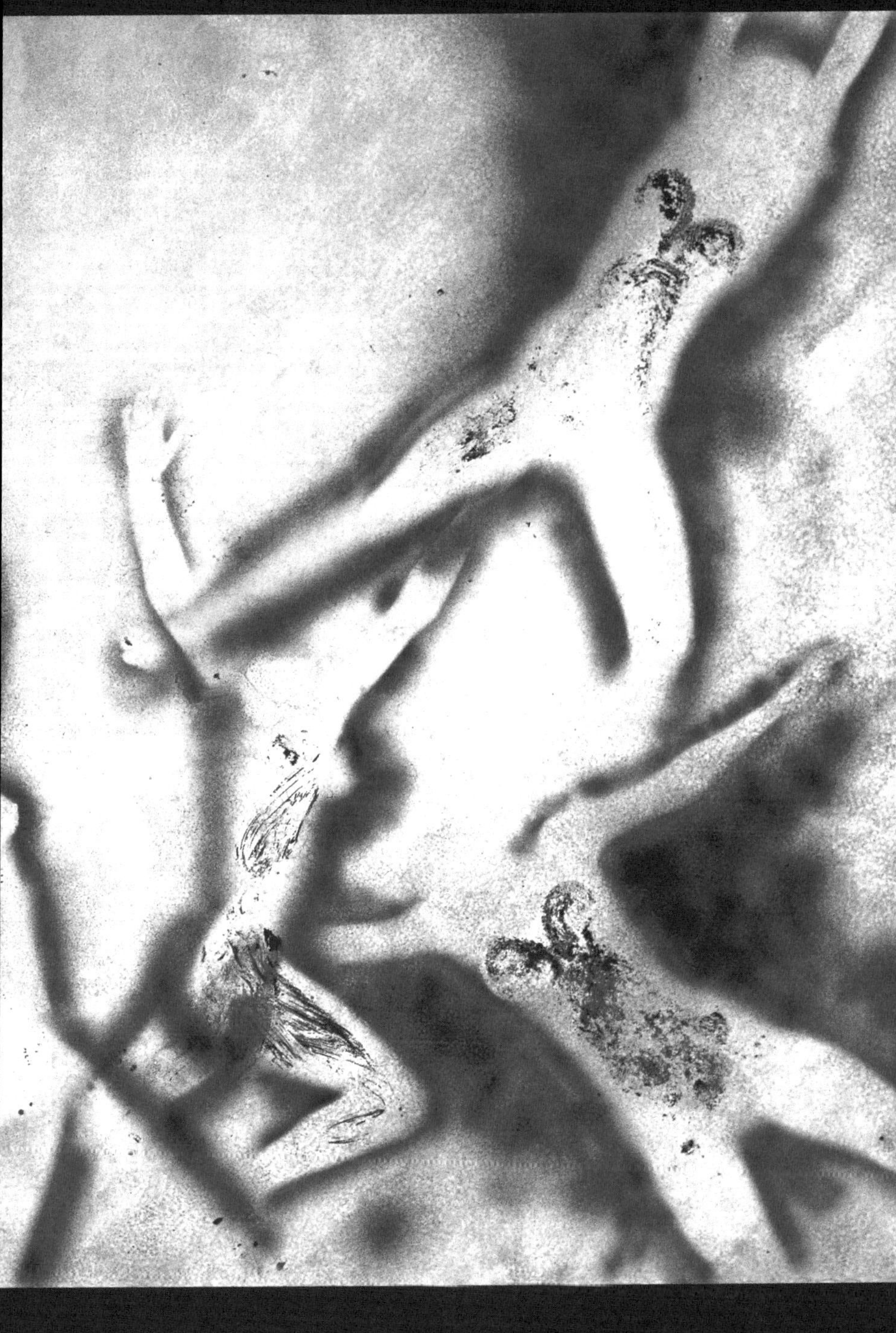

remained as "ashes" of the process. Klein made nearly two hundred of these "living brush" works, sometimes spraying paint selectively around the models to create negative prints.

The "Anthropometries," hovering ambiguously between the media of painting and print, restate Klein's rejection of genre categories. They may also be seen as parodies of the traditional craftsmanly art of the figure. But the anti-art aspect of these works is absorbed in turn by its opposite—an apparent affirmation of aesthetic value—through the living grace of the works themselves, which unlock the flat surface and drift or fly from the wall with a wispy transparency. The hollow centers and disintegrating edges of the figures invoke the theme of dematerialization, as their postures of flight, foreshadowing the age of levitation, return us to the Leap.

The theme of impregnation by Spirit mingles with the critique of art theory in a series of pieces that resist categorization. The International Klein Blue Nike of Samothrace expresses (by simultaneous appropriation and mockery) a rejection of the linear, masterpiece view of art history, and asserts (with blueness) the underlying sameness of all things. Appropriation, by blueness, of the Duchampian "Readymade" and oceanic dissolution of the boundaries between the art and non-art realms are also involved.

Klein's most commonly used personal title, "Yves the Monochrome," extends this universal impregnation to the artist and dissolves the boundaries between artist and art work as each is reciprocally absorbed into the other. If seen in terms of Conceptual and Performance Art, the adoption of the title was itself a "piece" or a "work," and as such it is characteristically self-canceling; the artist appropriates all space within himself, and at the same time, by designating himself an art object, takes his place as an object within space. A similar reading applies to the photograph of Klein gazing at an International Klein Blue globe of the world, which seems to float in midair: the world, which contains him, is appropriated by blueness and designated as a gallery object that he will display. The reciprocal appropriations and dissolutions of his works, his personae, and his world, form a shifting Conceptual/Performance piece whose inner life is the driving force of paradox and mutual containment.

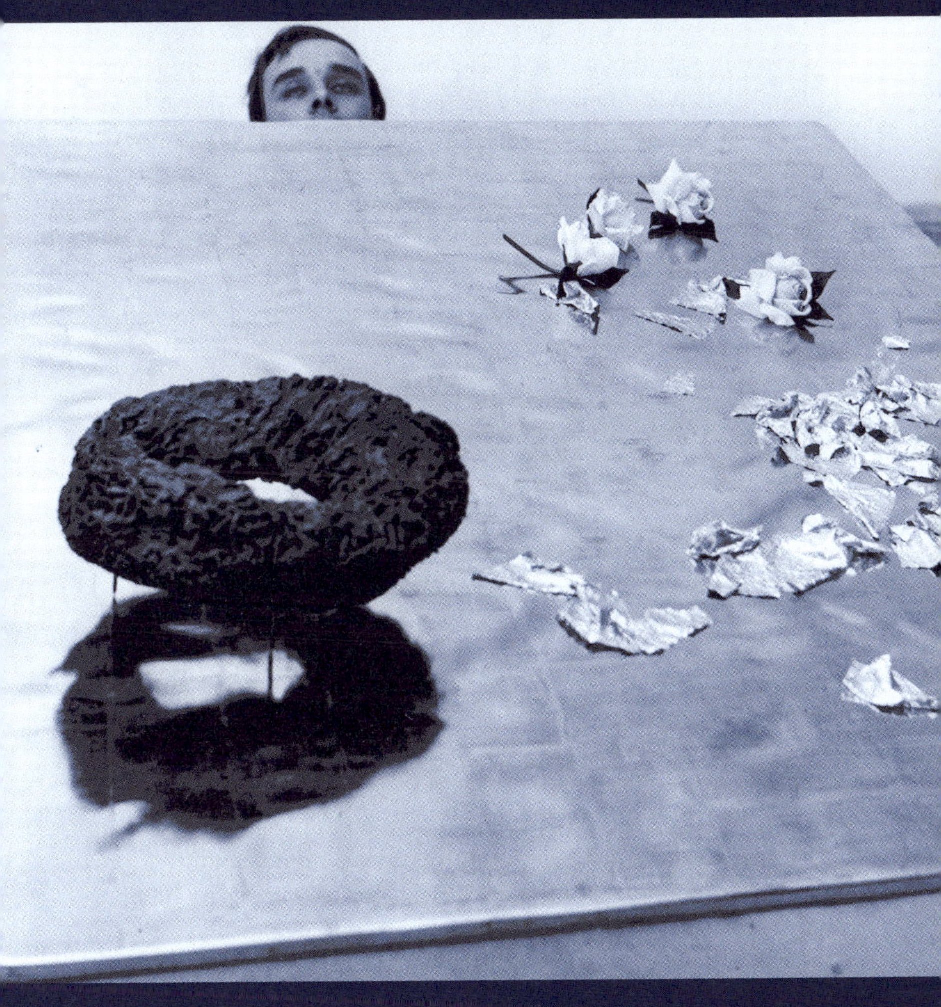

The Tomb—Here Lies Space, 1962.

For Klein all these works had the alchemical associations (rooted in Rosicrucian allegory) that culminated in the "Monogold" paintings, whose solemn and royal radiance suggests completion of the Great Work. Gold, alchemically, is a symbol of Spirit and as such equal to Space and a negation of separate individuality. One such work, *The Tomb—Here Lies Space* [*La Tombe—Ci-gît l'espace*], was the site of Klein's ritual burial in 1962 (just three months before his actual death). The photographed event—in which, characteristically, art object, Performance, and Conceptual piece are conflated—restates the theme of ego-death and infinite expansion, of the Leap beyond signature: "Here Lies Space," says the title; but it is Klein himself who lies buried there. By rejecting his personality and its role as artist, the artist has opened himself to the fullness of Space.

> *In our present materialistic period we have unfortunately lost the idea of all that lies behind that word Space… we have entirely lost the grand and holy significance of the word…. To the Rosicrucians, as to any occult school… space is* Spirit *in its attenuated form, while matter is crystallized space or Spirit.* —MAX HEINDEL[18]

> *I seek above all…to create…this transparence, this void immeasurable in which lives the Spirit permanent and absolute, freed from all dimensions…. The absolute void…is entirely naturally the true pictorial space.*
> *Space has given me the right to be its "Proprietor"…and has consented to manifest its presence in my paintings…my documents, my gestures.*
> *The Void belongs to me.* —YVES KLEIN[19]

THE HYPOTHETICAL ENVIRONMENT POSTULATED BY KLEIN'S conceptually expanded monochromes was Space itself. Painting was terminated (hypothetically) by dissolving/expanding it into volumetric ambience. But whereas Blue, according to Heindel, is the filmiest coagulation of Spirit that can be perceived by the senses, transparent space is more direct: it *is* Spirit itself. The artists of the incoming age, Heindel had said, will create immaterial works out of transparent space, which they will mold into specific configurations by projecting mental images onto it. These works will possess Life and radiate a more intense spiritual force than any material work has attained.

Klein had practiced Heindel's visualizations during his years in the Rosicrucian Society. In 1958, as the artist of the future, he began to act out this aspect of Heindel's prophecy, making, exhibiting, and offering for sale immaterial works in "the true pictorial space" of the Void. As always, the prophetic content was only one strand of his encompassing semantic net, beside a sophisticated critique of art, art history, and the artist as a self.

In April 1958, Klein presented the classic exhibition, *Specialization of Sensibility from the State of Prime Matter to the State of Stabilized Pictorial Sensibility*, known as *The Void (Le Vide)*, in which the Galerie Iris Clert in Paris was emptied of furniture, painted white, and exhibited empty. Neither "exhibition" nor "environment" quite describes this piece, which like all of his work hangs carefully on the interfaces between categories. As his paintings were conceptually expanded into environments, his environment flowed over its boundaries into the zone of the performance, and the performance in turn transgressed the proscenium arch and entered politics. At the same time, the anti-art gesture of exhibiting an empty gallery was tinged with something like the theosophical feeling that somewhat hiddenly underlay Late Modernism.

The invitations to *The Void* were mailed with International Klein Blue stamps, preempting government in the name of the Blue Revolution (and also presaging Mail Art). Two days before the opening, the windows of the Galerie Iris Clert were painted International Klein Blue, and an International Klein Blue canopy appeared before the entrance. Passing beneath it, Klein closed himself into the now-secret space, which no one else would enter until the opening. "Working carefully, as on a large picture," he painted the interior walls white to return the gallery space (through sympathetic magic) to the state of Prime Matter. Then he projected mental images onto the transparent space, creating immaterial paintings that were "stabilized" in mid-air by prolonged concentration. Meanwhile, his own presence filled the space with "an abstract but real palpable density existing and living in the space by and for itself."[20] The atmosphere of the place had now been purified, thickened, complexified, and stilled.

By prearrangement, Republican Guards in full array flanked

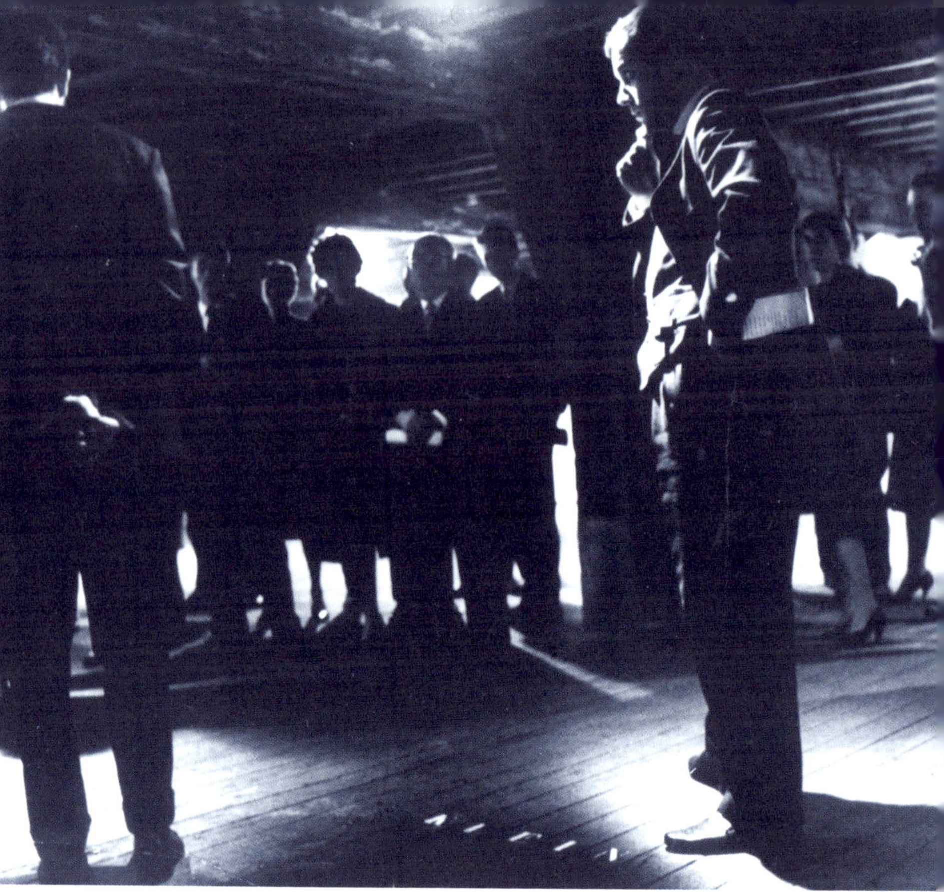

the canopied entrance at the hour of the opening, implying the presence of a government in the void space where Klein waited alone. As guests arrived they were served an International Klein Blue cocktail (gin, Cointreau, methylene blue) that would cause them to urinate blue for a week (a sign of their impregnation by Space); then they were allowed inside in groups of ten or fewer.

For one night it seemed that the whole Paris art world was eager to Leap into International Klein Nothingness. By 10:00 p.m. the narrow rue des Beaux Arts was jammed with two to three thousand people. Police and fire trucks were called to disperse the crowd. Inside, the Painter of Space bargained over immaterial paintings, concluding two sales. In a speech delivered about 1:00 a.m. at the famous Left Bank café La Coupole, he declared "in my modest person…four millennia of civilization have found their exhaustive conclusion."[21]

Like his gallery objects, Klein's immaterial works radiate meaning through various semantic directions and levels. The Rosicrucian allegory, as always, is obvious: it is an acting out of Heindel's prophecy of the imminent dematerialization of culture. But at the same time the facetious procedure of selling "pieces" of infinity subverts the Rosicrucian seriousness of the event, and the inner contradiction forces a semantic Leap to another level. On this new level also absences are reified. The act of displaying the gallery in which art works are seen rather than the works themselves follows from the Wittgensteinian/Duchampian "contextual" or "usage" definition of art. If placing an object in an art context, or otherwise designating it as art, makes it art, then it is in the context or designation, and not in the object, that the art-essence resides, and it is the context itself that should be exhibited, not an object within it. On this semantic level, *The Void* was a derisive critique of the art object, the art business, and the role of the artist. (In fact, Klein also reduces the Duchampian example to absurdity, by involving it in an infinite regress: the context is put in a context.) Spiraling down the semantic stack, this critique returns us to Klein's serious Rosicrucian strain: Space/Spirit is everywhere, he explained in an interview with Pierre Restany; it permeates the picture, the viewer, the gallery, the city, the universe. This permeation trivializes distinctions among objects and reveals the conventional art work as a mere entanglement of lines, desecrating both inner and outer space.

The Void, like *The Leap*, points toward the empty center of Klein's labyrinth, where all boundaries and divisions are dissolved. For Klein, the boundaries between art media and genres (abstract/figurative, concept/object, and so forth), or the wider boundary between art and life, were internal divisions within the stuff of Spirit by which the tangled self is strapped and bound. They were affronts to Life, which should be boundless like the sky through which the Painter of Space leaps into effortless flight. He parodied one boundaried zone after another, while contradictorily laying claim to each in turn. He invited all interpretations, in order to destroy them all. It is this, finally, that makes the moment of confronting his works a "moment of truth." And it is this (or so the Painter of Space hoped) that makes the attempt to categorize them impossible, because self-contradictory. Ancient mystical images of the knife trying to cut itself apply. By insisting, in his conceptual overlays, that each of his works drives past its own boundaries into the infinite, Klein extended them beyond the reach of differentiation and interpretation. By such strategy he hoped to terminate in his own person the entire preceding age of cultural evolution.

> *At the end of our present Epoch the highest initiate will appear publicly when a sufficient number of ordinary humanity desire and will voluntarily subject themselves to such a leader.... After that time races and nations will cease to exist. Humanity will form one spiritual fellowship.... Before a new Epoch is ushered in...the physical features of the earth will be changed and its density decreased.*
>
> —MAX HEINDEL[22]

KLEIN'S ATTEMPT TO WRAP ALL ART FORMS IN A NEST OF mutual containments reaches necessarily beyond art into politics: all boundaries and divisions are affronts to Pure Color and the Monochrome Spirit. (*The Void* had already inaugurated the age of Space.) In 1958 Klein sent a letter to President Eisenhower (Mail Art again) informing him of the termination of the French national government by the Blue Revolution. In the next year he undertook Heindel's project of decreasing the density of the environment for the age of spaced-out humans, in which levitation would replace gravitation. The "Architecture of the Air"—houses built of compressed air currents in which levitating humans would live in Edenic closeness to nature, passing through boundaries at will—was to be followed by the creation of a controlled climate over all of France. In a commingling of art and politics that prefigures certain of Joseph Beuys's activities, Klein exhibited maquette drawings for these projects at the Musée des Arts Décoratifs; and, in conjunction with the architect Werner Ruhnau, he carried out industrial experiments (which failed to produce the air roof). In 1959 Klein presented at the Sorbonne his plans for a World Center of Sensibility that would make obsolete the archaic educational modes of the age of matter and would prepare humanity for the age of space.

These gestures, or Conceptual Performance pieces, locate themselves, as usual, at a shifting place between art and politics. For Klein, the boundary between art and government, or art and science, was as petty and irksome as that between, say, geometric and figurative painting. Beginning in 1959, he acted out the establishment of the post-governmental age by the systematic selling of *Immaterial Zones of Pictorial Sensibility*, that is, blocks of the Void—immaterial real estate of the age of Space, paid for in the timeless currency, gold.

Meeting Klein on a bank of the Seine, the buyer paid pure gold (a different weight for each Zone) to the artist, who gave him a signed receipt. Then the buyer burned the receipt while Klein threw half of the gold into the river, to return it to the matrix of potentiality. Only then was the Zone permanently relinquished by the Proprietor of Space and transferred to the buyer, who was left with no visible object or documentation except—in some cases—photographs. The "relinquishments" satirize the business of art and the sanctity of the art object, which is falsely predicated on its alleged separation from Life.

In the same year, as the first citizen of the age of space, Klein participated immaterially in a group show in Antwerp, projecting a mental vibration into the space reserved for his work, then returning to Paris.

And the kaleidoscope of his interacting elements continued to shift. As Klein's paintings flowed over into conceptual environments, and his environments into political strategies, so his political pieces flowed into the zone of revolutionary theater—a theater that attempts to overleap all divisions and establish the "Kingdom of the Impossible *quickly.*"

> *The theater which I propose is not only the city of Paris, but is also the countryside, the desert, the mountains, even the sky, in fact, the whole universe.*
> *Why not?—*YVES KLEIN[23]

KLEIN'S ASPIRATION TO RID THE WORLD OF ART—AS OF ALL boundaried safe-zones—led him to postulate the whole universe as simultaneously his studio, his material, and his stage. The dateline of his personal *Newspaper of a Single Day* read: "Yves

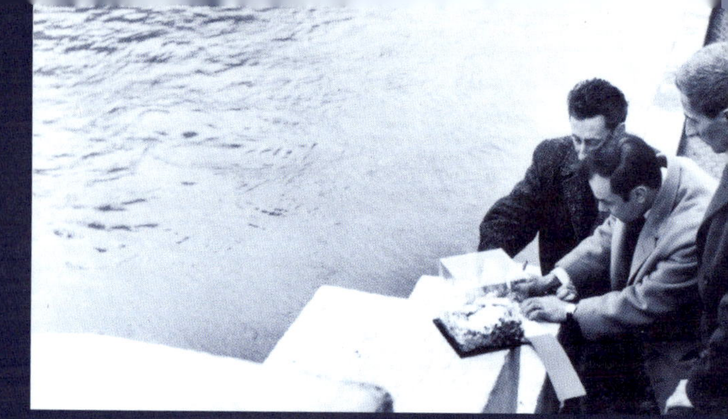

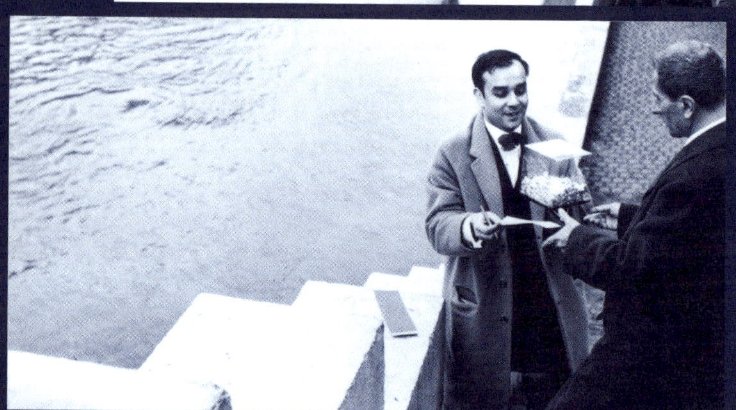

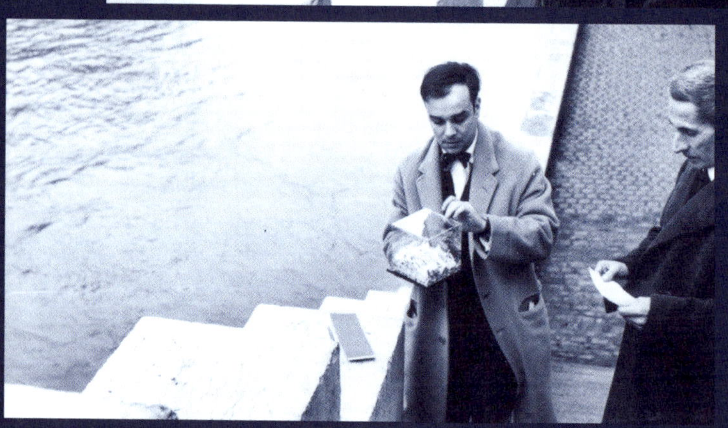

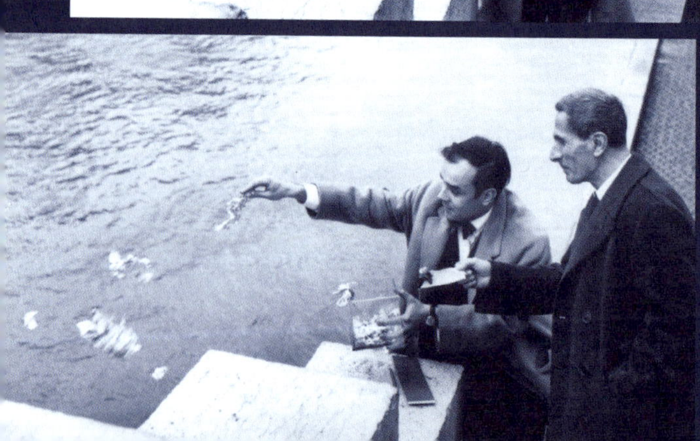

The ritual for an *Immaterial Zone of Pictorial Sensibility*. Klein with the writer Dino Buzatti, Paris, January 1962.

Klein presents Sunday, November 27, 1960." It is virtually a *Fiat lux!* The artist, through his power to designate-as-art, has become godlike. He transposes entities at will across the perpetually dissolving boundary between art and life. For one day, the lead story read, every person in the world was cast as both actor and spectator in Yves Klein's Theater of the Void. It was "an historic day for the theater," which now included everything. All distinctions between art and life were suspended as their arenas became coextensive. The world was an art work, or theatrical production, because it had been designated as such, the designation then being offered as Klein's "piece" to the Festival d'Art d'Avant-garde. Piero Manzoni's *Base of the World* and other works of Conceptual Art involving universal appropriation follow from this prototype. The world is, for a "moment of truth," "made strange," "defamiliarized" (in Viktor Shklovsky's terms); a Brechtian alienation device is placed as a framework around the All.

Klein correctly wrote on the front page of his newspaper that the Theater of the Void was "the culmination of my theories." Characteristically, this culmination does not assume a fixed form; the rest of the newspaper restates the vision in constantly changing terms. In his theater of Life the actors are "to live a constant art exhibition, to know the permanence of being, to be here, there, everywhere," like the constantly moving, and escaping, artist of the future (who instead of going underground went to the sky). In one of the many unrealized theatrical projects described in these pages, the theater is to remain permanently empty—empty subscribers' chairs facing an empty stage. Each night at eight the lights will go up and the curtain open on the empty stage. Actors hired for the event will be apprised of its nature, then will drift back into the world to portray human beings, with a new sense of the solemnity of this role. As new ones are constantly hired to replace them, the process of reversing art and life will move onward through the world. The world is asked, in effect, to throw itself toward freedom, into the void, like the Painter of Space who, having repealed the law of gravity, Leaps jauntily upward in the front-page photograph.

·   ·   ·   ·   ·

> *Today anyone who paints space must actually go into space to
> paint, but he must go there without any faking, and...by his own
> means: in a word, he must be capable of levitating...*
>
> *I have opened to the monochrome space...into the immeasurable
> pictorial sensibility.... I have felt myself, volumetrically impreg-
> nated, outside of all proportions and dimensions, in the ALL. I have
> encountered, or rather been seized by the presence of, the inhabit-
> ants of space—and none of them was human: no one had gone there
> before me. —*YVES KLEIN[24]

FOR KLEIN, LEVITATION, OR BODILY FLIGHT, WAS THE MOST
revolutionary of all acts. And as such it must deal in paradox and
circularity, which were the weapons of Klein's insurrection. Even
his famous Leap is tangled, on the front page of his newspaper,
in self-referential circularity. The caption above the photograph
says: "A Man in Space"; and below, in the only other photograph
on the page, one of Klein's blue monochromes is reproduced, in
black and white, with the caption: "Space Itself." That is: he Leaps
into his own painting, which is the open window leading out of
the closed room of art and the self. But leading to where? In the
photograph there is nothing but hard pavement beneath him.

In Paris in 1960 the rumor quickly spread that the Leap made
famous by the photograph was performed over a net, the upper
half of the scene then being montaged onto a lower half in which
the camera, in the same setup, had photographed the empty street.
Firsthand inspection of a print made directly from the negative
confirms this rumor, and original photographs including the
catchers have come to light.[25]

But the question does not end there and is not, in terms of
Klein's career, a trivial one. In a sense, the final definition of
Klein's intentions rests on the question of the historicity of this
"practical demonstration of levitation" (as he called it). Was he
sufficiently detached from his revolutionary theater to create it
out of conceptual whole cloth? Or was his dedication to his symbolic gestures so complete as to require the bone-crunching fall
after the devil-may-care "moment of truth" in mid-air? Clearly,
Klein believed that in some cases it did not matter whether his
projects were physically realized. But the Leap, in fact, was not

one of those cases. A recent investigation of all evidence, including interviews of all known witnesses, indicates that Klein did indeed make his Leap originally (in January 1960) above pavement alone, only later reenacting it over a net for the cameras.[26]

Here Klein's art stands firmly upon nothingness. The Leap opens vacancies at all levels of his intricate intentionality: the photograph, as a "trace of the immediate" (a term with which Klein described many of his works), indicts the art object as unreal. The locus of art is Life, the untrammeled expression of the immediate; the objects left behind are as dead as ashes and as distant as a photograph of a reenactment. For Klein, it was "indecent and obscene" to call objects outside oneself art; the artist is the location of the art event. "Painting is a mode of existence," he wrote; "the fact that I exist as a painter will be the foremost pictorial event of our time." In the Leap more plainly than in any other work, we see what he meant by *existing as* a painter. Aware of his responsibility, the man of the future ushers in the age of Space, demonstrating definitively the overleaping of all limitations.

> *I am proposing to artists that they pass by art itself and work individually on the return to real life, the life in which a man no longer thinks he is the center of the universe, but in which the universe is the center of each man.*

Klein then utters a prophecy that has something in common with Duchamp's prophecy (of about the same time) that the artist of the future would go underground:

> *The true painter of the future will be a mute poet who will write nothing but recount, without detail and in silence, an immense picture without limit.*—YVES KLEIN[27]

KLEIN ATTEMPTED TO TERMINATE CRITICAL CATEGORIES BY emptying them into one another. This approach was in part an attack on Modernism (which seemed old-fashioned to him), specifically on Modernism's attempt to erase content by selective seeing. In his work, form and content are not treated as two entities, of which it is feasible (or even possible) to elevate one above the other, but as a single bipolar continuum where the reality of each pole is continually passing into its opposite. Through selective seeing it is of course possible to focus on one end of the continuum alone (and that practice is at times useful); but it is not possible to rank them since each is equally dependent on the other. The two terms in fact form a dependent pair, like left/right, up/down, inside/outside, yes/no: neither element in such a structure can be real in a universe in which the other is not equally real. Like two sticks leaning on each other, if one is removed, the other falls too.

Klein's insistence on content ran counter to the zeitgeist of his time, which can be represented, for example, by Clement Greenberg's insistence that "a modernist work of art, must try, in principle, to avoid dependence upon any order of experience not given in the most essentially construed nature of its medium."[28] Clearly Klein's insistence on the prophetic level of his work violates this "principle." But on the other hand, Klein was very conscious of critical attitudes, and his work conspicuously fulfills the Modernist imperative that the artist's attention should turn "in upon the medium of his own craft."[29] There is, as always, reason to his duplicity.

The essentially dialectical nature of his work, in which content not only dissolves into form (as Greenberg and other formalists advised), but form into content as well, combines iconological allegorism with avant-garde criticism of the medium. Like a dedicated reductionist, he erases traditional signifying devices; then, playing the constructionist, he encodes this erasure as itself a signifier—of Prime Matter, or zero-expression—in a traditional metaphysical system. Dialectical balance affirms each limb and thus negates each by affirming the other. As in the ancient "Epimenides" paradox: if yes then no, and if no then yes. Klein empties the work while filling it, and fills it while emptying it. Paradox and circularity emerge as strategies to transcend the given terms, to reject the critical attitude that postulated an antinomy between them in the first place.

To a certain extent Klein, like Manzoni and Beuys, belongs in what some critics have called the Other Tradition in modern art—the tradition of artists whose work involves "extra-art [or anti-art] ambitions."[30] But this category also is of limited relevance. As always, it is difficult to say where Klein "belongs." He seems to have rendered dialectical the very distinction between formalist

Modernism and the Other Tradition, allowing each a place in his work so that each could destroy the other, attempting to point toward an art beyond these and all other critical distinctions.

The question of content, slightly contracted, becomes a question of the place of the artist's intentions. Klein attempted to conflate his intentions (expressed through essays, interviews, symbolic photographs, events, and rumors) and his "works," to put them on a single footing as equal and mutually interacting parts of a metastructure. Before the legitimacy of this tactic can be determined, it is necessary to answer a prior question: where does the artwork end (and who is to draw the line)?

Is the monochrome painting inside the artwork, and the photograph of Klein, in knight's suit, holding the same monochrome and preparing to do war against Line, outside of it? Is the text that Klein wrote to accompany this photograph inside or outside of the artwork? Are his various essays on the monochrome idea, and the titles of his shows, with their allusions to Heindel, inside or outside of it?

It should be remembered that in such questions we are not dealing with essences but merely specifying the rules by which the game is to be played. A few years after Klein's death—after the recognition of Conceptual Art and Performance Art as legitimate mediums—gestures, events, and writings could be catalogued or "indexed" into the status of art works.[31] Klein's own practice, foreshadowing the conventions of Conceptual and Performance Art, assumed that his photographed gestures and poses, his published writings, and his monochromes and other physical works were all inside the artwork, as interacting parts of it. The work itself was the set of complex interactions among these elements, not any one element to the exclusion of the others. Klein's idea was to fuse concept and sensum so that each would lose autonomy and the work become a vast shifting structure involving both conceptual and sensory elements in a meta-system. Insofar as his age was undergoing a transition from a sensory to an ideational aesthetic,[32] then Klein was indeed, as Tinguely called him, a Messenger of the incoming age.

Klein's strategy of placing concept and sensum in interaction was designed to compensate for the weaknesses that he felt were inherent in a purely sensory art. The zeitgeist had argued that abstract art has only semiotic, and not semantic, ability. It can refer around within itself, in a nonverbal sign system that a so-called faculty of taste then receives, decodes (nonconceptually), and appraises, but it cannot refer outside itself, and it can make no bridge with the world. It is, in short, artificially isolated and as such, to Klein, an affront to the wholeness of Life.

Faced with an art that (supposedly) lacked semantic ability, formalists accepted the consequences and focused on morphology, neglecting (or claiming to neglect) all conceptual overlays as outside the work. Klein made the Other Decision: to reject art as presently known and restructure it in a corrective meta-system that would restore its semantic capability. And lest this restructuring become reactionary, he submitted it in turn to a dialectical destructuring through inner contradictions.

A fundamental question is raised by these conflicting decisions. Critical insistence that the artist's intentions are separate from, or outside of, his works (and vice versa) may be merely self-indulgence on the part of the critic, who wishes to replace the artist as the creator of content. (For all criticism, no matter how formalist, has contentual implications.) From this point of view, perhaps the soundest critical strategy would be to regard everything that the artist deliberately presents to the public as inside the work. But from the formalist critic's point of view, Klein's attempt to saturate his works with his intentions may also be seen (as it has been in Duchamp's case) as a strategy to distract attention from their possible deficiencies, by clouding the critical gaze with intermediary concepts. Inevitably, the adherents of this latter view must emphasize, perhaps hopelessly, questions of appraisal (the faculty of taste) rather than of explication.

Like Duchamp, Klein despised the faculty of taste because its decisions are so variable. Produced, he reasoned, by cultural conditioning rather than by nature, they will be trivialized, or even rendered absurd, by the passage of time and the ascendancy of different cultural codes. In fact, the problem goes even deeper, since questions of taste are not tactically answerable; they are distanced, perhaps infinitely, by prior questions that they beg (and that in turn beg others). We must first decide, for example, about the place of the artist's intentions, the limits of the art realm, and so forth. And these decisions in turn must fall back upon the faculty of taste—or habit, or entanglements of lines—for these questions also beg others. For example, is the mind only a user of sense-data? Or is it also (as Buddhist psychology teaches) a sense in itself, with its own sense objects (concepts), and its own quite legitimate aesthetic delight in them? And that question in turn begs others.

Jean Tinguely called Klein "the greatest provocateur I have ever known."[33] And surely Klein's work, while answering every question, questions every answer, provocatively. This winding dialectical path leads, through infinite regress, to an unbounded free zone. Inner space opens with the realization that (as an ancient artist of the dialectic proclaimed), "Every opinion is nullified by an equal and opposite opinion."[34] Or, as Yves Klein the Provocateur put it: "It is necessary to be like untamed fire; it is necessary to contradict yourself."[35]

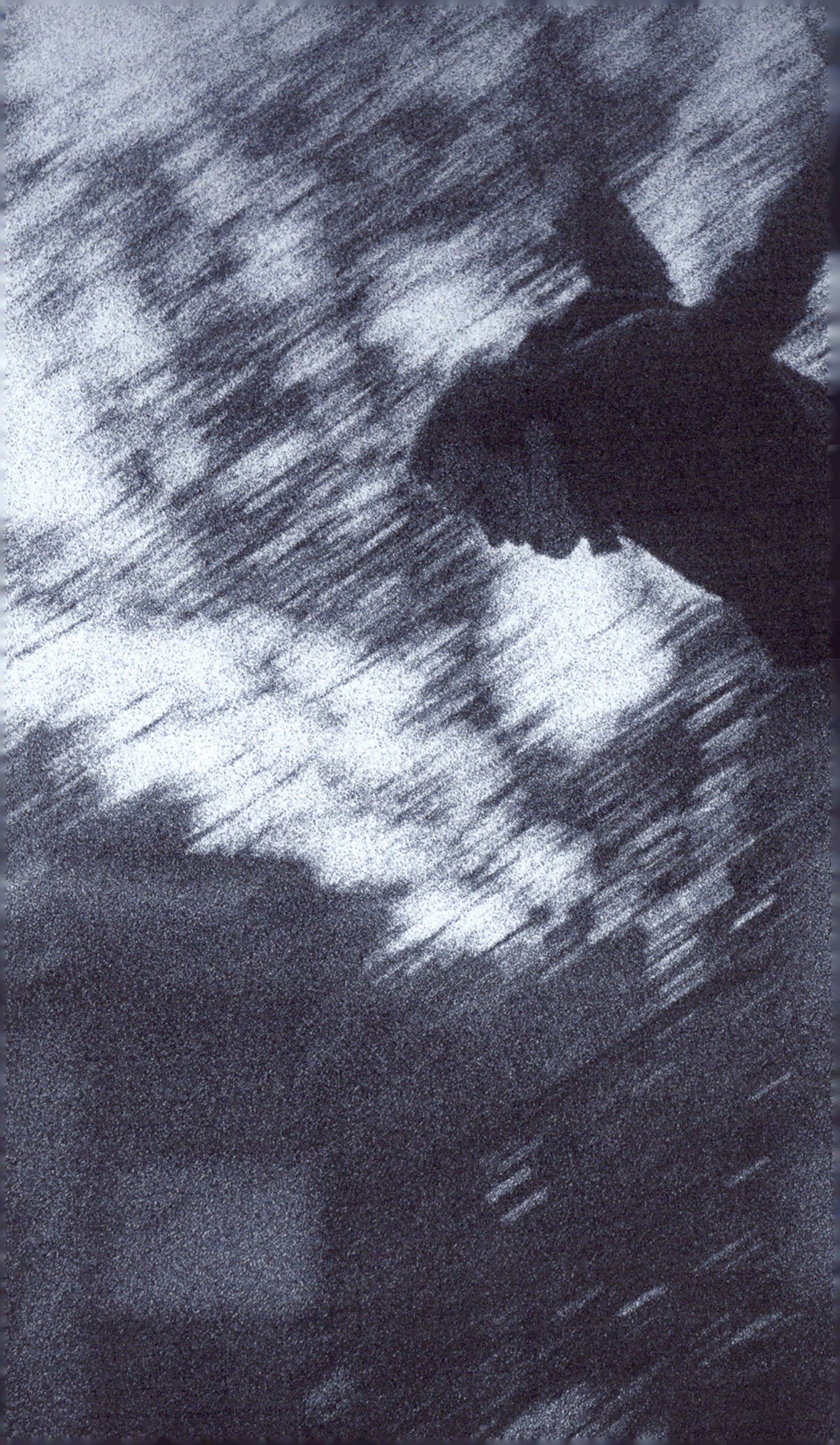

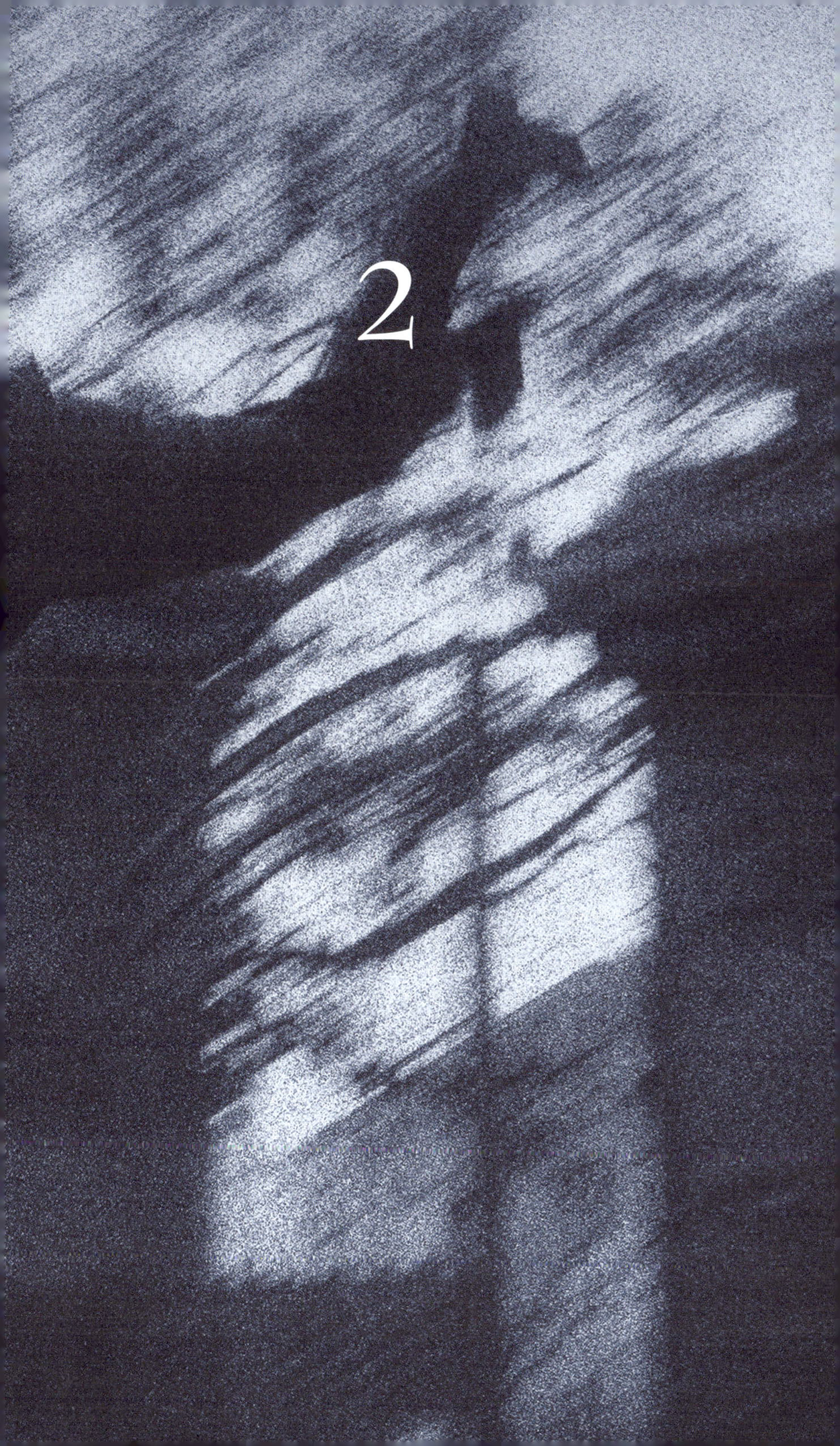
2

Yves Klein died prematurely. He is almost a heroic figure to the postwar art world of Europe. Legends and controversy still surround the artist and his extraordinary career....His life was a symbolic poetic act.

KYNASTON McSHINE[1]

Unlike most artists, Yves Klein was not inferior to his works. We consider them as the highlights of an exceptional adventure and to a large extent they bear witness to this adventure. But of many other stages only memories remain. For Yves Klein took as much trouble with what was to disappear as with what was to endure. That's why it's not proper only to show his paintings, his weldings, his prints, his fires, his golds; one must also try to recount that part of his work whose traces exist only in memory.

PIERRE DESCARGUES[2]

His influence has been exerted not so much through his paintings as through the character of his activities generally.

MICHAEL COMPTON[3]

He was like one who, in a state of sudden intoxication, fills life with meaning to the point of overflowing.

GIULIANO MARTANO[4]

It is not easy to follow him into his innermost spaces.... He had his own ideas, his own drunkenness.

PAUL WEMBER[5]

He didn't paint to paint, but to reveal his truth.... To grasp it, one has to...enter into his game.

PIERRE RESTANY[6]

Yves Klein:
Conquistador of the Void

1

*The painter only has to paint one masterpiece,
himself, constantly.*

YVES KLEIN

Yves klein was a myth-making artist. he declared that his *manner of existence* would be the foremost artistic event of our time; and his strategy for realizing this goal involved the propagation of an explicit personal myth, left behind as the trace, or ashes, of his life. So brilliantly was this myth presented, with such daring, charm, and (usually) good humor, that it caught fire at once in the public imagination; yet its real shape, its sources, its purposes, and its relationship to his everyday life have not yet been made clear.

Klein was a craftsman of myth, working directly with it as an artist with his material. With both deliberation and flair, he acted out the fulfillment of an ancient prophecy by incorporating its symbols into his life as a series of ideographic Moments or Kratophanies; these he proffered to the public like Stations or Labors of a sacrificial monotheater, to mark the stages of his progress along a path of transcendence. When he showed himself, he was often in costume, acting out one current or another of his overflowing mythic energy. At one such Moment he was the apotheosized Yves the Monochrome, at others the Proprietor of Color, the Champion

[67]

of Color, the Conquistador of the Void. By such apparitions he hoped to install himself in the realm of the archetypes, all traces of personal origin concealed.

Klein's writings supported these visual Moments by evoking related literary codes. Sometimes the sorcerer's:

> *I have manipulated the forces of the void.*[7]

Sometimes the messiah's:

> *My original goal [was]…to restore the lost Eden.*[8]

Sometimes the mystic's:

> *I, without the "I," became one with life itself. All my gestures, movements, activities, creations, were this life, original or essential in itself.*[9]

But Klein's myth was not primarily a literary product; it was rooted in what he felt were the deficiencies of his life. For as Roland Barthes pointed out, no myth is innocent; each tries to force reality into a certain shape, for certain motives. And to conceal its motivation "myth has the task…of making contingency appear eternal."[10] Just so, the contingent Yves Marie Klein was gradually submerged beneath the eternalized Yves the Monochrome.

Still, despite the compelling obviousness of its motivation, such a myth is not altogether produced, as an object, by the decision of a subject. It has a momentum of its own, like a game which "draws the players into its own realm and fills them with its spirit. The player experiences the game as an overpowering reality."[11] And just so, again, the historical Yves Marie Klein experienced the mythical Yves the Monochrome with the overpowering reality of a game which he could not stop playing until it stopped playing him. The myth and the man, reciprocally, created one another.

It is not easy to enter into the processes of this extraordinary adventure. The appearance of eternality must be reduced back to contingency. And the lost Eden of the myth's original horizon must be reconstituted from within.

2

THE VILLAGE OF CAGNES-SUR-MER IN THE SOUTH OF FRANCE fills, in the early summer, with the odor of the mimosa groves, the cries of children released from school, and the arrivals of summer visitors from the cities. For generations artists have gathered there, drawn by the Mediterranean light, the beauty of the seashore and the countryside. Renoir painted there, Modigliani, Braque , Soutine, and others. It was to figure prominently in Yves Klein's life.

Yves' grandfather, a businessman from Hanover, was established in Java as a planter toward the end of the nineteenth century. There Fred Klein, Yves' father, was born of a Dutchwoman whose grandmother was Javanese. Educated in Europe, Fred Klein became, in his early twenties, a painter in a pointillist neoimpressionist mode—delicate landscapes with gamboling horses, Monet-like surfaces of water. In 1925, at age twenty-seven, he bought an old ruin on a hillside just behind Cagnes and spent his summers there, restoring it as a studio.

Yves' mother, Marie Raymond, was from a middle-class family in Nice (her grandfather a buyer of flowers for perfume makers, her father a pharmacist). Rose Raymond, Marie's sister, married a medical doctor who often vacationed in nearby Cagnes. When Marie was fifteen she accompanied her sister and brother-in-law when he was called to Cagnes to tend to an ailing artist. It was her first exposure to the artistic milieu, and at once she recognized her metier. Back in Nice she bought a box of paints and began to work. In the following summers she returned to Cagnes on her own. In July 1926, at age eighteen, she met Fred Klein in Cagnes at an outdoor party where a guitarist was playing. That October they were married in Nice, and she returned to Paris with him.

Soon—perhaps sooner than penniless young artists would have hoped—she was pregnant. The child was due in April 1928, but there was no money to pay a hospital and a doctor. Fred and Marie drove to Nice and awaited the event in Marie's sister's house, where Marie's brother-in-law, the doctor, could preside. Here, in the bosom of his mother's family, Yves Klein entered the world on April 28, 1928, when the sun was in Taurus and Gemini was on the eastern horizon.[†] A handsome baby with unusual eyes—the Javanese strain left an exotic touch—he was hugged to the breasts of grandmother, childless aunt, and mother.

Having no money to set up a household in Paris, the Kleins retired to the villa at nearby Cagnes, where Yves spent his first months in a paradisal ambience of sunlight, flowers, and relaxed country living. His father painted; his mother took a correspondence course to become a drawing teacher and worked sometimes in the decorative arts center in nearby Nice. But in Cagnes, Fred Klein could not make the contacts which would be necessary to start selling his work. "A charming man, but absolutely in the clouds"[12] (words which might later have been spoken of his son), he successfully resisted wage slavery all his life. As years passed, they would sell the furniture in the villa in Cagnes to buy food, parting even with the Japanese cloisonné vases cherished by

---

† In the late 'forties Klein became interested in astrology and cast some horoscopes. This in itself makes his own horoscope relevant, and it was interpreted for researcher Virginie de Caumont on March 16, 1981, by one M. Berthon. The most salient feature he noticed was precisely the "temperamental duality" between the sun sign, Taurus, and the ascendant sign, Gemini, which he describes as "very contradictory signs." "Taurus is a patient worker,...[but] Gemini always wants to give the impression of playing, of irony, of being at ease... I think there was a kind of humor in his lifestyle but this humor was not free: it leaned on...the Taurean universe, which is...slow, patient, industrious.... He had two personalities....[In addition] a triplicity of fire gives much exuberance, vitality, and self-confidence; and alongside it...there is Saturn squared with Mars in opposition to the ascendant; this is a cyclo-thymic or manic-depressive situation, with periods of low energy, depression, inhibition. At one moment one is dealing with a strong man, sure of himself,...at other moments a depressed man, who is restless,...in anguish, who believes that the world is lost, that he is dying, and so forth.... The emotional relationships of his life were far from simple.... At the amorous level I think he must have had many problems.... In order to love intensely he needs anguish, drama, a kind of little cinema.... He was able to live intensely because he was a Taurus and as such was inside the role; but at the same time he was able, as a Gemini, to disengage himself from the role and change the game. He was a double man.... He is capable of speaking with ease, and at the same time is profoundly introverted."

Marie (which her sister bought), and finally with the villa itself. Their financial situation never visibly improved.

Before Yves was one year old Fred traveled to cities in the north, seeking contacts in the art world, and arranged a show in Amsterdam for 1930. Marie soon joined him, reluctantly leaving the child with her sister in Nice, where, at least, there was money to feed and house him. This was the first dislocation in a childhood which was to become increasingly confused and fragmented, with many comings and goings, many changes of residence, role model, and attitude.

Rose Raymond, childless and now divorced, was living in her mother's house again. She took Yves into her care with something more than willingness, more than affection. As she walked him in the pram, held him, doted on him, fussed over him, he became in a sense as much her son as Marie's. The infant had in effect two mothers, between whom a certain competition existed for his affections and the right to guide his development; the situation was as confusing to him as to the only child of divorced parents shuttling back and forth between their homes. As the years passed, and the parents came and went (to Cagnes for the summer, back to Paris at summer's end), young Yves was subjected to contradictory role conditioning. It was Aunt Rose who "had her feet on the ground," who had money and knew its value, who cared for schooling and hard work. "It was she to whom he would return each time he had some need for the rest of his life, because with her he could find himself on solid ground again."[13]

Yves' grandmother and aunt were devotees of the Italian Saint Rita of Cascia, whose miracle cult had many adherents in the south of France. Their attachment to Saint Rita provided the background for Yves' ritualism and religious ambitions, his obsession with magic and miracle. As a child he was ritually presented to a statue of the saint and consecrated to her care forever. (Ominously, perhaps: Saint Rita was known as the patroness of lost causes.) Years later, when Yves felt he needed heavenly intervention, he would ask his aunt to pray to Saint Rita for him. When he got what he wanted, he would say, "Saint Rita got it for me." Four times he himself would make pilgrimages to Cascia to leave gifts for the saint and make requests of her. This imprint of rustic piety never left him.

When Yves was two years old his mother "languished" from desire for him, and Aunt Rose ("in despair" at losing him) took him to her in Paris. For two years he came and went between Paris and Nice. Then at age four he was settled in Aunt Rose's house more solidly, to stay for almost six years. During most of the summers he was with his parents in Cagnes; for the rest of the year he lived in Nice and attended a Catholic school. He was living, really, in two worlds, and the contradictions between them became ingrained in his personality. For the rest of his life he would swing between the poles of the creative, free-roaming parents and the pious, respectable aunt, emulating both, but never making them one. Like the parents, he would avoid conventional employment, acquire debts, devote himself to art, learn to disappear. Like the aunt, he would practice religion, dress like a business person, and consecrate himself to a kind of respectability. It was his parents' world, where his imagination and sense of freedom and adventure grew almost pathologically intense, which attracted him most; yet each September this world would reject him, sending him back to the solidity and careful supervision of his aunt. As his two "mothers" competed for his affections, he learned to control them both and get what he wanted; the temper tantrum became a part of his arsenal for surviving. At once spoiled and rejected, he felt both in control of the world and outside of it. It was his parents whom he would finally emulate, finding a way into the Paris art world where he was to surpass them both quickly; but it was his aunt who would be called on, at the height of his adventure, to intercede with Saint Rita and to accompany him to the saint's shrine to give thanks for his attainments.

3

When I was young, I opened my arms to purity.
This was only a beating of wings in the sky of my eternity.

PAUL ELUARD

HE WAS A SORT OF HOLY CHILD," SAYS HIS FRIEND ARMAN: A person of special power and charisma from the beginning. "He had the power to convince people by his charm," says his mother. "He was always surrounded by a group of children who looked to him for leadership." In the summers in Cagnes they would come to the house in the morning, saying, "What will we do today, Yves?" He would organize treasure hunts and games of knights in armor. (The age of chivalry continued to fascinate him throughout his life. "Tintin seeking the Holy Grail," François Mathey would call him years later.)[14] He would go for long walks in the woods and come back, his arms filled with flowers. "The great freedom he enjoyed," his mother says, "certainly developed his sense of adventure, and his imagination." But already he was a fighter (*un bagarreur*), with a sense of military victory. At age ten, he would demand a written surrender from a beaten foe: "I lay down my arms. Signed, Antoine."

In the summer of 1937 there was an artists' festival in Cagnes for which Yves' parents decorated a pavilion with themes of air, earth, water, and fire (a structure he would later repeat in his own works). Someone organized a "racecourse of cockroaches," which he would also repeat, more than once, in Paris and Germany in his twenties. His admiration for his parents, his resentment of the time they spent away from him, and his desire to emulate their freedom and creativity were enduring parts of his character.

When his parents returned to Paris in September, he would return to Nice and attend the Catholic school. There things did not go so well. His thoughts were already far removed from ordinary things, and he fought with the priests and the other boys. The freedom of his summers undermined the discipline of his winters; he became a rebel. His attendance at the Catholic school ended with the year of his private first communion, May 27, 1937. The

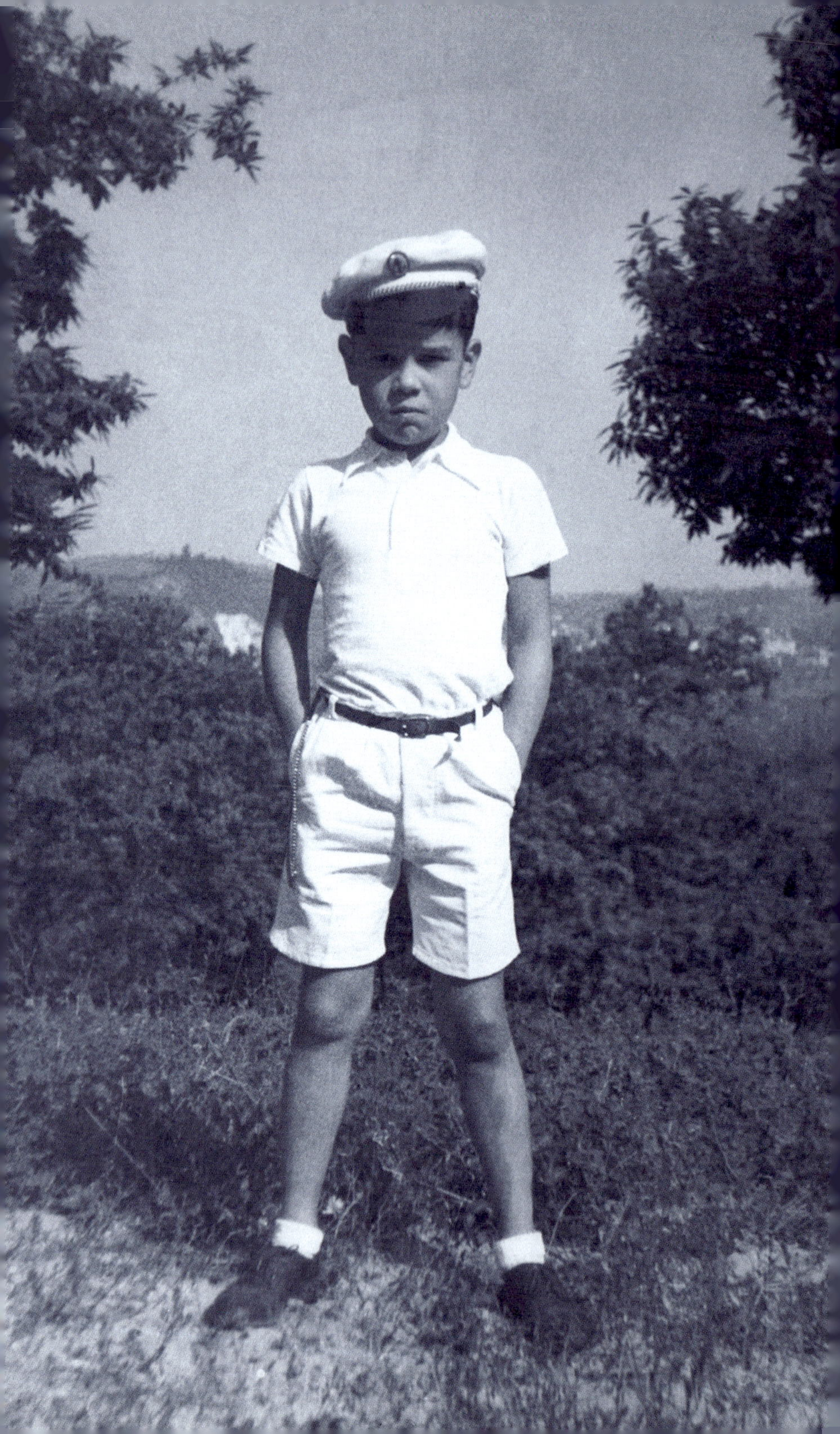

following year he attended a private (tutorial) school, and began to do better. Each evening he would sit with Aunt Rose while she patiently checked his homework. His education seemed about to get back on track—when his mother called for him in Paris again.

In Paris at age ten, he became a confirmed *bagarreur* and was asked to leave one school after another. In the summer of 1939 his family returned to Cagnes and was caught there by the war. For four years he lived with his parents in Cagnes, and though the "freedom he enjoyed" there set fire to his imagination, his discipline, in effect his formal education, was over for good.

Many artists left Paris for the South at this time, and many of them passed through the Klein-Raymond home. Yves was introduced to the Paris art world in exile. Hans Hartung and others were frequent visitors; Nicolas de Staël lived nearby.

Away from Aunt Rose's supervision, Yves ceased caring about school altogether, and spent more and more of his time at hero's games, or imitating the activities of the grown-ups. He wore a military cap which his mother had given him, and was known throughout the village as "the Captain." He and de Staël's son once took paintings from the artist's dustbin, grasped them by the stretcher braces, and used them as shields in knightly battles. He began to write little poems which gave a sense already of the literary power he would later attain. Painting itself, however, did not interest him. He was, in fact, "fed up with it," even "against it," because it had separated him from his parents for so long.[15] Instead he spent hours at the piano, learning to play basic jazz motifs by ear, and read comic books. His favorites were Tintin, who even as a boy achieved knightly adventures, and Mandrake the Magician, who wore a black tie and cape, read minds, and was a master of illusion.

In the summer of 1940, while France still drifted in the *drôle de guerre*, Yves organized a children's theater in the basement of the Maison Musée in Cagnes. While the village youths built benches of planks and stones and brought electricity into the room, he conceived and directed, making up sketches and rehearsing the other children in them. On the day before the performance he distributed invitations throughout the village, in the cafés and the streets. "Already he was able to organize everything and get his audience," his mother says. Many artists in the village attended; the Renoir family came from nearby; even the famous Valentine Tessier, who likewise was waiting out the war in Cagnes, appeared. The little Captain had won a choice audience indeed!

But the Captain was soon pubescent, and he became fiercely independent, beyond anyone's control. In the summer of 1942 his parents financed a trip to St. Dalmas, in the Alps, by renting out the villa, and left Yves behind in Nice. He sorely resented it. In the following summer, at age fourteen, he took off alone on his bicycle to see St. Dalmas for himself, and was gone for days. "I knew then," his mother says, "that he had gone his own way for good." He was terribly stubborn ("the freedom he enjoyed...") and would not take no for an answer. (Years later his friends would say, "He admitted no obstacle, tolerated no one who resisted him.")

But life in Cagnes was becoming difficult. Even food was scarce in the south of France. In the summer of 1943 the family moved back to occupied Paris, and Yves learned war, the black market, and the streets. Everything was difficult now. Fred Klein had to sell the villa in Cagnes, and Marie's parents sold a lot in Nice, dividing the money between Rose and herself. Mere survival was a problem. Debts accumulated.

Still Paris was fairly stable, and galleries began to open again in 1943. Fred Klein worked desperately to get a show and make some money. Occasionally he sold a painting, but the earnings came to little. Yves, in love with jazz, would play the piano with friends who came over on Sundays bearing trumpets, flutes, drums.

In June 1944, Yves went with a Boy Scout group on a camping trip to Normandy. They returned to Paris one day before the landing of a million and a half American and British troops. Fearing for his safety, his parents sent him to stay with friends in the village of Milhars (Tarn). He remained there for about three months, while they lived through the liberation of Paris—blockades in the streets, gunfire at their doorstep, Leclerc's tanks tearing down the barricades; by August 26 the Germans were gone from Paris, and soon Yves was summoned back. Sixteen years old, he returned eager to join the Resistance, carrying a hand grenade hidden in a loaf of bread. His mother kept it under the tiles of the kitchen floor until the war was over, then turned it in to the army.

The war had aroused his taste for adventure, and in the following year his troubles in school increased. More and more often he failed to attend, and no one could force him. He took to frequenting nightclubs and daydreamed of being a jazz musician and playing in the Claude Luther band (with which he was occasionally allowed to sit in on piano for an easy number). In 1946, his mother recalls, he presented himself for the baccalaureate exams and failed them. It was a disappointment which he felt increasingly as the years passed, and which he tried to compensate for by various mythic inventions. Even more serious was a consequence of this failure. Eager to set out on travels and adventures of his own, Yves had planned for two years to enter the Merchant Marine Academy. Now his failure at the baccalaureate rendered him ineligible for the entrance exam. It was a second major disappointment, which he later tried to rectify through invention. The common story that he attended the Merchant Marine Academy was created by Yves himself, who was ashamed, in later years, of his lack of formal education. Translating his early life into myth, he claimed imaginatively some credentials which cannot be seen by daylight. At the moment, the disappointment was softened by the opportunity to travel in the company of his parents.

As soon as the war ended, the art world came to life again. In 1946 Marie Raymond, who had begun painting abstracts during the war, began exhibiting at the young Galerie Denise René; Fred Klein was invited to show at the Anglo-French Art Centre in London. In July, Marie and Fred went to London, but had difficulty obtaining a visa for Yves. A month or so later the visa was cleared, and Yves joined them. For several weeks they stayed with friends who had a handicapped son. Yves befriended the boy and showed the graciousness and kindness which throughout his life would coexist paradoxically with his arrogance and egocentricity.

Back in France after a taste of travel and freedom, Yves found himself, at age eighteen, living in his aunt's house in Nice again. She had remarried (becoming Mme. Taramasco) and was running a Phillips appliance store and doing well. Yves was already at a kind of dead end in the world. His education had been aborted by familial instability, poverty, and the war. He could not enter the Merchant Marine or any school of higher education. His personality was already too brilliant, too strong and assertive, for conventional limits. And though physically an adult, he was still wrapped up in the dreams of his childhood, still reading Tintin and Mandrake the Magician.

Hoping to groom him for a career in commerce, his aunt set up a bookshop for him to run in one room of her appliance store. Yves was "very competent," she says. But inwardly he dreaded becoming the next generation's Phillips dealer. He played the piano desultorily and began to tell his friends that he had been a member of the Claude Luther band. (He had never perceived a clear boundary between his imagination and the world of plain facts, and never would.) In the evenings he strolled on the promenade by the sea and went to dances; he was an excellent jitterbugger and was popular with the girls. Occasionally the bandleader would let him sit in on piano. Life was pleasant enough, but dull; he yearned for the more exciting world of his parents and openly resented the fact that they had sent him away from it. The restlessness which would become so famous in later years ("He was the most restless man I have ever known," says Tinguely) began to show.

Outside of his fantasy life (where he was Mandrake and Tintin and Perceval and Claude Luther and a famous artist all rolled into one), nothing that he had experienced was really his own. It was his parents' world, from which he was repeatedly sent away, or his aunt's world, which tempted him with a suffocating security. The confusion of his childhood was maturing into a kind of desperation. The paradox of being simultaneously neglected and spoiled was a difficult one; the neglect left a residue of anger, the pampering a false sense of omnipotence. He wanted a world of his own, a reality which would assuage his inner anger and reflect his inner sense of omnipotence. He wanted to go "beyond" everything he had seen.

4

I am a child of the Earth and the starry Sky,
But the Sky alone is where I belong.

ORPHIC INSCRIPTION, CIRCA 300 BC

IN 1947 SOMETHING MOVED YVES TO JOIN THE JUDO SCHOOL at the police headquarters in Nice, where courses were offered to the public. He met Claude Pascal, and two weeks later Armand Fernandez (later simply Arman). These were the most important friends of his life. With them in the next few years he underwent a "mystic crisis" (as Claude Pascal calls it) which introduced him to his personal myth and established, once and for all, the governing symbols of his life—the symbols of "spiritual space."

Yves was quick and strong, though not large, and the combat on the judo mats aroused his energies fully for the first time. Judo, he would say later, was his first experience of spiritual space, that "sensorium of god," as Henry Moore called it, which was to preside over the end of his adventure as much as its beginning. The straining of muscles, the flying through the air, the landing unhurt—these released him from the limitations of "plain facts," and made him feel free and powerful.

He was to seek the unobstructed freedom of empty space for the rest of his life—to evoke it in his art of emptiness, to activate it with his immaterial works, to mark its flight and fall in his Imprints, to consummate his sex-and-death relationship with it in his Leap—even to sell it, though the proceeds went into the river of time, not his own pockets. Space, transparent and shining, whole and without blemish, which contains Everything but is Nothing—this was his embarkation and his terminal, the prelude of the sermon he preached with his life and its peroration.

But judo by itself was not enough for Yves and his friends. They wanted hardships and adventures, explorations in the nighttime world of magic and lunar vision. They were ready for a teacher; and when the student is ready, says the occult tradition, the teacher will appear.

"One day [late in 1947 or early in 1948]" says Claude Pascal,

"Yves arrived saying, 'Look, I have found it!' He showed me the *Cosmogonie* of the Rosicrucians. We tried reading it and found that without a master it could not be understood. We asked everyone, 'Do you know anybody who understands the *Cosmogonie* of the Rosy Cross?' After about two months, as we were leaving a judo class, Yves said, 'I have found someone.' We went to a house at about eleven o'clock at night, which in Nice at that time was very late, and knocked on the door. When it opened, we saw a very old man in a white shirt, who said, 'What can I do for you?' Yves showed him the *Cosmogonie* and he said at once, 'Ah! Come in, my children.'" This was Louis Cadeaux, a man in his seventies who operated inconspicuously as an astrologer, occultist, and proselytizer for the Rosicrucian Society. Through some inscrutable dispensation, he acted as the artificer of Yves' Icarus-like adventure in fiery space.

For almost a year the three youths visited Cadeaux's apartment twice a week. He gave them lessons in casting horoscopes and meditating, lectures on Rosicrucian doctrines, on the rising of the world of forms out of formless unity—and on the taming of the ego that is necessary to return to that unity.

Yves underwent a dramatic change. This at last was schooling which aroused not only his interest, but his passionate dedication. In June 1948 he and Claude joined the Rosicrucian Society (Arman did not) and began to work the biweekly lessons that were sent from Oceanside, California. With surprise and pleasure Aunt Rose saw him working studiously at this "homework" (as she calls it) every evening.

The central source used by Cadeaux, and by the Rosicrucian Society in general,[†] was Max Heindel's *La Cosmogonie des Rose-Croix*. In this book Yves found his myth. The shock of recognition made a believer of him, and for years he read the *Cosmogonie* daily with what can only be described as religious faith. As late as 1952, says his mother, "he would read this book for hours every day. He would read it for entire nights. You could see the light in his

---

† The Rosicrucian Society of Oceanside, California, should be distinguished from the Rosicrucian Order (or AMORC); it became a separate organization, under the leadership of Max Heindel, around the beginning of the twentieth century.

window from the street. At two or three in the morning he would still be reading. He was deeply penetrated by Rosicrucianism." In fact, Yves was still, as far as books went, an intellectual child. His mind had rejected what was taught in school and remained empty, even innocent; and it was through this emptiness or innocence that the doctrines of the Rosy Cross penetrated to his very depths. He was never to forget them.

Yves did not read many books, but those he did read (or read parts of) influenced him deeply, Heindel's *Cosmogonie* above all. Yves' own writings, which he began to publish while still a Rosicrucian, show an increasing cleverness at balancing several cultural codes, or finding interfaces between them, so that he could retreat, when pursued on the basis of one interpretation, into another. The first of these, and the most basic to the very end, was the Rosicrucian code as set forth in the *Cosmogonie*. The structure of Heindel's thought became basic to Yves, and other codes, when he learned them, were fitted to it. Heindel's dogmatic certainty recompensed Yves' lack of higher education. Rosicrucianism was, in effect, his baccalauréat and his university.[16]

"The Spirit penetrates all things, even the most solid bodies," says the *Tractatus Micreris*, an alchemical text. Max Heindel's Rosicrucianism is a psychological alchemy which aspires to set spirit free from solid bodies and restore it to the Eden of unity— to render it one with the seamless transparency of Space before the first "Fiat" was uttered. This dream, of a self-transcending fecundity which can be attained by ascending the Great Chain of Being, arose before European occultism in the Platonic schools, before them in Orphism, and before Orphism it was shadowed forth in Egyptian afterlife myth and shamanic rite. It has captured many spiritual adventurers, and now it captured Yves.

What Yves learned from Heindel was that he "had a rendezvous with the end of an age."[17] We are now, Heindel says, approaching the end of the Age of Matter, when Spirit lies captive in solid bodies, and the beginning of the age of open Space, when Spirit will exist free of form, at one with the boundlessness of Space. The law of gravity is about to be rescinded. Soon solid bodies will levitate, and personalities will be able to slip out of matter at will and travel, in an immaterial or "ethcric" form, through invisible realms, traversing great distances in the wink of an eye. This airy body will be equipped with an immaterial sensibility empowered to read the "Memory of Nature," which is inscribed on empty space, and, by manipulating its circuits, to exercise a godlike power over the world of form.

Here was a path which led "beyond" the limits of things, a magic which would dissolve the boundaries which separated Yves Klein from Tintin and Mandrake and the Knights of the Grail. Here was a way to make (or believe) one's fantasies real. Yves' face brightened as he read this, and his inner world became both excited and still. He was a child of the imagination, after all. (As late as 1960, Tinguely says, "he would tell us stories of knights and the Holy Grail.")

Yves was one of those who do not feel at home in the world of facts ("His passion," says Tinguely, "always went beyond, beyond the plain state of things"; "He had a great, an amazing, power to live an imaginary life," says Bernadette Allain), one of those for whom life in a body seems, by reason of its limitations, an insult and a punishment. He had lived in many homes, but none was his. Now Heindel's words seemed like a message from his true home, summoning him back at last. That he should be a citizen of infinity, should have a limitless home with no barriers, no inside and outside, no owner and no stranger, seemed right and natural. It was what he had always felt without realizing it. ("For Yves," says Tinguely, "megalomania was just a natural state, not something added on.") At the time, being reminded that his true home was in infinite space and that the central purpose of his life was to find his way back to it was enough. It was later, when forced deep into myth by the "plain facts" of life, that he assigned himself the messianic role which Heindel calls the "highest initiate," who will be the first to attain immaterial sensibility, and who will pass it on to others, ushering in the new age. Night after night Yves sat by the reading lamp until the early morning hours, recognizing, and then recognizing more strongly, his own hidden face, in that infinity where the omnipotence of the spoiled child may expand to fill the universe and the anger of rejection dissolve into invisibility.

Yves' Rosicrucianism was no passing fancy. "It gave him his

foundation," says his mother; and one's foundation does not change. He read Heindel daily and worked the Rosicrucian lessons faithfully (far more faithfully than he had ever done schoolwork) for four or five full years, the duration of an ordinary college education. Even after that, Heindel's idea system remained his "foundation." A friend of almost ten years later describes him then as still "passionate" about the Rosy Cross.[18] At that time, when he returned to Paris after his wanderings and began publicly promoting his myth, he would say that he was "an initiate," that he had "undergone an initiation," and would mysteriously say no more. This was a reference to his year of working with Cadeaux and his all-night sessions with the *Cosmogonie*, after which the world seemed entirely different to him. His art works, his writings, and the series of symbolic personae he adopted were all attempts, more or less serious, to embody this myth in his life. As his "beautiful megalomania" (as Tinguely calls it) grew, he would even try (or pretend to try) to enforce it on the history of his time. How much of the latter activity was dandyism, how much Dadaism, how much religious faith, and how much personal pathology, no one precisely knows. Yves became a master of the poetic act, and clouds of interpretations surround him. These range from Harold Rosenberg's "able to make a good show out of nothing" to Pierre Restany's "the latest prophet of Europe."

5

From the sky moved the charms of my dreams
And came to eclipse the banner of the real.

MAX JACOB

ON THE PRACTICE MATS AS IN A KIND OF THEATER YVES ACTED out the role of spiritual warrior which was to become central to his self-image. This "holy child," remember, was a *bagarreur*, deeply drawn toward power and domination. The attraction of judo was not simply that it gave one power, but that it made power beautiful and harmless; it made it a game, a dance, an art. He gained the black belt in the school at Nice and would in time write a book on judo and operate judo schools in Paris and Madrid. Judo and Rosicrucianism were for ten years the center of his life. His sense of manhood, his sense of "being at home in the world," came to be based on generating, through judo, the ability to dominate others and, through Rosicrucianism, the self-restraint not to do so.

Claude Pascal, who was a couple of years older, had a room of his own, and Arman, who was already involved in art, had made a studio in his parents' basement. A room in the basement was prepared as a "cave" or "temple," with one wall painted blue (for Heindel's new age and the sky) and imprinted with their hands. Gathering every day in one of these places, or on the roof of the apartment house where Arman's parents lived (Aunt Rose's house was "too bourgeois"), they would practice judo, study Zen, and cultivate the ability to sit properly for meditation. At this time Yves revealed again the stubbornness which, at age fourteen, had sent him off to explore the Alps on his own. He learned to endure physical pain until he could sit in the difficult full-lotus position for up to three hours without moving his legs. The three would concentrate their minds on "holy places" in India and Japan and practice the tantric-style visualization exercises prescribed by Heindel. (Yves' long practice of visualizations was the basis, in later years, of his "art of the immaterial.")

Also on Heindel's instructions, they became vegetarians (for about five years) and abstained from alcohol, cigarettes, and sex, feeling a certain guilt when, on the summery streets and beaches of Nice, an erotic urge would overtake them. And they fasted ("very seriously," says Arman) for one day each week, one week each month, and one month each year.

On the roof of the apartment house, during the long summer fast of 1948, they would meditate without pausing for two or three days at a time, lying in shavasana and walking in the Zen fashion. High on fasting and concentration (in the pre-psychedelic age), they talked of leaping from the roof and flying into the full moon overhead. Yves especially was lost in the dream of flying. The Rosicrucian texts said quite simply that it could be done by anyone with proper training. The Catholic church recognized flight as an activity of saints. Sorcerers, shamans, monks, yogis, and alchemists could all, their traditions claimed, fly without wings. There seemed no reason why Yves himself could not fly; his intense personal feeling of its rightness was like a guarantee. His lack of grounding in history and science made it easy for him, as for a child, to believe his fantasies.

As the months passed and the ascetic life seemed to dissolve their old limits, they adopted new names, like knights at the commencement of their official adventures. Armand Fernandez (thinking of Van Gogh) became Arman; Yves Klein (getting back at his parents?) became Yves; Claude Pascal (lover of paradox) became Pascal Claude.

Lying on the beach one afternoon, their adventure—and so the whole world—still unspoiled, they divided the universe among themselves (as Zeus, Poseidon, and Hades had done at the beginning of their careers). Arman, procreator and protector, maker of fullnesses, took charge of the animal realm. Claude, gentle and slow of memory, gathered to himself the safety of all plants. And Yves, harder, more abstract, and less at home in the world than the others, defined his realm, the mineral, as the blue emptiness of the distant sky.[19] Ascending mentally into the empyrean, he signed his new name on the other side of the sky—the side with no birds, no planes, no clouds, only pure and irreducible Space. It was the signature of an omnipotent creator: "The blue sky is my first art work," he said.[20]

This ambiguous act (or fantasy) of his twentieth year, with its resonances of Plato's *Phaedrus* and shamanic myth, became the central symbol of his life. He had come from beyond the sky, and he was going to return there. A kingdom as vast as the cosmos, spreading unimaginably far beyond the boundaries of his body-and-ego, of his personal history, of his parents' home and his aunt's, of Nice, and France, and all the closed-in spaces of ordinary life, awaited him—it was the destruction of the world, the matrix of the immaterial, the destination of the Leap into the Void.

"The daydream," wrote Gaston Bachelard (an author who would later influence Yves greatly), "transports the dreamer outside the immediate world into a world that bears the mark of infinity."[21] But for Yves it was more than a daydream; it gripped him too strongly to be that. The belief that he might one day ascend to his aerial kingdom, expand through all space and become one with it, never really left him. In 1959, giving a talk at Tinguely's exhibition in Düsseldorf, he declared (secretly referring to Heindel's prophecy),

> *We will all become aerial men, we will know the force of upward*
> *attraction, toward the void and the totality at one and the same*
> *time; when the forces of terrestrial attraction have been dominated*
> *in this way we will literally levitate to total physical and spiritual*
> *liberty.*[22]

And in 1960, when Russian cosmonauts were threatening to encroach on his dominion, he set them straight:

> *Today anyone who paints space must actually go into space to*
> *paint, but he must go there without any faking, and neither in an*
> *airplane, a parachute, nor a rocket; he must go there by his own*
> *means, by an autonomous individual force: in a word, he must be*
> *capable of levitating.*[23]

And again:

> *I would like to present myself on the stage of a theater hanging in*
> *space several meters from the floor without any gimmick or hoax,*
> *hanging for five or ten minutes at least without any commentary*
> *at all.*[24]

"The sky," as Eliade says, " 'symbolizes' transcendence, power and changelessness simply by being there... The whole nature of the sky is an inexhaustible hierophany."[25] This hierophany transformed Yves' sense of the meaning of life; he had been given a purpose: he had been shown the sacred space toward which his current flowed.

It is a fundamental (and common) error to disregard the mystical and miraculous tone of Yves' writings as an empty posture or a display of Dada. It is an error which his own behavior sometimes seemed to confirm, but it is still an error—because, as Arman says, "he was a very special and complex character" and as Tinguely adds, "he was very contradictory inside." His systematic mixing of codes, designed, as we will see, to protect his inner world from the dangerous intrusion of uncontrolled facts, was confusing. He used forms related to Dada to express ideas which were absolutely counter to it. He caricatured himself, yet resented ridicule.

"Yves knew how to joke," says Tinguely; "he would roll on the ground laughing—but at the same time he was taking himself very seriously."

And Claude Pascal; "Yves was not a Dada. He was a mystic. He laughed all the time and joked so people didn't take him seriously—but Yves was always dead serious."

And Arman: "A mystic yes. He was shy, and his showing off was to hide shyness. He was always a mystic."

And Rotraut Klein: "He was absolutely a mystical man. He was like Jesus."

6

Follow my tracks,
You can come,
My best friends
The road is open
The sky is clear.

JULES SUPERVIELLE

YVES' DESIRE TO TRAVEL, TO CLAIM FOR HIMSELF THE FREE-ROAM-ing life of Fred Klein and Marie Raymond, had not ended with his failure to enter the Merchant Marine Academy. In the summer of 1948 he hitchhiked through Italy, staying at convents to save money. Costumed in a shirt imprinted with his hands and feet, he visited museums and monuments. Rosicrucianism had done what school had utterly failed to do: had aroused his interest in the past. He began to regret more deeply his lack of academic ground-ing; he dreamed of being a traveling writer, sending back to France his impressions of the world, and began to study languages.

The army could offer travel, if less than the Merchant Marine, and in November 1948 Yves entered military service. He was sent to French-occupied Germany, where he stayed for eleven months, training in artillery. There he imitated what he had seen of his parents' life, making a race course of cockroaches to amuse his fellows, and visiting museums and galleries during his furloughs. The Rosicrucian lessons still came from Oceanside and still were faithfully worked and returned.

Meanwhile he dreamed of a more radical adventure, fit for knights in armor. Two roads beckoned, one to Oceanside to live with the sages of the Rosicrucian Society, the other to Japan to pursue the "spiritual space" of judo. Japan was the more attractive, for it offered scope for an adventure worthy of Tintin himself: the Grail knights would go first to Ireland (which seemed to the three French youths a land of horsemen and horsemanship), learn to ride, and then, mounted on good steeds, crusade across Europe and Asia climaxing the great adventure by sailing from Korea to Japan and entering a judo academy. Yves returned to Nice on furlough and discussed it with Claude and Arman.

Arman, who was already busy with art work and had just met his wife-to-be (and who no longer read Tintin), begged off the lengthy adventure. But late in 1949, when Yves was discharged from the army, he and Claude crossed the Channel to London to learn English before proceeding to Ireland and their private *fiana.*

In London for about four months, Yves and Claude shared a room near Earls Court, attended judo classes and Rosicrucian meetings, and took English lessons three times a week from James Shorrocks. They continued the mystical life, conscientiously working the Rosicrucian lessons and maintaining the Heindelian discipline. Claude worked at a tuxedo rental firm, and Yves, calling on contacts of his parents, worked in the shop of the framer who had prepared his father's exhibition in 1946.[26] Yves' parents sent some money when they could, and Aunt Rose was often called upon.

In London in 1950 Yves' "vocation" as a painter began to force itself into his awareness. He was still, and would remain for several years, "fed up with painting" as Claude Pascal puts it, even hostile to it. His desire to differentiate himself from his parents, to create his own world rather than tamely enter theirs, led him to judo, to an assertion of warlike individuality quite distinct from their artistic receptiveness. But an inner discord was involved here. Yves' talents as an artist were enormous and his rejection of art did violence to his inner nature at the same time that it freed him outwardly from his past. While moving judo and Rosicrucianism into the foreground as the coordinates of his personal identity, he began to catch hold, in the background, of the threads of his own artistic direction.

By his own later account, Yves began painting monochromes in 1946; but there is no witness who confirms this. In 1948, however, not long after signing the sky, his first art work, he attached a round blue disc to the notebook in which he did his Rosicrucian work. When Arman inquired about the disc, he was told, "This is what the paintings of the future will look like." Now, working at the frame shop in London, Yves found himself attracted to the powdered pigments, which for him were always the 'pure' colors. One day, Claude recalls, Yves disappeared into the bathroom for a long time and emerged carrying monochromes done in various pastels on small squares of cardboard. "I have found what I want to do," he announced to Pascal Claude. And so attuned was Claude that he credited the news at once, replying only, "Of course!"

Such was the beginning of Yves' extraordinary career—hands smudged with color, eyes glowing, "a man infested with dreams,...overtaken by the divine infection."[27] Carefully he placed the paintings on the table and bed and, fastidious, washed the color from his hands. Soon he tacked the cardboards to the wall and invited Shorrocks and two or three other friends to see them.

But Yves' return to the occupation of his parents was not to be so easy or so quick; the London monochromes are merely the first stage of a difficult change of direction which represents, in effect, the end of Yves' prolonged adolescence and his adoption of an adult vocation which truly satisfied his inner needs. For him the monochrome was from the beginning an expression of Rosicrucian thought (Arman associates it directly with the influence of Cadeaux's teachings), but on another level it was an attack on the whole world of painting as then known—an attack on the figurative painting of his father and the abstract painting of his mother. It made both seem unnecessary and by implication mocked them. "Everyone who saw these monochromes," says Claude, "died laughing; and Yves and I laughed too." Yves still "detested" all paintings except for the monochromes; but he was gradually becoming, as Claude Pascal says, "an involuntary painter."

In Yves' later mythic record of his early life this event is recorded as his first exhibition of monochromes—described sometimes as a public and sometimes as a private showing. Earlier than Rauschenberg's 1951 exhibition of white paintings, it became, in Yves' mind, an event of art historical weight and importance. To an immaterialist, to one who scorned the "plain dull skin of a man,"[28] who wrote that it is only when "transported by the Imagination" that "we attain to the immaterial space of Life itself,"[29] the "factual" record is a contemptible thing, not equal to describing Truth. However slight the event in worldly terms, it grew, in Yves' mythic theater, to its proper size—not merely a young artist's first tentative experimentation, but an announcement, like the prophecy of John the Baptist, of a turning point in human history: the first public signal of the dawning of Heindel's Age of Space. This exhibition, Yves was to declare in 1957, marked the beginning of the "Age of Bypassing the Problematics of Art." The monochrome painting had no problematics because it represented not a selection of objects from the All, but the All Itself. "*Solvite corpora et coagulate spiritum*."[30] In the monochrome all bodies are dissolved into the pristine ground where spirit coagulates into chromatic fullness. The Age of Form ends, and human evolution begins its ascending Return to Space. Thus the event in the London boardinghouse bathroom overflowed Yves' mental space, passed through the channel of his private myth, and began its appropriation of the universe: the future of human evolution became a ramification of his private thoughts.

7

Flee as far as possible from murderous Conceits,
Cruel Wit and impure Laughter,
Which make the eyes of the blue sky weep.

PAUL VERLAINE

IN APRIL 1950, YVES AND CLAUDE WERE READY TO PUSH ON to Ireland. Emulating wandering monks, they left their goods (except for the *Cosmogonie*) with English friends and set out hitchhiking, with only three pounds, a loaf of bread, and a bag of sugar between them. ("We were afraid of nothing in those days," says

Claude.) In Ireland they simply wandered into the countryside, found their way to the horse-breeding area, and inquired until they found work. For three months they lived on a horse farm, cleaning stables in return for riding lessons. (Yves would later describe himself as "an experienced trainer of horses.")

But the equestrian life was not smooth. They received few lessons in return for much shoveling, and in time tensions set in between them. Yves kept a journal, written in his left hand, largely in English;[31] in his determination to make up for years of neglected studies, he was memorizing ten English words a day, practicing English composition, and learning to write ambidextrously. The journal shows a sensitive and decent youth who was remarkably aware of his own shortcomings and seriously trying to soften the corners of his one-day-to-be-famous ego. The glimpse it offers of his character should be carefully considered by all who would understand clearly the record of his later life.

> Weds, the 11th of July and Thursday the 12th of July.
> Last night after the ride, or more exactly after the practice in the ring, I felt happy and in Peace with myself, and suddenly when we were dining the idea comes to me that I had not told Claude about the money I was going to receive from my parent, and also that I had to get it in New Bridge as quick as possible.... So I broke the usual silence, telling Claude all about; and asking him for his advice how to ask the permission to Allan [the farm manager]!!! First he said that it was no need that he comes and second—well, a bad interpretation of dry answer from me made him furious and angry!
> Now, that book here, will be never read by somebody else without my permission—I will be very strict—so I can speak clearly about ourselves and our two difficults caracters—then Claude these last days was in the very same bad period which I was a month ago—I have watched him for a fortnight quite intensely—my purpose was not to be happy looking at an unhappiness, but just to try to find how and why, you are catch so strongly by this "Discord Spirit" without any apparent reason at all.

Yves' effort to study the Discord Spirit in himself went to the roots of his psyche; it may be that he never solved the matter, and that his failure to do so cost him his life.

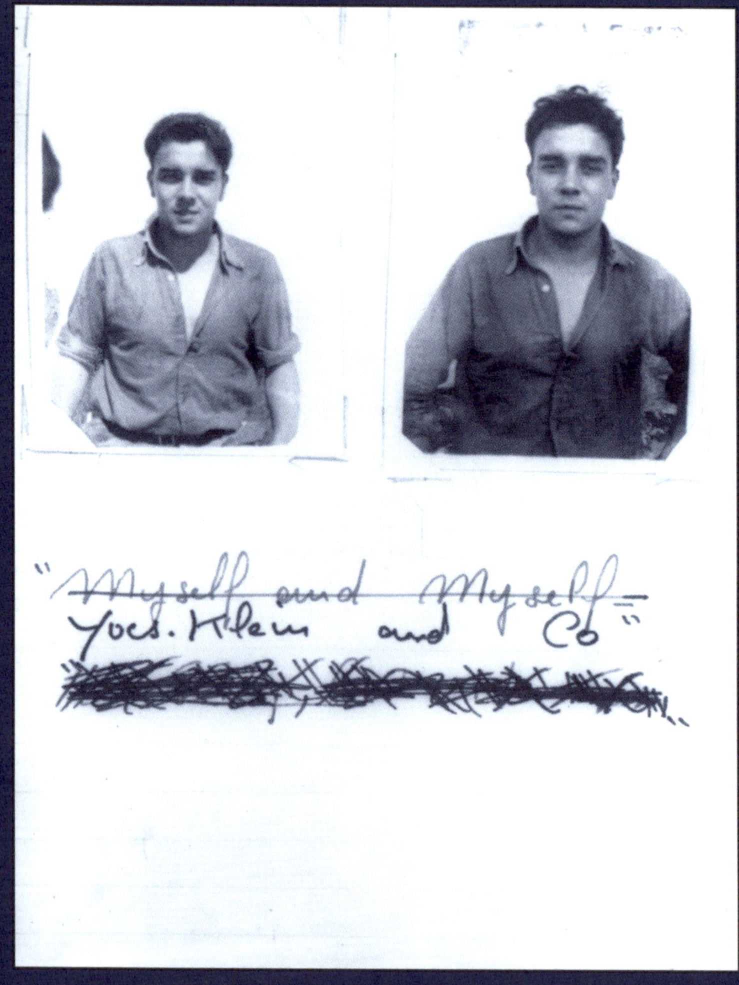

Frontispiece of Yves Klein's Irish journal, 1950.

Claude after that prelude cloudy—start a deep complaining speech about our comportement one to each other. I was listening, recognizing myself in the same bad state of mind in which I was a month ago—"It's something to become mad, he said, we must do something for it;" I said the very same words in this dayry in the pages of about one month ago. But it was nice and I was happy to heard that because I could understand him so well. I know many people would laught at something like that—but just to give an idea of the strength of that Spirit—when you look at your friend just without any purpose and then when suddenly you see him ugly, bad, dirty fellow, etc... at the point then when you want to speak to him you are so upset that the words stay in your throat, no there is no laughing matter....

...Now I just know that 'to be in peace with oneself is to be [in] peace with everybody else' that means when I you do in everything, every gesture, what the little voice of conscience tell you to do inside, everything goes well.

And I realize now that if we beat all that we will be *free* really in the world!!!

Making up their dispute, the young men went to a local party, and Yves remarked in his diary:

Very funny this world....I was not shave and looked very wild among these fraiche and white skins girls! They do not mind at all.

In fact, Yves was discovering, during these years, that sexuality was not to be easy for him. His impatience and overexcitable nature brought with them a proclivity to premature ejaculation which encouraged the Heindelian practice of sublimation. It was a heavy burden for a young man who was attractive to girls and disposed to their company. It did not help in his struggles against the Discord Spirit, which were always intense—sometimes unbearably so—and seem never to have gotten easier.

When the Discord Spirit comes it is a strange feeling, this is exactly a fact, that this spirit appear suddenly as quick as a flash—I have no idea at all how and from where he comes, I just know that it is very hard to take it away. When it comes I make me cold and absolutely without any emotion in order to analyse all the facts and reasons who might have bring this spirit... All the day I was again angry, not against Claude and not against somebody else, but just against everything—the reason was silly, again a question of no control of myself....I should be able to ignore an unsmart and ugly gesture like that now! No, I can't, I fall in the snare every time and the anger live in me for as long as it want.

Still, he learned much, in those months, of gentleness and nonviolence toward life situations in general:

> Friday the 13th of July—
> ...An amazing ride on Pat tonight, has again proved to me that softness and softness again is the only way in everything! Remember!

If only he could have remembered!

> Saturday the 14th of July
> ...I don't want to say anymore about him [Allan] because I know too well now what it cost to judge our fellow creatures and never one's self.

Throughout this period the Rosicrucian lessons arrived with their worksheets to be sent back to Oceanside. After the day's work, Yves and Claude ate their vegetarian meal (sometimes in monastic silence) and worked at the Rosicrucian studies into the night. Yves read the Bible along with the theosophic interpretations of Max Heindel, and was often moved to longing for a gentler, freer, less ego-serving frame of mind;

> Sunday the 15th of July—
> ...How to do all my possible for everybody? how to help everybody as much as I can? Just following the little voice... I know that it is the only way now, but in spite of that I still turn my head and I still look aside Knowing perfectly well where is the Good—I look at the Bad or not especially the Bad but I should say that I still make calculs and follow my cunning instinct, which is very clumsy. Oh God, if I could only forget for a little while the World Wisdom, the Civilization Wisdom and go in the natural love-way perhaps I would be able afterwards to carry on, looking a foolish at the everybody's eyes but happy inside myself knowing that I am doing my Best Sincerely—
> My left hand start to write better now—

But alongside his pious desire to "do all my possible for everybody" he was also developing his wicked satanic mask, partly in imitation of the farm manager, Allan, whose personal style he had earlier loathed:

> Friday the 11th
> ...I have perfectly understood today the laught of Allan—when
> he chuckle sometimes as a devil—I know now what that means
> exactly and I start to take a plaisure to do it either!

With the characteristic ambivalence of spiritual seekers raised in dualistic traditions, he fancied himself both potential devil and potential saint:

> "To challenge the evil" that should be my motto—I dont think
> I can really have hatred against anybody now but still too many
> voices hum in my innermost—If only my jaw could remember me
> each time swallow a mouthful, that am eating the Christ's body! I
> am still not rife [ripe] at all!—too young!

(His ten English words for Friday, August 11, included motto = devise, to challenge = défier, evil = mal, to hum = murmurer, jaw = mâchoir, mouthful = bouchée, rife = mûr")

Yves' desire that his jaw would "remember" him "each time swallow a mouthful" reveals a spiritual program related to the "self-remembering" of Gurdjieff, the "Attention!" of Zen, and the "mindfulness" practice of southern Buddhism.

> The 5th of August 1950[32]
> Many persons are like l am, when relaxing my mind and my body
> I start to dream about. I don't know... just about the first picture
> who come into my mind—then my eyes look completely mad and
> lost in the space—if someone speak to me when I feel like that it
> may get the impression so unpleasant of a person who does not
> listen at all and pay any attention at what it is said!
> This state is the result of a simple lasyness, I realize that now,
> as well as we have some difficulties to keep our back straight as
> well we have difficulties to pay constantly attention at everything
> around,...that question goes very far and can't really [think] about
> it tonight properly—but I feel that it might be a big question—I
> have to think about—because I am afraid it is a little negative to
> be like that—so now I have to keep a back straight a permanent
> vision of everything!

Clearly Yves had not yet begun to doubt Heindel's assurances that the human being is perfectible through his own effort, which no external force (such as childhood experiences) can countervail. Throughout these years Heindel presided over his life with minutely detailed instructions: what to eat, how much, and how often; how to breathe; even how to dream. The accumulated force of these disciplines, Heindel promised, maintained for at least seven years, would not only tame the "cunning" ego, but would actually "transfigure" the physical body, atom by atom, into a nobler creature, able to float at its ease through silken space and decipher at a glance the rebus of nature.

This laborious "transfiguration" was the organizing purpose of Yves' life for nearly ten years and, goaded by Heindel, he invested much effort and expectation in it. Many of his later works are (among other things) attempts to translate this purpose into symbols and, in effect, escape from it. But during the period of the Irish journal the promise was still newly made, too fresh and sweet to be doubted; as late as 1954 Yves wrote:

> *Transfiguration*
>
> To be transfigured is to think at each instant of the very essence of the purity of sanctity, and the breathing does the rest—that is, it spreads through the body a new life which enters into every separate atom and remakes each infinitesimal particle of the ordinary body into a body transfigured.
>
> What is necessary then is to breathe with joy an atmosphere and a climate intensely spiritual, which creates in the ego the power to purify the physical body and the astral body and the body of desire.
>
> Every instant
> every act
> every word
> every perception
> of my five senses
> must be for me
> steeped in joy
> a joy perhaps
> artificial and
> a little too self-conscious
> at first, but
> which will be little by little
> a continual
> illumination
> to drink to eat to breathe only joy
> It is necessary to breathe the divine everywhere.[33]

These themes of his journal at age twenty-two—the struggle with the Discord Spirit, the acceptance of the satanic laughing mask, the belief that transfiguration would come in the not-too-distant future—all remained prominent in Yves' life until the end. Later, after he had assumed his mythic role in public, when his "omnipotence" was challenged (or, worse, mocked) he reacted with violent anger; but when his claims on the cosmos were not in question, he was profoundly gentle. The ambivalence between the worldly life, in which he was forced to defend his appropriated zones of reality, and the life of the "innermost," where no claim was at issue, is expressed most poignantly in a brief entry toward the end of the stay in Ireland:

> It is better to have no friends and so no enemies
> I am afraid it is World-Wisdom
> And I don't want World-Wisdom
> > Do I?

8

And then he mounted upon his horse, and rode into many strange and wild countries, and through many waters and valleys.

SIR THOMAS MALORY, *Morte d'Arthur*

ONE DAY WHILE WORKING IN THE STABLE, YVES ENTERED A deep daydream. In his mind's eye he had mounted on horseback, cantered across Europe and Asia, passed through the gateway of a judo school, and donned a kimono, when, roused from his daydream, he saw Claude grimacing unhappily at him over his manure shovel.

He forced a departure, returning to London by himself at the end of August; Claude joined him there about a month later. By the end of the year they were back in Nice. But the long ride could not get started. Arman had other involvements, and just as Claude was applying for a passport, he discovered he had tuberculosis. Almost two years passed before the pilgrimage got under way, but Yves didn't sit still. ("He was too impatient," says Tinguely.

"There was such anguish in him, such longing for paradise, that he could not wait for anything.")

On February 3, 1951, he left for Madrid alone, to study Spanish. There he joined a judo club, and when the instructor got sick was asked to replace him. This was Yves' first employment as a judo teacher, which was to be his source of livelihood for much of the rest of his life. He became very friendly with the director of the school, Fernando Franco de Sarabia, whose father was a publisher.

Meanwhile, his subterranean vocation as an artist continued to thrust itself upward toward awareness. He wrote in his diary (February 18, 1951) an idea, neither an actual plan nor a mere daydream, of exhibiting monochrome paintings with unspecified musical accompaniment.[34] Very probably this was a reference to the idea of one-note or one-chord music (later the *Monotone Symphony*), which, according to Claude Pascal, Yves had "discovered" in London not long after "discovering" the monochrome, and which he specifically regarded as the musical correlate of the one-color painting.

Yves, the international traveler, now reversed roles on his parents, inviting them to visit him in Madrid. The money was difficult to find, but in June, at last, Fred, Marie, Aunt Rose, and Yves' maternal grandmother (the instigator of the family's devotion to Saint Rita) traveled to Madrid and spent ten days or so touring Spain. At the end of June he returned with them, on a steamer by way of the Balearic Islands. But first Arman, who needed a job, was summoned by Yves to Madrid, and took over for a while Yves' "professorship" of judo.

Throughout his travels Yves wrote to both his parents and his aunt, often to ask for money, sometimes just to keep in touch. His closeness to his mother's family, and above all to his Aunt Rose, never ceased. His letters are almost childishly affectionate. When his mother shared the Kandinsky Prize in 1949, he wrote from England: "Hurray for Mama! Both abstract and famous!! Bravo!!" To Aunt Rose, from London: "A thousand thanks for the candied fruits! With thousands of big kisses and a great big hug!"[35] in fact, he was finding it difficult to break away from his mother's family and strike out on a path of his own. His adolescence was unnaturally prolonged both by the excessive care of his aunt and by his own refusal to follow his increasingly frequent impulses toward a career in art.

From January 1951 until the end of summer 1952, Yves lived in Paris in a rented room a hundred yards or so from his parents. Away from Claude and Arman, he felt himself an outsider and began to worry about finding a place in the world. Because Paris frightened him, he sought anchorage in Rosicrucianism, which he studied through the night: Rosicrucianism, like judo, was his own, not something given to him by his parents or his aunt. Twenty-three years old now, he was ready for the second time to try to enter the adult world.

His mother's reputation was then very high, and she held a weekly open house ("Marie Raymond's Monday") through which much of the Parisian art world passed. Yves attended regularly. ("He loved those gatherings," says his mother. "He loved the ambience of artists.") His sense of the art historical moment could not have been more finely tuned than by alert attendance at these salons. It was here that he grasped his second code, that of twentieth-century avant-gardism; later, in his writings, he would conflate it, with deliberate ambiguity, with the Rosicrucian code.

Among the avant-garde activities which Yves now witnessed at first hand were those of the Lettrists, who professed to continue the tradition of Dada and surrealism through concrete poetry, glossolaliac performances, and multimedia projects. He met young artists such as Raymond Hains who were about his age and already had careers under way. "I am a little afraid," he wrote to Aunt Rose, "to be so hesitant before life, to be still and always in so much doubt....I still dream of Japan."[36] Still hoping to remedy his lack of education, he attended the School of Oriental Languages informally, studying Japanese. ("I have no diploma," he wrote with a touch of desperation in a letter never mailed. "But have been studying Japanese furiously for months.")[37] The great question was whether or not to seek entrance into his parents' world, hitching his carriage to their train. But the little Captain was too independent for that. He remained fixed in the desire to make his own way, in a profession as close to a Knight of the Grail as he could find—as a judo master!

In the summer of 1952 he arranged contacts in Japan through his parents' circle, asked his aunt to pay his steamship fare ("Of course, I said yes"), and set out alone, not on horseback, but on the *Marseillaise*, through the Suez Canal, cruising the warm seas around India, by Singapore and Hong Kong, arriving in Yokohama on September 23, 1952.[38] He was met by Takachiyo Uemura, an art critic acquainted with his parents, and stayed briefly in Uemura's house. "My dear aunt," he wrote, "See! I'm in Japan at last!" Soon he moved on to Tokyo and on October 9, 1952, enrolled in the Kodokan Judo Institute, the most prestigious judo center in the world.

9

"Sirs," said the youth, "you would do well to be still, for I will not be stopped for anything or for any man in the world."

CHRÉTIEN DE TROYES, *Perceval*

YVES STAYED IN JAPAN FOR FIFTEEN MONTHS. ROSE RAYMOND sent money regularly, and in addition Yves tutored two French children and taught French to Japanese and American students. Investigating the art world, he arranged three shows of his parents' works. At the same time he pursued his experiments in monochromy, making small cardboard monochromes, as he had done in England, and inviting Japanese friends to his (characteristically empty) apartment to see them. As in England, he received no encouragement from their reaction.[†]

Still thinking of a career as a traveling journalist, Yves wrote an article on Japan which he sent to his mother, asking her to try to place it in a magazine, and promising more ("I have written a lot") if they were wanted.[39] The article is very interesting by way of contrast both with the Irish journal and with the mythic essays

---

† Mr. Shinichi Segi of Tokyo (interviewed by Jean-Yves Mock of the Centre Georges Pompidou in August 1980) met Klein at the exhibition of his parents' works at the Bridgestone Gallery, Tokyo, and attended the private showing of monochromes at Klein's apartment. He notes that Klein employed only primary colors in these pieces, a practice which he would later return to.

he would begin to publish in 1958. When Yves wrote of his own feelings, as in the Irish journal, he was often charming, in a rather touchingly innocent way. When he wrote his self-glorifying essays of the late fifties, he had found a voice (partly from Bachelard) of power and poetic beauty. But in writing on a subject outside of himself, such as Japanese culture, he is a deadly bore. There is none of the passion, none of the flashes of exalted mood or imagery, none of the taut phrases, of his essays on himself. Wisely, Marie refrained from forwarding the essay to any editor; its voice is that of a schoolboy trying to sound grown up.

Above all, Yves practiced judo, flying through "spiritual space" for hours a day at the Kodokan Institute. With characteristic grandiosity he was fiercely determined that upon his return he would be the foremost *judoka* in Europe. The plan had two parts. First was the publication of a book which would clarify through photographs the set of *judokata*, or slow movements, which are the basis of the training. (With relentless determination Yves would practice each of these movements for a thousand repetitions at a time.) No European book really made the positions clear. With borrowed camera equipment and a cameraman, he managed to have a film made from which the stills for such a book could be derived. But the second part of his plan was of the essence. In Europe there were many *judokas* with the third degree, or *dan*, of the black belt, but of the fourth *dan* there were very few. Yves was determined to return to France with the fourth dan black belt from the prestigious Tokyo Kodokan, win the European judo championship, and take over the French Federation of Judo.

Laying down his French belts, which were not recognized in Japan, he started over again from the beginning and worked at the almost pathologically high energy level which would come to characterize his activities more and more as the years passed. His judo master, Tashiro, wrote to Aunt Rose that "he has practiced judo so intensely since his arrival in Japan that his friends have sometimes been worried about his health."[40] In fact, Tashiro's concern for Yves' health was justified. Following the examples of Japanese sumo wrestlers and *judokas*, Yves began taking various stimulants to prepare himself for judo performances. These included calcium injections and amphetamines, which were legally obtainable at that time in both Japan and France. The regular use of legally obtained amphetamine products continued until the end of his life and may have contributed to the apparent change—toward greater intensity and grandiosity—which his personality underwent in Japan, and to the inability to sleep for which he was famous among his friends in later years.[†] His letters to his family from Japan show a growing strain and an increasing rigidity of ambition.

On Christmas day, 1952, he wrote to his grandfather about his grandmother's death (which had occurred the previous July): "Her photo is constantly on my table in my bedroom. I look at it as often as possible….I am absolutely certain that she protects and helps us without us being aware of it….She will fence off from me all possible dangers and for that I thank her often." His grandmother, who had first entrusted him to the care of Saint Rita, seemed now to share in that saint's activity.

In January he wrote to Aunt Rose, asking for money to relieve him of the need to give French lessons so he could "work judo from morning till night…. I think of nothing else right now." Receiving it, he replied, "You are truly a Fantastic Tantine!" Hoping to hit it rich on his own, he entered a business arrangement for importing kimonos from Indonesia to Marseilles, and was gypped.

[†] Klein was later to complain (to Marcel Boulois, Jean Laffont, Edouard Adam, and others) that these stimulants had weakened his heart. Edouard Adam recalls Klein taking amphetamines "in connection with judo performances" after his return from Japan. Marcel Doulois agrees, adding that "all students took Benzedrine in those days." Rose Raymond recalls that Klein frequently took Maxiton, an amphetamine product. Rotraut Klein-Moquay recalls that "Yves had some capsules which he always took when he was tired or starting to work. He would say that they were a mixture of calcium and something. I don't know who gave him these capsules; he always had them." It would be ill-advised to ignore the influence which this practice may have had on his lifestyle. Claude Pascal, in speaking of the years in which he knew Klein most intimately (1948-52), recalls that Klein slept a good deal—usually eight, sometimes nine or ten hours a night. But those who knew him after his return from Japan declare unanimously that he slept very little. George Marci says: "That boy never slept. I would leave him, to go home to bed, at eleven at night, and when I met him the next morning at eight or nine he would tell me all the things he had done in the meantime." Tinguely agrees, saying that Klein complained often that he was tormented by lack of sleep. Rotraut Klein-Moquay recalls that usually when she awakened in the night Klein would already be awake and out of bed.

Again Aunt Rose came to the rescue. Yves replied, "Thank you, thank you a thousand times as always.... You have again saved me from catastrophe, with those brigands. I have the most formidable Tantine in the world."

But the strain of his effort, and the difficulty he was encountering at succeeding in anything, were showing. "It is hard here," he wrote to Aunt Rose, "and I constantly remember how sweet life is in Nice, well taken care of by Tantine. But I absolutely must work at this damn judo and return to France a Grand Master and Champion. It is my future!" ("I have no diploma!")

After a year he requested the fourth *dan* belt (his "future") and was told that he qualified only for the second. He wrote to Aunt Rose in a frenzy:

> I am fed up with this country. I am a nervous wreck and desire only one thing, to return to France as soon as possible. But I desire above all to obtain what I came for; it is absolutely necessary that I get the 4th dan from the Kodokan. Without that I could not return, would have lost everything, because today in France if I wish to be someone in Judo I must have the 4th dan, the third, which is offered me [!] is insufficient, there are too many third dans in France at present (about sixty), but there are only five fourth dans, and you see I will not be the very foremost even if I extract the fourth dan from them. . . I am regarded as the best foreign student and all the professors think I deserve the fourth dan, and even the fifth. But alas they are against foreigners and have decided not to give promotion to a foreigner without his having won at least ten times or their being tempted by money, But this last way does not please me. I have been too sincere in judo up till now; I do not want any trafficking in money to buy my rank. But there is a way, that is to impress them, to make them understand that on my return I am going to be a very powerful figure in France, and that it will be to their advantage to keep me on their side by doing me this special favor, of giving me the 4th dan before I leave. To this end have asked the Spanish Federation of Judo [through his friend Franco de Sarabia] to recognize me as their technical director; they have very kindly done that for me and at present the Kodokan is aware that I will be the master of Judo for all of Spain... I have explained further to the Kodokan that I am going to establish in Paris the largest and best Judo club in the city and perhaps in Europe... and that I will devote it exclusively to the Judo of the Kodokan (BLUFF) if I get the 4th dan.

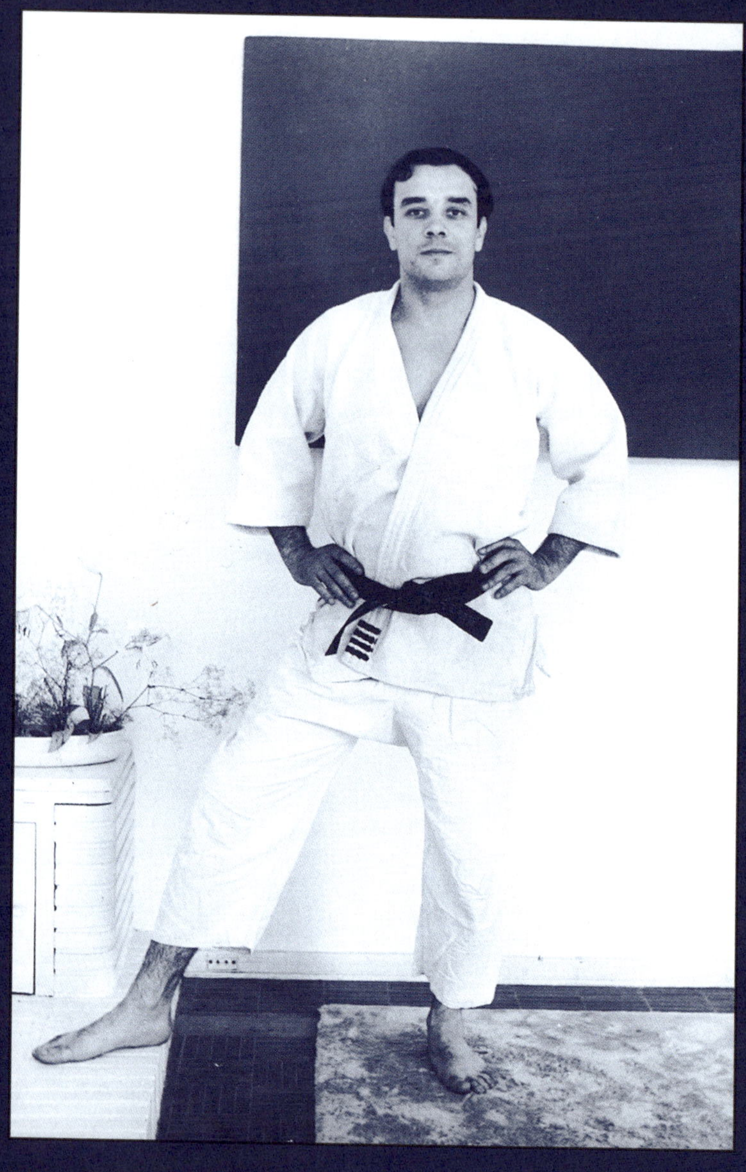

Fourth *dan* black belt in judo, 1960.

Aunt Rose's complicity in the "bluff" was requested. She was to write to Tashiro and inform him, "clearly and discreetly," that if and only if Yves received the fourth dan,

> I will have at my disposition three or four million francs for the establishment of my Judo club in Paris....This letter must be genteel and familial but unhesitating in its request for the 4th dan, and about the three or four million francs....If I lose this, I do not think that I will ever get over it....Write quickly, tantine, but construct your letter well....I am in a hurry to see you again; embrace Grandpa for me, and for you hundreds of thousands of big kisses, BRAVO TANTINE

On November 18, Tantine did as she was asked: "My heart is filled with hope that I have the honor of addressing the master of the prestigious Kodokan Judo Institute, famed throughout the entire world, so that he might deign to honor with his attention the situation of one of his students, my nephew Yves Klein."

Yves, it turned out, had read the psychology of the Kodokan well. On December 7 Tashiro replied to Aunt Rose in a letter that is a masterpiece of doublespeak. "Yves," he wrote, "has become a second Dan in a very short time: his progress is truly impressive." But the shortness of time is precisely the problem: "Myself, I began to practice Judo at the age of fourteen and after three difficult exercises a day for eight years finally became third Dan." Having established the necessity for rejection he slips out of it with amazing ease: "I understand well your affectionate concern and that of Yves' parents. But, to speak frankly, the situation being as above described, it is impossible to give him the fourth or fifth Dan in so short a time that is to say, before the end of this year." Before the end of *this* year—the date of writing being December 7! Eleven days later, on December 18, the Kodokan issued Yves' diploma—fourth *dan* black belt.[41] A diploma at last! On February 9, 1954, on the *Marseillaise* at Hong Kong, en route to France, Yves wrote to Aunt Rose, "And so I am fourth Dan, which is the highest in judo in France, it is truly marvelous…I hope that I will be at the very top in Judo….You are, without exaggeration, the only Tantine of your class in the world!"

Behind the record of this successful "bluff" several tendencies lie: a determination to be *first* in whatever he did ("in Paris, or perhaps in all of Europe"); a refusal to recognize boundaries between fact and fantasy when the fantasy was intense and personal ("I think if I don't get this I will never get over it"); a desperate dependence on childish appeals ("a thousand big kisses for Tantine"); and, perhaps most important, a tendency to "set himself up" for disappointment by nurturing unrealistic expectations ("I hope that I will be at the very top in judo"). Combined with his unwillingness to admit any obstacle, this latter trait, in years to come, would join forces with the Discord Spirit.

In fact, Yves seems to have undergone an important change in Japan. In Ireland he had not been thinking of power and primacy, but of "softness and softness again." ("Remember!") But now he was impatient to make up for lost time, to overtake those of his generation who had entered careers more easily and quickly—in short, to assume at last the destiny of a hero. Early in 1953 he stopped communicating with Oceanside, and six months later his membership in the Rosicrucians lapsed. There were still darknesses inside him where the Discord Spirit waited. But his mastery on the judo mats deceived him. He was a champion already. He could now demand a deeper response from the world. He was no longer a mere seeker, but One Who Has Attained.

10

Patience, patience.
Patience in the blue sky.

PAUL VALERY

EARLY IN 1954 YVES RETURNED TO FRANCE, AND AT ONCE Franco de Sarabia invited him to Madrid to teach. But Yves had greater things in his sights: the European championship beckoned. He traveled to judo clubs in France and Italy, giving talks and demonstrations. The advertisements—written, it seems, by himself—are almost sinister in the intensity of the demands they make upon the world:

> There are in the world heroes of adventure whom the public at
> large does not know. Yves Klein is one of these....
> It is not every day that one has the chance to meet and even to
> watch at work one of the great masters of judo...[42]

Unfortunately, this approach was not the right one. The situation was more delicate than Yves had thought, and his reading of French psychology less precise than of Japanese. Judo was a big business in France already, and the French Federation of Judo, which had no master trained in Japan, was teaching it commercially as a sport. Yves, who had been disappointed by the lack of mysticism in the Tokyo Kodokan, was deeply offended by the commercialism of French judo. Rashly he took on the establishment, talking against the Federation in the clubs. *He* represented the lineage of the Tokyo Kodokan. *He* had the highest rank in Europe. And *he* believed that he, not the Federation, should be the guiding power of French judo.

Predictably, the Federation did not like him. Yves may indeed have been, as he claimed, "the most advanced judo expert in France," but the Federation, claiming that his Japanese belts were not recognized in France, nevertheless demanded that he take a new examination.[†] He refused, in self-righteous anger, and was prohibited from participating in the European championships and even from joining the Federation. Privately it was said that he was a grabber, a troublemaker—he advertised himself too much.

Suddenly the goal for which he had worked with such determination, which was the basis of his differentiation as a self, and on which all his expectations were placed (*"It is my future!"*), had disappeared from sight. His *Fundamentals of Judo* was published by Bernard Grasset in Paris in November; but despite the book, he saw that he could not be a real judo master—with the prestige which, in his eyes, the position entailed—in France. The most he could hope for was to run a private club. His first and, he thought,

---

† Actually Klein's competence in comparison with the members of the Federation cannot he evaluated precisely. Arman and Bernadette Allain feel that for a year or two after returning from Japan he was probably the best in France. But Marcel Boulois, a judo teacher himself, says: "Yves was a mediocre *judoka*. There were members of the Federation who, although they were only first *dan*, were five times better than he was."

best option for a career of his own was over before it had begun. Filled with bitterness and preferring to endure his humiliation away from French eyes, he made plans to move to Madrid—"out of sheer disappointment," says Arman.

As usual in a time of need, he called on Aunt Rose. "I need a car," he said, "to organize my kingdom of judo in Spain." "I went to Paris" she says, "and bought him a little four-CV Renault, with which he was enchanted." ("My dear Tantine…the car's absolutely Sensational!…and thank you for the card of Saint Rita, in which I truly believe.") Soon thereafter, promising her (or himself) that this was "your last surge of spoiling me," he left for Spain. There he poured the energy of his frustration into teaching, and made a powerful showing.

Clearly, Yves did return from Japan a more impressive figure than before. "Judo gave him strength and life," his mother says. And Bernadette Allain, who practiced judo with him in Paris in the following year, says: "His true métier was as a *judoka*. On the judo mats he was serene, strong, and inwardly at peace. He had learned in Japan the true judo, which was nonexistent in the French schools—judo as an intensive discipline and ascesis, which confers on the body itself a knowledge that has never passed through the intellectual mind." Yves had that "other" knowledge, that infraverbal, pre- or postintellectual knowledge; his body and countenance, as long as he remained a true *judoka*, radiated strength and self-confidence. He developed the Spanish Federation of Judo from a mere name into an ongoing institution and obtained accreditation from the Kodokan to leave a lineage of black belts, the first in Spain.

But this did not supply what he had wanted, or needed: preeminence of some sort in Paris itself, in his parents' milieu. During the months in Spain he planned a second attempt at the conquest of Paris, this time on another flank. He would develop his second career option, the one for which his attendance at his mother's Monday salons had prepared him. The dead end of his career in judo pointed him toward art. ("He did not so much come to painting," Edouard Adam says, "as come back to it.")

There was, however, a problem. He was now twenty-six years old and had honestly acquired a profession already. To return to

Paris as a beginner, as, in effect, a child, so far behind Hains and Villegle and others of his own age who, unobstructed by a parental example to rebel against, had started in art a decade before, was too humiliating. It is beyond doubt that Yves had at least conceived the idea of the monochrome painting as early as February 1951, when he mentioned it in his journal. Almost certainly the first primitive examples had been made as early as 1949, as Claude Pascal recalls—perhaps as early as 1948, as Arman says. The physical record is gone—at some point Yves destroyed the earliest works—and the documentary record has been deliberately tampered with. The latter date is perhaps the most plausible, since Yves, who claimed to have painted monochromes in 1946, seems to have commonly backdated his "discoveries" by about two years. In any case, he decided to date his career as a painter of monochromes from 1951, and, in company with Claude Pascal, who now joined him in Madrid, set out to produce evidence to support the claim.

He was in fact still engaged in the making of little monochromes of pastel on cardboard, as he had done in England and Japan. It had become his practice to put such objects on the walls of his environments, a kind of Rosicrucian icon beside the pictures of his grandmother and Saint Rita. Now, in Madrid, he hung monochromes in the hall where he taught judo. Judo, Rosicrucianism, and the monochrome, three approaches to "spiritual space," were all "his"—they did not bear the taint of parental example. Now the monochrome began to come to the foreground and offer itself as his ticket of admission to the adult world.

With money supplied by Rose Raymond, Yves and Claude prepared, in Franco de Sarabia's father's print shop, a book of reproductions of monochromes. In a gesture with distinct Dada overtones, they published two versions, one entitled *Yves Peintures*, the other *Haguenault Peintures* (after a brand of gingerbread, Yves was later to say). Inside both was a preface of blank lines, divided into paragraphs and signed with the name of power, Pascal Claude, and ten color plates of monochromes in green, yellow, blue, pink, red, and orange—each dated (1951-54), some with city names and dimensions indicated, and each signed, at the lower right, "Yves."

Clearly these reproductions were meant to imply a group of larger originals made in various cities between 1951 and 1954. Back in Paris Yves would use the book[†] to establish the "fact" that he had already been for some years a practicing painter, and that his work was already mature enough to warrant publication. Yet each of these claims is highly questionable. There is no evidence that Yves had yet made monochromes as large as the reproductions imply. In fact, these plates have been identified not as photographic reproductions but as pieces of inked paper tipped onto the page;[43] if this identification is correct, then there is no guarantee that the implied originals ever existed.

Yves' deception here (if indeed it was a deception) is of great interest in revealing his style as trickster, for every feature of the little book can respond to either of two interpretations. For example, the attributions ("London, 1950," "Paris, 1951," "Tokyo, 1952") seem to have been secretly justified by Yves not as details of manufacture but as titles. Aldo Passoni relates a story, probably originated by Yves in reference to this pamphlet, that Yves had organized in Madrid an exhibition of ten monochrome paintings, each one dedicated to a different city."[44] Thus "Tokyo, 1952" may be read as meaning "This is my impression of Tokyo in 1952." The "exhibition" seems to have been no more than the hanging of small monochromes in the judo hall.

In any case, Yves had prepared himself, by the end of his period of exile, to make his second "entrance into Paris" with a revised strategy. The decision was of crucial importance. Judo, the passion of his youth, was thrust to the background; into the foreground stepped the alchemical artist, keeping his rendezvous with the end of an age.

---

† The preface of blank, paragraphed lines was, says Claude Pascal, Klein's idea, and Klein later explained it in terms of heraldry: "You know that horizontal lines in heraldry mean 'blue'... At the time I did not know that, and the coincidence is curious" (MS 12174, Klein archive: fragments of an interview of Klein by Pierre Restany).

11

*"This is Tintin speaking. I've just put on my spacesuit and am now
standing in the air-lock. They're just going to reduce the pressure to
a vacuum in here."*
                HERGÉ, *The Adventures of Tintin: Explorers on the Moon*

IN DECEMBER 1954, AUNT ROSE VISITED YVES IN MADRID.
He returned with her to France, moved into his mother's Paris
apartment (she was now living separately from her husband),
and began to experiment with materials and methods for more
mature monochrome paintings. Rose and Marie sold a lot they
jointly owned in Nice and used the proceeds to help set up the
Judo Club of Montmartre on the Boulevard de Clichy, in a studio
formerly used by Leger where, between his judo classes, Yves
began, says Arman, "to paint like mad." From this base he began
at last to drift away from his mother's family and acquire a new
circle of associates.

At this point Yves' horizon expanded, and his remarkable and
variegated talents began to flower. He underwent, in the next
two years, a transition from boy-in-family to artist-in-world, and
he must be seen increasingly as a public rather than a private
figure. But the child remained unusually prominent in him until
the end; in fact it gained strength. In ferocious compensation for
his late start in the art world, Yves asserted his grandiosity with
increasing insistence. In effect, he transited from a "kingdom of
judo in Spain" to claiming (with a certain sense of dynastic right?)
a kingdom of art in Paris. Now, and increasingly in the following
years, he drew on the ability demonstrated at age twelve in the
children's theater at Cagnes to mobilize other people for his own
purposes.

One important friend and adviser was Robert Godet, a colorful
figure on the edge of the Paris art world. An occultist and Gurd-
jieffian who was interested in Eastern religions, avant-garde art,
utopian prophecy, and the martial arts, he and Yves were kindred
spirits. A pilot and, like Yves, a worshiper of the "inexhaustible
hierophany" of the sky, Godet lived in a fairly sumptuous style

which was rumored to be based on gun-running activities. For years he was at Yves' side in La Coupole, the famous Left Bank café, urging him always to "go beyond" the present state of his work. They were close until Godet's death in 1960, rumored to have occurred while Godet was piloting a load of guns to Tibet in his own plane, after the Chinese invasion.

Godet in turn introduced Yves to Bernadette Allain, a precocious young architect who for years lived with Yves and helped him with the techniques and materials of his work. Yves introduced her to judo and she guided his experiments to find a binder which would fix powdered pigments without "murdering their color," as Yves and Bernadette said. She found him, in 1955, still "passionately devoted to Rosicrucianism," in which the "world of pure color" represents the higher metaphysical realm (the realm of the "astral" body) which it is the goal of the initiate's labors to attain. She also, she recalls, was "passionately interested in pure color" at this time, and together they spoke of the mysticism of color, of "going beyond the limits, beyond the gamut of sensations," of finding out "what would happen if one's personal intensity increased beyond known frontiers." They were convinced that there was a "certain hypersensitivity" which would permit one actually "to enter into the world of color" and exist as color. It was "a physical matter, a question of vibrations, wavelengths, and resonances." (Bernadette identified herself with ultramarine blue, the color with which she was "exactly in resonance.") Finding, after much experiment, the necessary ingredients, they made the first exhibited monochromes together, in Yves' mother's kitchen, painting with rollers on vellum mounted on wooden panels.

It is important to dwell upon Bernadette Allain's insistence that she and Yves regarded "entering into the world of color" as "a physical matter, a question of vibrations, wavelengths, and resonances." For this is pure Rosicrucianism, of the same stuff as Heindel's insistence that one can literally learn to fly. Yet the phraseology, divorced from its Rosicrucian sources and viewed in terms of Parisian culture of the 'fifties, sounds like phenomenology, as Bachelard or Gadamer, for example, will speak of entering into the world of a work of art. This example of a phrase which relates simultaneously to two existing codes, hanging ambiguously on the interface between them, foreshadows many such careful formulations in Yves' writings. Phenomenology, at first picked out of the Paris air, later buttressed by a superficial reading of Bachelard, was the third of the three codes which Yves was to weave together in his rich literary statements of 1957 and after.

In these writings Rosicrucianism provides the basic structures of thought to which the other codes are fitted to create the multidirectional ambiguity which, as in the Madrid pamphlet, was Yves' artful way of mediating between his desires and the world of facts. Whether this constitutes a belief or a habit is perhaps not a proper question. But if one judges by Yves' writings and by the persistence of certain ideas (such as flight or levitation) in his life, then the Rosicrucian code would seem to be a belief system, a structure to which his inner self-definition was inextricably bound.

Although Yves stopped working the Rosicrucian lessons in early 1953, he continued to read in Heindel's book until at least 1956, by which time he had it virtually memorized. Upon returning from Madrid to Paris, he spoke openly of his Rosicrucianism within the art world and was mocked for it. He did not make that mistake again. Henceforth, phenomenology mediated his Rosicrucianism to the outside world, and Neo-Dada provided an escape route from explanations and demands for consistency. "Yves' culture," as Pierre Restany says, "was very personalized and had many gaps in it. But in a sense it was the very gaps which made his personality remarkable."

During the period of the first monochromes, Yves was also teaching in the judo club of Montmartre, where Bernadette Allain demonstrated the judokatas with him. Yves' personal charisma attracted many of the neighborhood hoodlums and delinquents; they made up perhaps half his students. He sympathized with their rebelliousness, their violence, their resistance to formal education; they were better potential warriors than the bourgeois students. He in turn influenced them deeply. As Allain says "When the neighborhood tough is thrown to the mat time and time again without exception, in three months this eighteen-year-old boy will be transformed, because he has come into contact with a *force*." He taught them the ethic of the Kodokan, the fraternity of the *judokas*, the quietness of the judo master who when he walks on the street looks like anyone else. "Already," says Bernadette, "he had an insane need to be admired," but in the hero cult of this "pure judo period" he had not yet begun to caricature himself. He was peaceful and dignified. He was, in her eyes at least, at his best.

Yves' "insane need to be admired" never abated. The shock of his near "failure" at judo had alarmed him. He began to feel, perhaps as a kind of compensation, an inner conviction of his own importance which grew more rigid and fanatical as time passed. Always a devotional personality drawn to the supernatural, he began to regard his life, through its secret connection with Rosicrucian prophecy, as sacred history. He assimilated himself to Jesus Christ, telling Bernadette that he would die at age thirty-three. ("In fact," she says "he died every time he didn't get what he wanted....Yves Klein, mental age: ten." She laughs.)

When he wanted to rush into the art world at once, confident of his success, she tried to pull him back. ("I knew how they buy, how they manipulate, how they sell.") His head was still filled with Tintin and knights in armor. He was "too naïve, too infantile—and too fascinating. He had a certain...power." Competing for attention in the avant-garde, he was in danger of throwing away whatever degree of inner peace he had gained in judo. It was the first of the disputes which were to bring their relationship to an end.

Nevertheless, impatient, as always, for paradise, Yves submitted an orange monochrome to the Salon des Réalites Nouvelles in 1955. When he refused to add an element of drawing, the painting was rejected (though the judges disliked barring the son of Marie Raymond, who had participated in the exhibition for several years). Rejection only increased Yves' energy level. ("He would not tolerate anyone who resisted him," says Bernadette.) He arranged a show of monochromes at the Club des Solitaires in October 1955. The exhibition went almost unnoticed except by the young critic Pierre Restany, whose work was to be linked with Yves' for their mutual benefit. As the years passed, Restany would write Yves' catalogues and, on at least one occasion, arrange for his shows. "Restany," says a mutual friend, "wanted to *become* Yves."[45] "I owe him very much," says Restany. "I owe to him both the structure of my thought and the conduct of my life, my style of life." Yves in turn found in Restany the educated voice which he himself lacked but deeply desired. When words were required, he interposed Restany between himself and the world, while secretly searching (through Voltaire, Hugo, Flaubert, Proust) for a writing style of his own.

Equally important was Yves' meeting with Jean Tinguely (who had been standing by the judges' table when Yves' orange monochrome was rejected). Tinguely was beyond convention and as the years passed would greet Yves' increasingly flamboyant mythic gestures with delight. The little Captain, with his childlike beliefs and laughing intensity, made life into a poem overflowing with good humor, and that was a magic beyond questioning.

In the next years several young artists from Nice (the "School of Nice," actually formed in 1961) would arrive in Paris: Arman, Martial Raysse, Cesar. They all had a certain intensity, or "anguish," as Tinguely calls it. "It was astonishing," he says, "to see such anguish coming from the Cote d'Azur. But Yves Klein was absolutely the champion in every category of anguish. He was the most anguished man I have ever met. He had too much positive force in a climate of materialism which was impossible for him to bear."

The little group which would become the New Realists was forming. Yves' glowing eyes and inexhaustible childish energy propelled him toward its center. ("He was," says Tinguely, "a superb companion," as well as the "champion of anguish.") With supreme—indeed, exaggerated—self-confidence, he promised the others that he would quickly become famous and then sponsor their careers.

In 1956, after an introduction by his mother, he exhibited monochromes of various colors at the Galerie Colette Allendy; the preface to the catalogue was written at his request by Pierre Restany.[46] Restany suggested that Yves was carrying to its conclusion the adventure begun by Malevich (a comparison which would disturb Yves more and more as the years passed), denounced *l'art informel*, and characterized the monochromes as icons of "asthenic silence" and "pure contemplation." But there is an interesting contrast between Restany's "pure contemplation" and Tinguely's description of Yves' state of mind as he made the paintings: "He had no contemplation, no calm, no inner balance. While he painted the monochromes he was going crazy with anxiety about whether the three materials he was using would mix properly." The discrepancy between Yves' high-voltage personal style and the ideal of pure contemplation would become more pronounced as time passed.

But the show did not satisfy Yves. The effect of several colors was too decorative to express the profound sensibility of pure color. In the following year he would use only one color, ultramarine blue (later International Klein Blue)—Bernadette's color, and the color of his first art work, the blue sky of Nice.[47]

Prowling the galleries in search of a dealer, Yves appeared one day at Iris Clert's, a blue monochrome under his arm. At first, like the judges of the salon, she denied that it was a painting. But after hanging it (at Yves' insistence) for several days, she realized that it had "a certain power," a certain "positive force," like its maker. It was the force of "spiritual space," of the "upward attraction" toward limitless blue freedom in the sky. It was the force that would draw Yves more and more strongly back toward his infinite home.

12

I am obsessed! The Blue! The Blue! The Blue! The Blue!

STÉPHANE MALLARMÉ

AT THE TIME, IRIS CLERT WAS NOT YET A DEALER TO WHOM SERIous artists were offering their work. But she was ambitious and excitable and wanted to be part of the avant-garde. For this she needed a group of "anguished" young artists, and Yves was offering her one. The arrangement was advantageous to both. In the next few years she exhibited the works of Yves, Tinguely, Arman, and others who would become the New Realists, at times (e.g., the exhibition *Le Vide*, 1958) performing curatorial heroics. Fired up by the youthful exuberance of her new associates, she encouraged their tendency toward radical innovation, as opposed to a slower deepening and maturing of vision, to the point of psychological strain. Yves in particular underwent pronounced personality changes as the game of avant-gardism became an overpowering reality. He grew increasingly hungry and manipulative ("No one could refuse anything to Yves," Iris Clert says). He became, she remembers, "a kind of Nietzsche of painting"; the "hypertrophy of his ego" became overwhelming; he was *"un gras bébe,"* *"un grand naïf,"* and, above all, *"un dictateur."* Their ruptures as time passed were passionate and nearly hysterical.

In collaboration with Robert Godet, Jean Tinguely, Pierre Restany, and Iris Clert, Yves began the process feared by Bernadette Allain, the process of becoming a caricature of himself; he began to make his personal myth public by stages, along with his work. At once he found that the technique brought him worldly success, and he pushed on with it regardless of what it was doing to his inner world. The presentation of a mythic persona which at times he seems to have literally believed, but which, in self-defense, he buffered with the fashionable codes of the day, became increasingly a game which had its own momentum, which pushed on toward its conclusion with a ruthless dynamism, a game from which the player himself could not simply escape by an act of choice.

But concealing his Rosicrucian "foundation" concealed the inner coherence of his *oeuvre* also, and opened him to constant misinterpretation as a mere showman or opportunist. This blindness to his inner seriousness frustrated Yves deeply, and as in his rash decision to challenge the Judo Federation, he responded with more and more assertive claims. And as his claims became more extreme, Yves found himself increasingly caught up in them.

Perhaps the first of the symbolic Stations or Labors were motivated primarily by an opportunistic desire for publicity. But as his self-image came to depend more and more on the status of his claims, his commitment to the myth became less playful, his identification with it more complete and more dangerous. As Yves' identification with his symbolic personae grew, his mood became increasingly doomed, heroic and tragical.

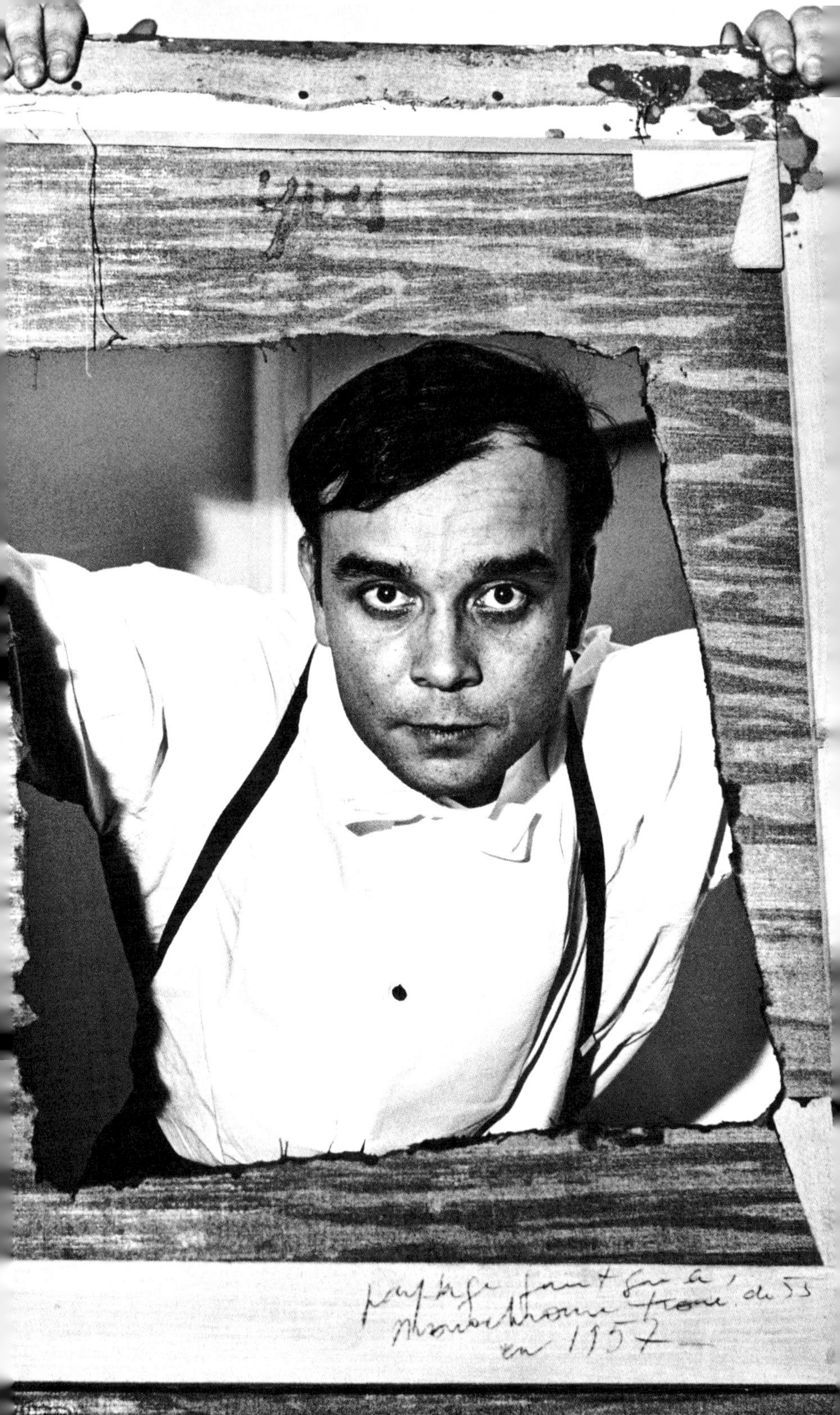

Those who watched him undergo this process evaluated it differently. Tinguely, for example, romanticizes it and regards Yves' self-crucifixion (through self-caricature) as beautiful poetry. His mother chooses to regard it as unavoidable, a "destiny that had tracked him from the day he was born." Bernadette Allain, on the other hand, regards it as a growing pathology, brought on by over excitement and loss of inner balance and intensified by the encouragement of those whose careers would profit from his drama of self-immolation.

In 1957 Yves began to act out his mythic function as Messenger of the incoming age. The Blue Epoch was inaugurated by an exhibition of identical blue monochromes at Guido Le Noci's Galleria Apollinaire in Milan. Yves' artfully interpenetrating code system was now solidly in place on several levels. The title of the exhibition, *L'Epoca Blu*, makes ironic reference, in art historical terms, to Picasso's famous Blue Period; but in Rosicrucian terms it indicates the age in which matter will be dissolved and humanity will return to the bodiless Eden of space-as-pure-spirit, which Heindel symbolized by blue. The blue monochromes themselves represent the melting of forms into prime matter beyond internal differentiations, while in terms of art history they are a sharp (and timely) rejection of *l'art informel*; phenomenologically they deny the subject-object dichotomy by forcing the "observer" to participate in the creation of their meaning. The fact that the paintings were hung about eight inches in front of the wall is also a conflation of codes; in Rosicrucian terms it indicates the end of the age of gravity and the beginning of the age of levitation (Yves began at this time to speak "obsessively" about levitation); in art historical terms it relates to the project of "proclaiming... the activity of painting in real space... [and revealing] the picture as an object within that space."[48] As Yves was to write in "The Monochrome Adventure,"[49] he wanted the painting to "invade the space of the observer," both by controverting habitual modes of perceiving a painting and by signifying the Rosicrucian doctrine of the onrushing invasion of all matter by spirit.

The fact that the paintings were more or less identical is again

---

Left: Yves Klein, 1961.

an expression of the triple code: in Rosicrucian terms it refers to the underlying sameness of the absolute or ground of being beneath all individual beings; in art historical terms it is anti-illusionistic, "insisting upon the material 'thinghood' of the components";[50] phenomenologically regarded, it is a strategy to break up the viewer's complacency of perceptual habit.

It must be stressed that these paintings could very well have been exhibited without the implied claim that they ushered in not only a new age of art but a new phase of human evolution. But Yves' grandiosity required the myth. Art in and by itself, without exalted spiritual implications and claims, was never enough for him. He was later to say to Claude Parent that "the monochromes are me": they were his calling card as Messenger from the Blue Void, the heraldic emblem of his ethereal kingship in the sky.

In purely art historical terms they were as timely at that moment in Europe as the more or less contemporary works of Newman and Reinhardt, or Rauschenberg's white paintings were in America. But it was not only the perfection of the gesture at that moment that put the blue monochromes in the art history books; the brilliant presence of these paintings cannot be denied. Each of them preserves still its maker's magnetic gaze and high-voltage surface. Quite without any myth they exerted an immediate influence on serious artists. In Milan, Fontana bought an International Klein Blue monochrome and subsequently moved his own work further into monochromy. Piero Manzoni was converted by the IKBs from a figurative style to his "achromes." In the following years he made repeated trips to Paris to knock on Yves' door and hang around Iris Clert's gallery. His *oeuvre* became a strange parody, or deliberate inversion, of Yves'.

Later that year the blue monochromes were exhibited at Iris Clert's. In conjunction with the exhibition, Yves showed at Colette Allendy's an astonishingly varied group of works which presaged not only much of his own later career, but in a sense the next ten or twenty years of Western art. There the first blue sponge sculpture appeared, alluding to the Rosicrucian doctrine of the permeation of matter by Spirit and foreshadowing the development of new media in the sixties; blue painted screens gestured both toward Japanese influence and toward the sculptural transformation of the painting; upstairs, a room was left empty as an exhibition of "the surfaces and volumes of pure pictorial sensibility"; and on the evening of the opening, Yves performed a "One-Minute Fire Painting," made up of four rows of four signal flares each, mounted on a square plywood support. As the exhibition of blue monochromes at Iris Clert's was the announcement of the beginning of Yves' career as self-appointed art messiah or Messenger of the New Age, the show at Colette Allendy's laid claim to the whole range of art as his domain.

Still later in 1957, groups of monochromes in various colors were exhibited in Düsseldorf and London. Though London and Paris remained unconvinced, the effect in Düsseldorf was as positive as in Milan. Young German artists (Heinz Mack, Otto Piene, and others) were electrified by directions implicit in Yves' work and, after meeting him, by his "man of destiny" style. The groups N in Milan and Zero in Düsseldorf purveyed his influence and, when they came to know it, his myth.

Ten years or so earlier, Yves Marie Klein had rejected his personal origin and history, becoming simply "Yves," and like an Orphic devotee had chosen a mythic origin and cast his true home beyond the sky. Now, launching the Blue Epoch in which all humanity, catalyzed by him, was to recall and regain the Sky-nature, he called himself "Yves the Monochrome." It was in part a knightly title for his adventures in the infinity of color-space-spirit. But in part it was a claim, perhaps ill advised, to a seamless wholeness like that of his paintings, to an inner space uniformly and serenely blue, where no darknesses or entanglements of lines might conceal the Discord Spirit.[†]

[†] Klein also asserted "the glaring obviousness of my paternity of the monochrome in the twentieth century." In fact, it was not all that obvious. Miro's blue monochrome of 1925 may be regarded as an exception. But around 1950 a number of artists had seen that twentieth-century painting was headed toward the monochrome as one of its ultimate expressions. In 1951 Rauschenberg exhibited white monochromes; in 1953 Reinhardt confined himself to a monochrome style. Others were quick to follow.

13

Shall we admit that in the blue void
is limitless pleasure?

LU KUEI-MENG

YVES' ESSAYS COMBINING PROPHECY, THEORY OF ART, AND CLAIMS of occult attainments began to be written in 1954 (the year of exile and wounded pride) and began to be published in 1958. The most accomplished of these—"Truth Becomes Reality," "Due to the Fact That," "The Monochrome Adventure"—reveal a poetic talent and have a certain interest as pure literature.

The earliest of them, "The War: A Little Personal Mythology of the Monochrome" (parts of which were written as early as 1954), presented a mythic interpretation of the monochrome exhibitions.[51] The Rosicrucian opposition between Space (unity) and Form (multiplicity) was translated into art historical terms as the Battle between Color and Line. As human evolution, according to Heindel, is on the verge of a return from Form (separateness, limitation) to Space (wholeness, infinity), so the artist, Yves wrote, should reject Line (division, entanglement, neurosis) in favor of Color (unity, openness, enlightenment). Whereas Line divides and fragments space, Color fills it completely and becomes one with it:

> *It is color which bathes in cosmic sensibility.*
> *The line does not have the ability to impregnate, as color does.*
> *The line cuts space.... Color impregnates it.*
> *Line rushes through infinity; color just "is" in infinity*

Color, as Heindel taught, is Spirit when it has coagulated enough to become visible in space, but not enough to fracture into forms;

> *Before the colored surface, one finds oneself directly before the matter of the soul.*[52]

The dichotomy between Delacroix (color) and Ingres (line) was the paradigm of this battle. Yves had discovered Delacroix's *Journals* in 1956 and it remained his bedside book for the rest of his life, the record not only of a comrade in arms but of a spiritual brother. He was drawn by the romantic mysticism of this painter who wrote, "In some people the inner spark scarcely exists. I find it dominant in me. Without it I should die—but it will consume me."[53] This Werther-like spirit, Yves wrote, "sought the total expression of himself in and by color,"[54] and was in a sense the first prophet of the return to Space. But it was above all Delacroix's insistence on the "indefinable" factor that aligned him, Yves thought, with the alchemical approach to art.

Alchemical texts speak of a real, although invisible and ineffable, substance which distinguishes the "gold of the philosophers" from "common gold," the "fire of the philosophers" from "common fire," and so forth. Control of this substance, symbolized by the Philosopher's Stone, was the goal of the Work; by isolating it in his own person, the alchemist gains the power to inject it into other entities at will. Guided by Heindel, Yves had been seeking this power for years:

> *The gold of the ancient alchemists can be extracted from anything. The difficult part is uncovering the gift of the Philosopher's Stone, which exists in each of us.*[55]

Now, inspired by Delacroix's "indefinable," he transposed the alchemical doctrine into artistic terms; a true painting contains an invisible, indefinable "substance" which transmutes it into an eternal absolute:

> *Painting is alchemical, and beyond time. It represents nothing.*[56]

An immaterial substance, which Yves called "pure pictorial sensibility," is injected into the art work by the alchemist/artist who has isolated and purified this sensibility in himself; it can be experienced in the painting, after any number of years, by a viewer whose own sensibility is sufficiently developed. Art, then, is not a sensory but an extrasensory experience. Of two visually identical paintings, one possessing this substance is art, and the other, lacking it, is not. A sensitive viewer can distinguish at once.

The theory was based on Heindel, but Yves heard resonances of it in Delacroix, who said, "It is not a painting if it doesn't point beyond the finite; the value of a painting is the indefinable factor."[57]

Yves read Delacroix's "indefinable" as equivalent to his own "pure sensibility," and both of them as equivalent to Heindel's "Spirit." The indefinable, said Delacroix, is "what the soul [of the artist] has added to the lines and colors to reach out to the soul [of the viewer]."[58] Similarly, Van Gogh (whom also Yves enlisted on his side in the Battle, because he "foresaw the monochrome") wrote to his brother Theo that "paintings have their own life which comes entirely from the soul of the painter."[59] Heindel, the ultimate authority, also had said that a true work of art has a soul like a living creature. The artist, then, is truly godlike. Said Yves:

He puts a soul in his creation.

A synopsis of art history emerges which consists of Yves and his "precursors," to wit, Giotto, Rembrandt, Delacroix, and Van Gogh, all of whom had managed to "put a soul" in their creations.

Such claims are, of course, grandiose. As Bachelard put it, "Alchemical gold is a reification of a strange need for royalty, superiority and domination which animates the solitary alchemist."[60] This "strange need" may reach back, through the "timelessness of the unconscious," to the child in the cradle, bawling his claim to omnipotence.

Yves' alchemical theory of art might be discredited on the ground that, since (it seems) he "could not hold a pencil,"[61] he was forced to argue for a non-visual criterion of value. After all, if Yves claimed—as he did—that he had isolated the Philosopher's Stone in himself, that his inner world was open and clear, and that he had injected "pure sensibility" into his works, who could deny it? Yves would simply retort that his critic's sensibility was not sufficiently developed. The theory of the immaterial essence, in other words, could be a charlatan's disguise. But it is not so easy to dismiss either Yves' work or his theory.

Iris Clert relates that in the year after showing Yves' "monoblues" she exhibited "monoblacks" by another painter which aroused no response at all: they lacked the magnetic gaze of "pure sensibility."[62] Indeed, many have discovered that, face to face, these paintings have "an unmitigated, pure, but very sensuous beauty."[63] An IKB monochrome viewed out of context on the other side of the world still breathes the fierceness of Yves' ego and his fiery drive toward transcendence. Such vibrations seem, quite as he said, to cling round his work, or emanate from it, invisibly.

Finally, it must be noted that Yves' art is hard to define—thus hard to criticize. ("Am I a painter?" he asks in "The Monochrome Adventure"; "oh all right then, I'm a painter.") He was not in fact devoted to any single medium, but to the general aim of giving a body, a voice, and a soul to the absolute—of making it a living mythic presence in our time. This was a composite project, for which Yves intended to employ the arts and sciences in general. At the time of his death he had already employed painting, sculpture, event art, photographs, music, and literature, and had clear plans for works in theater, ballet, and film (not to mention the various scientific, political, and economic projects conceived in the name of the Void).

14

The eyes in the countenance of the young barbarian were bright and smiling. Though no one who saw him thought him other than mad, all found him handsome and noble.

CHRÉTIEN DE TROYES, *Perceval*

AT THE COLETTE ALLENDY EXHIBITION OF 1956, YVES MET A FRIEND of his father who was involved with heraldry and an order of "archers," the Knights of Saint Sebastian, which traces its origins to the time of Charlemagne. He invited Yves to join, and Yves was delighted: here was a Round Table still active in his own day.

Yves was accepted on a Friday, rented a cape and sword on Saturday ("He loved costumes," says Arman; "He loved disguises," says Claude Pascal), passed the night in a vigil with the other inductees, and on Sunday, in the presence of his parents, at the touch of a bishop's hand he was made a knight, at last!

A cartoon panel, Station, or Labor, of the Myth: Yves, Knight of Saint Sebastian, stands trim, compact, straight, in the plumed hat and black cape with Crusader's cross, a veiled challenge in the famous Javanese eyes as he stares into Space poised for combat. He holds in his right hand a blue monochrome painting which his left hand points to as the symbol of the kingdom he serves. "Having been made a knight of the Order of Saint Sebastian," he proclaims in a hero's ringing voice, "I espouse the cause of Pure Color, which has been invaded and occupied guilefully by the cowardly line and its manifestation, drawing in art. I will defend color, and I will deliver it, and I will lead it to final triumph."[64]

(In the following year he asked his aunt for a new costume to wear each Saint Sebastian's day. She sent a red velvet waistcoat with "Italian trousers." The Champion of Color, ever a child to his aunt, replied: "What a formidable red velvet! Really this time I have been re-spoiled and super-spoiled by my tantine! It is getting terrible, everyone tells me that I am spoiled rotten.")

15

"Moon rocket calling Earth... This is Tintin here. I am no longer subject to ordinary gravitational pull."

Explorers on the Moon

JEAN TINGUELY: "YVES WAS VERY EARTHY. HE LOVED TO EAT WELL. He loved the good things of the earth. But at the same time he was transported toward the opposite—the ethereal, the immaterial, the void. He was very contradictory inside. I think that at a certain age this contradiction began to take over his personality. He would spend an entire evening trying to convince someone that the earth was flat and square. It was hard, at that time, with satellites orbiting the earth, to prove to people that the earth was flat and square. But he managed to do it. He would spend insane amounts of energy to convince some fellow—it didn't matter who—someone he had met by accident in La Coupole. He would even search for victims to persuade. And they believed him. He had such fire, such force, in conversation, he marshaled so many proofs of an unrecognizable metaphysical character, that the idiots would leave feeling sure he was right.

"This was not a man who was interested in material things. He was profoundly non-materialistic. For him money meant a good meal, and he always shared what he had with a friend as a sign of respect. Once Eva and I did not have a cent. Yves said, 'I have twenty thousand francs. I'm giving you ten thousand.' It was like Saint Martin's cloak.

"He had an aerial walk that created a happy mood around him. He would go out walking in May still wearing his winter coat (I don't think he even noticed). He would stride into La Coupole, the Saint Sebastian cape flying around him, his eyes shining, with the new Tintin book under his arm. He shocked the intellectuals.

"He read comic books and talked about knights and the Holy Grail. Those marvelous things that exist in the world of a child still worked for him."

16

"Greetings, spirit of the air, greetings, spirit that penetratest from heaven to earth and from earth to the uttermost abyss, greetings, spirit that penetratest into me and shakest me."

Great Magical Papyrus of Paris

SITTING AROUND LA COUPOLE, TINGUELY, IRIS CLERT, ROBERT Godet, and others encouraged Yves to "go beyond" the monochrome. In a sense, he already had, for he had already declared his belief in the immaterial essence of the art work which of course implies the irrelevance of color quite as much as of line. Clearly the unbroken field of color was not the ultimate symbol for Prime Matter before it has separated into forms. In 1958, aware of these problems and encouraged by his friends, Yves redefined his kingdom. No longer bound to any ordinary human experience—such as the visual experience of the blue of the sky—it was now the actual emptiness which had been hinted by the blue, the immaterial itself. He and Iris began to prepare for the classic exhibition *Le Vide*.

(Just prior to the opening of *Le Vide*, at the beginning of April 1958, Yves rooted the event in the basal level of his religious personality—the nourishing and protecting female deities of his mother's family—by flying secretly to Cascia and visiting Saint Rita at her own shrine for the first time. There he prayed to her for an ability to penetrate Rosicrucian magic without losing his soul. As he explained later to his Aunt Rose: "I said to myself, 'I think this exhibition of the Void is rather dangerous.... It is necessary to go to Saint Rita....'")

Station or Labor: it is April 1958. Yves is alone in the Iris Clert gallery. Moving quickly, carefully, and silently, on feet accustomed to "spiritual space," he carries the furniture to storage, sweeps the floor, and slowly, through two long days, paints the interior walls white. Concentrating his mind as in the old days of meditation on the terrace in Nice, he gains access to the first immaterial realm and begins to manipulate its forces. Projecting images onto its Prime Matter, he draws them up from potentiality and stabilizes them in the space of the room. It is his thirtieth birthday, an occasion traditionally associated with the commencement of spiritual ministries.

As evening falls, crowds of thousands gather in the narrow street—the Void itself is about to open its secrets to them. Guards of the Republic flank the doors to the *sanctum sanctorum*. Glasses of blue liquid are passed out like a communion drink ("The blood of the body of sensibility is blue").[65] The door opens and Yves-the-Sorcerer appears in formal dress. He guides small groups into the Void while striving "to create a magnetic current and enthrall or enchant the guests."[66] Many laugh and leave at once. Some stay silent for an hour or more. One man "trembled and couldn't hold back his tears."[67] Camus himself enters and writes in the guest book, "With the void, full powers." (Casual flattery? Or did he feel a power in that room?) Yves' judo students try to keep order. The fire trucks come, and then the police. As the crowd disperses, many people who went inside emerge strangely excited or moved. They walk away "impregnated" with the new sensibility of the incoming age. At midnight, at La Coupole, Yves proclaims that four millennia of civilization have been culminated; a new age of human sensibility has arrived. He quotes Socrates and Cicero, denounces Einstein and Roosevelt, and announces that henceforth "leprous France" will be governed by Blue, concluding with a magician's prayer to reify his words: "May this be said and done." (And remember: "Yves was always dead serious.") Still, inside, despite the protection of Saint Rita and his grandmother, he feels a little frightened at what he has done; he feels, somehow, that he has contacted his own death that night.[68]

For a week all those who drank the blue "cocktail" urinate blue, the blood of pure sensibility issuing from their bodies.

Other Void or Immaterial works followed, as Yves pursued the project of eliminating the visible art object altogether. The artist of the future, he wrote (following Heindel), will only leave his vibration in a space, to be picked up later by the immaterial antennae of others walking there.[69] In the following years he demonstrated the art of his invisible kingdom, opening the door to the age of immateriality.

Station: it is 1959. Yves is asked to participate in a group show (*Vision in Motion—Motion in Vision*) in Antwerp. At the opening, he stands for a while in the place allotted for his piece, recites a passage from Bachelard on the color blue, then returns to Paris. An empty space in the gallery is his work—a vibration left hanging in the air, a bodiless magnetism with his ego patterns in its waves. In Paris, he works on plans to sell invisible paintings and to give a public demonstration of flying.

17

In the bright crystal of your eyes
Show the havoc of fire, show its inspired works
And the paradise of its ashes,

PAUL ELUARD

YVES UNDERSTOOD THAT HIS WRITINGS WERE AS ESSENTIAL TO the program of mythic theater as were his art works and events. Yet his Heindelian belief system was an anachronism, with its wholehearted commitment to the priority of unchanging essence. It could have no place in the Paris of Sartre, Barthes, Levi-Strauss, and Robbe-Grillet (whose 1958 essay "Nature, Humanism, Tragedy" simply pulverizes the "spiritual" approach to art). Yet it was a part of Yves' genius—indeed, his method—to be archaic while seeming ultramodern. He found his strongest link to modern thought in the works of Gaston Bachelard.

Bachelard was superficially much like Heindel; he too wrote about alchemy and the four elements, about spiritual space and the soul's voyages in it. Yet his modernism was guaranteed by none other than Sartre, who praised him for several pages in *Being and Nothingness*.[70] Yves read (or read parts of) Bachelard's books on the four elements and space, deriving from them a thin overlay of phenomenology with which to soften his Heindelian literalism.[71]

"We can classify poets," said Bachelard, "by asking them to answer the question: 'Tell me what your infinite is...: is it the infinite of the sea or sky, is it the infinite of the earth's depths or of the pyre?'"[72] Yves, the child who had no home on earth but, he suspected, a whole kingdom in the sky, seems nevertheless to have regarded himself not as an air but a fire type: it is fire which burns away limits, which produces change, which converts solid matter to spirit-like ash on the wind. "The alchemist," of course, "is a 'master of fire.' It is with fire that he controls the passage of matter from one state to another."[73] "In comparison with the intensity of fire," said Bachelard, "how slack, inert, static and aimless seem the other intensities that we perceive. They are not embodiments of growth. They do not fulfill their promise. They do not become active in a flame and a light which symbolizes transcendence."[74] "I hold that in the heart of the void, as in the heart of man, fires are burning,"[75] wrote Yves, echoing the ancient image of the universal soul as a central fire whose scattered sparks are individual souls. "Fire is dialectical in all its properties," said Bachelard; "...it only has to flame up to contradict itself."[76] To Yves this became a desperate moral imperative:

> One must be like untamed fire....One must know...how to contradict oneself.[77]

For the same fire which burns through into the void is, says Bachelard, the fundamental symbol of sexuality. (Consider the ithyphallic angle of the flame-thrower in the photographs of Yves making fire paintings, consider the interplay of sex and death in those works.) "My paintings are only the ashes of my art," said Yves.[78] "He was always speaking of ashes," says Tinguely. "Whatever he did, he would say, 'It's the ashes that interest me.'" There is danger in this preoccupation. As Bachelard said, "In the last analysis, all the complexes attached to fire are painful complexes."[79]

"Repression," wrote Bachelard, "is a normal activity, a useful activity, a joyous activity," when it is performed in the service of an "absolute sublimation."[80] "Sublimation" of course is an alchemical as well as a psychoanalytic term, denoting the ascension phase of the Great Work ("It rises from the earth to the sky and again descends into the earth," says the *Emerald Tablet*). Yves' dreamed flight to the other side of the sky was an analogue of alchemical sublimation; but his life partook of psychoanalytic repression and sublimation as well. His Rosicrucian belief that sexual energies must be stored up for the great burst of the Transfiguration never completely left him. It was perhaps sustained by his ongoing problem in sexual performance. "Eroticism, for him, was something transformed," says Tinguely. "It had nothing of the pornographic in it." And Arman recalls: "Sublimation was a key word in his vocabulary."

Indeed, Yves borrowed Bachelard's term "absolute sublimation" to describe his own inner alchemy:

> *I seek the effective liberation of the personality in all its aspects in*
> *the individual, by the exasperation of the Me practiced to the point*
> *of an absolute, purifying sublimation.*[81]

We can recognize still the archaic and painful ascesis of Heindel, only superficially tamed by the stylish Bachelardian terminology. Art remained for Yves a ritual of self-sacrifice and self-liberation, the cannibalistic communion rite of a dying god:

> *The painter, like Christ, says the mass while painting and gives his*
> *body and soul as nourishment for other people; he realizes a little*
> *the miracle of the Last Supper in every painting.*[82]

In fact, Yves had a growing problem with Heindel, to which Bachelard seemed to offer a solution. As the years passed and Yves found himself still not *"free really in this world"* (as he had written with boyish enthusiasm in the Irish journal), he came to doubt more and more the radical Transfiguration which was promised in the *Cosmogonie* and in which he had invested a decade's faith and effort. But Bachelard dissolved all such goals into symbols; magic he called imagination; ascension and transfiguration he called the glories of reverie, not of the physical body. All value, in fact, he shifted from the objective to the subjective pole of the intentional vector: it is the inner disposition that matters, not the outer act.

Yves pricked up his ears at this. Here was a door through which he might escape the devouring sky. But what if Heindel was right—Heindel through whom a thousand sages spoke? What did Bachelard know of the lonely truth of the hermit and yogi? In his writings Yves plays sleight-of-hand with these two, now making the absurdly literalist claims which made him seem to many an imposter, and again retreating from literalism into Bachelard's "imagination." In the end, however, there was no contest, for only one truly promised omnipotence and transcendence.

The same problem besets the "invitation to a voyage." Every poet, said Bachelard, proffers to the reader an "invitation to voyage" into his imagination, into "the land of the infinite," "the realm where the imagination…is free and alone,…[and] the reality of unreality asserts itself."[83] Yves' career as an artist is a long and often-reformulated invitation to voyage into his kingdom of infinite space beyond the sky.

> *Now I want to go beyond art, beyond sensibility, beyond life; I want to go into the void.*[84]

Clearly this is a dangerous desire, this sublimation of oneself right out of the world. But on the very danger of it hung its amazing heroism, and on its literal truth depended its glory. Yves was not ready to abandon ontology for epistemology, to give up heaven for dreams of heaven, to consider Heindel merely one of Bachelard's "poets." Perhaps if he had lived longer…. But he was still devastatingly innocent. He was still burning too brightly to touch. He still wanted to live with untamed fire.

So the question, as Bachelard put it, was whether "to seize fire or to give oneself to fire, to annihilate or to be annihilated, to follow the Prometheus complex or the Empedocles complex."[85] Surely Yves (the Conquistador of the Void!) thought he was acting out the Prometheus complex; as events would show, however, he was an Empedocles walking toward the mouth of the volcano.

18

ANDRÉ FRENAUD

YVES HAD BEGUN TO MEET THE ARTISTS OF THE ZERO GROUP IN 1955, and his exhibition of monochromes in Düsseldorf in May 1957 brought him more centrally to their attention at a propitious moment. On the day of the opening, the city of Gelsenkirchen announced a competition for the commission to decorate its new opera house. Norbert Kricke, a young German sculptor, invited Yves to join a group of artists taking part in the competition. Yves accepted eagerly and was introduced to the architect, Werner Ruhnau, who became fascinated by him. Over the following months, Pierre Restany says, "Yves gradually, imperceptibly, took over Kricke's place as the leader of the group." Following the directions of his shows at Iris Clert's and Colette Allendy's, he proposed for the foyer of the opera house a set of monumental paintings and sponge reliefs in ultramarine blue.

Characteristically he mobilized his forces (primarily female) in pursuit of the commission. Bernadette Allain was set to work on the maquettes, and Aunt Rose was asked to intercede on high. "How I prayed to Saint Rita," she recalls. Several months later Yves phoned her, saying not, "I won it," but, "Tantine! Saint Rita won it!" Soon, however, the Gelsenkirchen commission was to bring about a shift in his relationship with the female deities.

In the summer of 1958, not long after the exhibition of the Void, Yves traveled to Nice and in Arman's house met a beautiful eighteen-year-old German girl, Rotraut Uecker (sister of the Zero Group artist Gunther Uecker, and herself a painter), who was babysitting young Yves, Arman's son and Yves' namesake. They locked archetypes at once, and he began to expose to her that side of himself which felt profound and tragical and secretly doomed. (Yves' "technique" with girls, says Marcel Boulois, was to appeal to their motherly, protective impulses.) He was offering Rotraut, in effect, a front-row seat in his mythic theater. The first emblem of his identity he extended to her was the myth of his imminent dematerialization in the Void. "He was leaving Nice soon," says Rotraut, "and he said, 'I don't know if I will see you again. I have made an exhibition that has led me onto a very dangerous path. And I think that I may have to die for it.'" His eyes had a darkened, almost tearful look; the prophetic intensity of his voice frightened her.

He was in fact about to leave for the Gelsenkirchen project, which had him traveling a good deal. In September he went with Aunt Rose to Cascia for his second, and her first, visit to the saint's own shrine, to thank her for winning the commission for her favorite. He left among the ex voto objects a blue monochrome, once again involving the patroness of his art in Rosicrucian mysticism. The monochrome represented both thanks for success so far attained and a promise of greater things to come. In October he was back in Gelsenkirchen and found himself in need of an assistant and a translator. He phoned Rotraut and asked her to join him. She came at once.

Soon he was at work on the huge sponge reliefs which, according to Tinguely, "were his death." He soaked the sponges in polyester resins to harden them before applying the color, working without a mask, and at high intensity, for twelve hours a day. "At that time," says Tinguely, "no one was aware of the dangers of synthetic resins."

Back in Paris in June, Yves showed the *Bas Reliefs in a Forest of Sponges* at Iris Clert's—sponge reliefs like those for Gelsenkirchen but smaller, and blue sponges mounted like the foliage of trees on metal stems. Like the blue monochromes and the immaterial pieces, this exhibition seems to have roots in Heindel, in whose writings the saturation of sponges is a standard image for the permeation of all matter by Spirit—and blue the color most closely connected with Spirit. The mounting of the sponges on slender stalks again suggests Heindel's description of saturated sponges floating in empty space, and, like the mounting of the blue monochromes away from the wall, was a sign of Yves' ambition to make truly levitating art, sculptures which would float in the air, freed from any base.

Shortly after the opening of the *Forest* Yves travelled for a third time to Cascia, leaving four tiny ingots of gold for Saint Rita. In an accompanying prayer he dedicated the forthcoming Gelsenkirchen paintings to God the Father and the sponge reliefs to Saint Rita herself, praying fervently "that the impossible may arrive and establish its kingdom quickly."[86] In December 1959, Yves attended the impressive Gelsenkirchen opening with his mother and aunt. "The president of the German Republic was there," says Aunt Rose. "How proud I was." Yves seemed really to be achieving the ambition (to be at "the very top") of which he had written to her on the voyage back from Japan.

Yet his success, ominously, did not bring much financial reward. Rotraut, who returned to Paris to live with him, recalls that their first dinner together after Gelsenkirchen was on credit at La Coupole. The experience would become familiar in the years that followed.

Yves' conjunction with Rotraut, both charmed and tumultuous, lasted until the end of his life. Rotraut's sweetness of temper and childlike openness to the imagination mingled happily with the same qualities in him, though his infantile and tyrannical angers drove her at times toward estrangement. "He was a child," she says, "who was both very happy and very sad at the same time."

Rotraut became both presiding goddess and chief spectator of his monotheater, the spectator who watched both from backstage and from front row center. Further, she is present in his works in the most direct way: many of the classic imprints are of her body —her tissue, texture, heartbeat, in the "trace of the immediate" in the paint.

More Stations of the Myth: alone at home with Rotraut Yves puts on a vampire cape, makes paper fangs, marks her throat with red ink. She removes the cross from her neck, and he pretends to drink from her throat. "Don't worry," he says, "I just took a little. I'm the vampire who will die by self-starving."

Arman hailed this "very special and complex character" in free verse:

> *Master of the Blue Sky*
> *Monogold vampire*
> *O! Great master of the school of Nice—*
> *Let the school of New York be over*
> *and all the American renunciations.*[87]

Spurred on by accelerating success, Yves made his gestures of appropriation more extensive and fantastic. On May 29, 1958, he wrote to President Eisenhower announcing the termination of the French national government by the Blue Revolution. Receiving no answer, he sent the same message to Premier Khrushchev, again receiving no answer.

To the astonished architect Werner Ruhnau, he proposed plans for altering the earth's climate and building cities of compressed-air currents which would neither break up the visual unity of space nor obstruct the flight patterns and telepathic communications of the levitating, mind-reading humans of the Blue Age. The power of Yves' personality is demonstrated by the fact that he often convinced people that he might actually be able to do such things. Ruhnau carried out experiments with him at a factory near Hamburg and soon concluded that the air roof was impossible. Yves, however, was by no means convinced.

Station: fighting his inner war, he fills pages of his notebook with the word "humility, humility, humility…"

19

The alchemist is a dreamer who wishes, who enjoys wishing, who magnifies himself in his 'wishing big.'

GASTON BACHELARD

AFTER THE SUCCESS OF *LE VIDE* IN 1958, YVES DID IN FACT BRING Arman and Tinguely and others to Iris Clert to launch their careers. Still eager to "do all my possible for everybody," he delighted in advancing his friends. He encouraged their work in the directions that seemed natural to them, introduced them to dealers in Paris, Milan, Düsseldorf, lent them the aura of his burgeoning fame, praised their works to critics, became a kind of beneficent patriarch to his own contemporaries. But the "Proprietor of Color" had to come first in all things—that was his condition. As Restany says, "I would see that from time to time a new carriage would be added to Yves' train." There was no question about who was the locomotive. As he helped his friends, he also created a school of followers around (and behind) himself.

Soon, problems arose. In collaborating with Tinguely for their joint show, *Vitesse pure et stabilité monochrome* (1958), he referred to their work as "mine." But Tinguely, a bit of a samurai himself, did not want to be owned. Yves wrote at torturous length, explaining that for one who has gone beyond ego, the word "mine" was quite different in intentionality. In the egoless Age of Space, all art belongs to all artists. One must resist "the temptation to materialize pure spirit," and the consequent fall into passion. "The Sabbath Queen, Iris," was invoked to write an affidavit, specifying the "domain" of each of the collaborators, much as Yves, Claude, and Arman had once divided up the world. "The air, the atmosphere," Iris declared, "are the domain of Klein, while the magnetism, that is the earth...is the domain of Tinguely."

This controversy with a close friend was of serious moment to Yves. He was depressed by the clash of egos. Contemplating his dematerialization in the Void, he wrote wearily of life:

> Is it then a game, that it is necessary to live in the skin of a plain
> dull human? and in society as a pure spirit which has put on a
> costume and plays on the stage of a theater one role as well as
> another?

He even offered, in the context of his deep friendship for Tinguely, a prophetic Station of the Myth, forecasting more publicly now his own death, which he saw draw nearer in his incursions into the Void:

> The immaterial blue color presented in April '58 at Iris' had
> rendered me...inhuman. It had excluded me from the society of the
> world of tangible reality. I was outside of society, living in space,
> and unable to return to the earth. Jean Tinguely saw me in space
> and signaled to me by speed to show me the path of volumetric
> return to the ephemerality of material life. This is what I call my
> "salvation" by Tinguely.[88]

This pattern of disturbing ego clashes followed by tense reconciliations became a constant feature of Yves' last years; he quarreled over priority, at one time or another, with virtually all his friends. Still, he remained a "superb companion" much of the time, eager for collaboration with his friends.

In October 1960, after Iris Clert had exhibited the work of Yves, Arman, Tinguely, and others, Pierre Restany forged them into an official group, the New Realists. The manifesto was drawn up and signed in Yves' apartment. Yves exerted a strong influence (stronger even than over the others) over Restany, who soon came to see him as the central figure in the group, and whose book, *Yves Klein le monochrome*,[89] is the main external support for Yves' myth of himself as prophet and superman.

For in 1959, buoyed by the onrushing success of his adventure in the world of Blueness, Yves had taken an irrevocable step into the horizon of pure myth. Pol Bury, in Belgium, published a collection of Yves' writings[90] which required a wholehearted commitment to live up to, or which were, in plain fact, impossible to live up to. There for all to see were the announcements of the new age and his role in it, his plans to replace Keynesian economics, his prophecies of immediate evolution into the age of levitation, telepathy, and immateriality. It was a severe case of developmental forcing. His "beautiful megalomania" and "delusions of grandeur"[91] (the fantasied omnipotence of the little Captain: "I lay down my arms. Signed: Antoine") were now in the public domain. There was no longer much possibility of escaping from the myth and becoming a "plain dull human" among the others. In Germany and Italy his myth was received with good humor. But Paris did not make peace with him until 1965, three years after his death. Many were fascinated or amused by his provocation of the public mind; others considered him a braggart and awaited his downfall with pleasure.

He began to live with a sense that "the public" was daring him to carry the myth all the way. If he backed down from it, he would be considered a "phony." And the myth began at some point to reveal a negative side. At first he had thought only of the scenes of the hero's victories; later the sacrificial ending came to the foreground. He was writing a beautiful poem with his life—but the poem had a tragic ending. Sooner or later he would have to face it.

Increasingly as the fifties rolled on Yves felt the strain of his uncompromising self-advertisement. When Rotraut awakened at night she would find him already awake (or not yet asleep), writing or meditating to calm himself. In 1959 he tried to raise money for a full-page advertisement in *Paris-Match* declaring, in ultramarine blue, "The greatest painter in the world, Yves Klein, is a Frenchman." "His great naïveté and his exacerbated ambition," wrote Iris Clert, "frightened me. They made him fragile. The least setback shattered him."[92] He projected now a sculpture magnetically suspended in the air, now an IKB Stations of the Cross (fourteen blue monochromes in an all-white chapel). As his territory became more complex, boundary disputes arose. He quarreled over priority constantly.

This in itself was not unusual. It was one of the dangers that Bernadette Allain had tried to warn him about. "The whole artistic milieu," she says, "forced people to do something new every time. If someone else had done it before, then your work was worth nothing. In other words, the work itself had no value; it was only a publicity device. One had to do something new, to say something new, rather than deepening one's work and reflecting on its quality. One fabricates a legend about oneself for publicity, and before long the legend takes possession of the man and the man is forced to behave in conformity with the legend, to do what publicity requires. And it is from this that he died."

"He had none of the qualities you would expect of someone who made monochromes," says Tinguely, "—a kind of quietude, a capacity to contemplate himself, a kind of balance. He made monochromes as an iconoclast, an anti-painter. He was fighting his mother, he was fighting his father...."

Since the "mystic crisis" with Claude and Arman in 1948, Yves' inner world had expanded for about ten years, then had begun to contract and harden around certain contradictions. The serious and likable youth of the Irish journal, conscientiously and quietly striving for inner growth, had hardened into the apotheosized "Yves the Monochrome" whose inner world was now, supposedly, all of one texture. Yet that inner oneness was belied by his ambitions, his jealousies, and, above all, his "celebrated temper tantrums."[93] For the Discord Spirit was still with him, ambushing him with increasing frequency. "He had a violent temper but almost always controlled it," says Rotraut. "He would turn white in the face, and then blue. You would think he was going to explode." And Claude Pascal, his oldest friend: "His biggest problem—and I think in fact he died of it—was those terrible angers that seized him; his face would go completely, *completely* white. And sometimes for nothing. It was something that came out from inside him and he could not resist it. And I think that's what destroyed him."

The myth of the clear blue sky was proving hard to live up to. In fact, it was a trap. He had drawn for himself a role of prophet and perfect master and struggled desperately to fulfill it. "The Void belongs to me," he insisted—and it was a hard claim to live up to. He wrote:

> I am in a spiritual state which grows from day to day; my only problem is to keep it pure and authentic and not allow it to be contaminated by the psychological domain.[94]

The "psychological domain" is the bound thrashings of ego, with its "cunning" and its "*calculs*"; the "spiritual state," the unlimited freedom which (according to Heindel) underlies it. This "only problem" which Yves mentions so lightly was in fact a terrifying inner battle:

> My fundamental nature is at war with the psychological multiplicity of my personality.[95]

For Yves, the true artist had to be a kind of saint or yogi who has purified his essence beyond all contamination. He sought to unify his character, life, and art by rooting them all in the stratum of pure Spirit. This inner unity is, as the alchemists said, the Great Art:

> The fact that I exist as a painter will be the most formidable pictorial work of our time.[96]

But what would one be, or would one be anything at all, after attaining the psychological mono-state? Yves ruminates along Zen lines, not knowing:

> The author of a play lives his spectacle, his creation, he is his public and his triumph or disaster. And gradually even the author is not there anymore, and still the play goes on.[97]

20

*I saw the tremendous sky, the beautiful look
of people deprived of everything.*

PAUL ELUARD

IN AUGUST 1959, WHILE VACATIONING IN GREECE, IRIS CLERT received a note from her assistant in Paris: "M. Klein came to take all his works. He told me that if a customer wished to buy one, I should say that his paintings are invisible, because immaterial, in the space of the gallery, and that if he wanted to buy one, it would suffice to write me a check. He was clear that the check should be quite visible. I think that M. Klein has gone mad."[98] Yves, his career now under way, was abandoning Iris for the more established dealer Jean Larcade.

But such was the charm of Yves the Monochrome that the first customer to whom the gallery attendant actually said these words[99] replied that he did indeed want to buy an invisible painting, asking only for a receipt signed by Yves. Yves showed his seriousness by rejecting the chance to make a Duchampian gesture. The transfer of immaterial realities had profound implications, and Yves understood them. In a few months he had devised the "Ritual for the Relinquishing of Immaterial Zones of Pictorial Sensibility, 1957-59" (note the two-year backdating), including a sharp reprimand to the customer for wanting something visible to indicate possession:

> *Every possible buyer of an immaterial zone of pictorial sensibil-*
> *ity must realize that the fact that he accepts a receipt for the price*
> *which he has paid takes away all authentic immaterial value from*
> *the work, although it is in his possession.*
>
> > *In order that the fundamental immaterial value of the zone*
> *belong to him and become a part of his life, he must solemnly burn*
> *his receipt.*[100]

(There it is again, the fire which burns through into the Void—as Taoist priests would send a message to Hell by burning it, as Paracelsus says the soul must be raised to the highest vibration by burning.) An immaterial zone, after all, is more or less a *soul*. Only gold can buy it (since "spirits are commixed with gold, and by it fixed"), and nature must receive its due (since "transmutation is the work of Nature, only aided by the Art").[101]

> *Yves Klein must, in the presence of…witnesses, throw half of the gold received into the ocean, a river, or some other place in nature where this gold cannot be retrieved by anyone.*[102]

Station: November 18, 1959 the bank of the Seine. Yves, in bow tie and overcoat, smiling and energetic, even businesslike, sells a ticket to the other side of the sky, a zone of pregnant emptiness, for gold which flows away upon the river, The event is recorded in photographs. ("Was this," asks Iris Clert, "the birth of Conceptual Art?")[103]

21

> *The fire in the clouds*
> *The fire in the birds*
> *The fire in the cellars*
> *All empties and refills*
> *In the rhythm of the infinite*
>
> PAUL ELUARD

THE SWARM OF WORKS AND IDEAS WHICH YVES PRODUCED without pause after becoming, in 1955, "an involuntary painter" was not simply the result of trying "to go farther each time, because it was necessary to be avant-garde," as Bernadette Allain suggests. While that compulsion did of course enter into it, Yves' *oeuvre* displays an underlying wholeness of program. At the foundation was Heindel's Rosicrucianism. But it is questionable whether after a certain age Yves should be called a Rosicrucian. There is something to Arman's statement that "he was not a Rosicrucian, he was not anything; he just used whatever was useful to him." As Bernadette Allain says, Yves had "a certain flair or intuitive knowledge of what he could use, in regard to people, books, materials. He nourished himself on things, which he made into food and then intuitively transformed. When by chance he found a text he could use, even a paragraph he could make into food, or on which he could lean, then he became an enthusiast."

But the point that must be made clear is that Yves did not "use" just anything; he exercised a refined and intelligent choice. First of all he was nourished by Heindel, and his artistic program was to translate Heindel's Rosicrucianism into visual terms, as a kind of sympathetic magic to induce the dawning of a new age in which Yves himself might feel more at home. But in artistically articulating Heindel, in giving Heindel poetic rather than dogmatic force, Yves was secondarily nourished by Gaston Bachelard. He found in Bachelard many passages which he could use as food because they seemed to parallel Heindel. By overlaying Bachelard on Heindel, Yves could more clearly see Heindel in artistic terms.

Yves' first public acknowledgment of the influence of Bachelard occurred in April 1959, at his immaterial exhibition in the Hessenhuis in Antwerp, where he read a passage of *L'Air et Ies songes* from the chapter entitled "Le Ciel bleu":

> *First there is* nothing, *then there is a* deep *nothing; then there is a blue* depth.[104]

In December of that year, at the Gelsenkirchen opening attended by his "two mothers," a text purportedly by Yves but in fact consisting of passages from the same chapter of Bachelard was read for Yves in German. The lack of acknowledgment was not unusual. Only once in his extensive writings does Yves mention Max Heindel. His desire to give the appearance of excelling at all things (great athlete, artist, lover, and man of intellect) became especially fierce in areas in which he did not in fact excel. ("He had such desire," says Edouard Adam, "to be what he was not—it ate him away.")

In June of the same year, in his lecture at the Sorbonne, Yves was careful to assign a date for his first reading of Bachelard: April 1958.[105] The date, which is called into question by the very fact that he published it, may yet reveal more than he intended. April 1958 was the month of the opening of Le Vide at Iris Clert's. Clearly for Yves that exhibition had Rosicrucian associations. But in addition, the transition from blue-as-absolute to immaterial is specifically mentioned by Bachelard in the chapter from which

Yves quoted repeatedly in the following year. After discussing "*l'azur*," Bachelard notes:

> *The mark of a true aerial [or ethereal] nature is found, among us, in another direction [i.e., other than blueness]. It is based, in effect, on the dynamic of dematerialization. The substantial imagination of air is only truly active in a dynamic of dematerialization.*
>
> *It is in surveying the degrees of dematerialization of celestial blue that we can see the ethereal revery in action...the* fusion *of the dreaming being in a universe as little differentiated as possible, in a universe blue and sweet, infinite and without form,* with the least possible structure.[106]

Yves later, in fact, referred to *Le Vide* as an exhibition of "an immaterial blue color." It is possible that he had read in Bachelard earlier than April 1958, and the transition from blue to immaterial may reflect in part the convergence of Bachelard and Heindel, both of whom felt that blue was the last veil over the face of the Void. Yves' conception of the Battle between Line and Color may also reflect the influence of Bachelard's claim that "the feeling of the blue sky appears as an expansiveness without line."[107]

In general, Yves' "method" was to respond to convergences between Heindel, Bachelard, and his immediate environment. His attempt at an architecture of the air is a clear example. Heindel specifically calls for the dematerialization of the human environment (through a union of science, art, and religion) for the incoming age of the "etheric" body. This remaking of the environment is one of the duties of the highest initiate, who must lead the way. This is the mythic or "prophetic" basis of the architecture of the air (Yves' works all had a mythic or prophetic basis), made explicit in the levitation Imprint called *L'Architecture de l'air* (ANT 102). Yet Yves seems not to have turned his attention directly to this part of the Rosicrucian system until he was stimulated by an apparent parallel in Bachelard. *The Poetics of Space* (of which Yves owned six copies when he died) was published in 1958, the year in which Yves first mentioned the architecture of the air; in the second chapter (section 6) he found the following lines;

> *My house...is diaphanous, but it is not made of glass. It is more of the nature of vapor. Its walls contract and expand as I desire.*
> *An immense cosmic house is a potential of every dream of houses.*

> *Winds radiate from its center....A house that is as dynamic as this*
> *allows the poet to inhabit the universe. Or, to put it differently, the*
> *universe comes to inhabit his house.*†
> *...houses that integrate the wind, aspire to the lightness of air...*
> *...wind house, abode that a breath effaced...*

Bachelard then set the hook in Yves by noting that such houses would "be rejected by a positive, realistic mind." To Yves—the man who would spend an entire evening trying to convince a listener that the earth was flat and square—this was a challenge; he proposed a universe opposite to that of "the positive, realistic mind," a universe based on inspired irrationality.

Yet Iris Clert says that Bernadette Allain gave Yves the first vague suggestion of the architecture of the air, and Bernadette Allain confirms this, saying, "I was the precursor of the architecture of the air." In fact, Werner Ruhnau makes a similar claim for himself. But it should be pointed out that such assertions show an incomplete understanding of Yves' method—understandably, since his method was so ambiguous and secretive. From the "prophetic" point of view, it is Heindel who was the precursor, and Bernadette Allain or Werner Ruhnau, or someone, merely acted as the trigger to set Yves' energy loose on that aspect of Heindel's prophecy. The fact that, as Bernadette Allain says, "he was the least intellectual person I have ever known" should not obscure the more important fact that he was influenced by certain books to an extraordinary degree (primarily the *Cosmogonie*, secondarily the works of Bachelard). His ideas seem to have arisen not simply from his environment, but from the interplay between events (or remarks) in his environment and the patterns of thought imprinted in him by these books.

In fact, many of the claims on Yves' work seem to arise from an incomplete understanding of his method. Bernadette Allain, for example, feels that she suggested to Yves the priority of blue among colors; Iris Clert, on the contrary, feels that it was she who

---

† Compare Klein's wording in *Dépassement* p. 19: "the real life in which a man no longer thinks he is the center of the universe, but the universe is the center of man." Whereas the substance of Klein's writings is primarily from Heindel, his style contains many artful echoes of Bachelard.

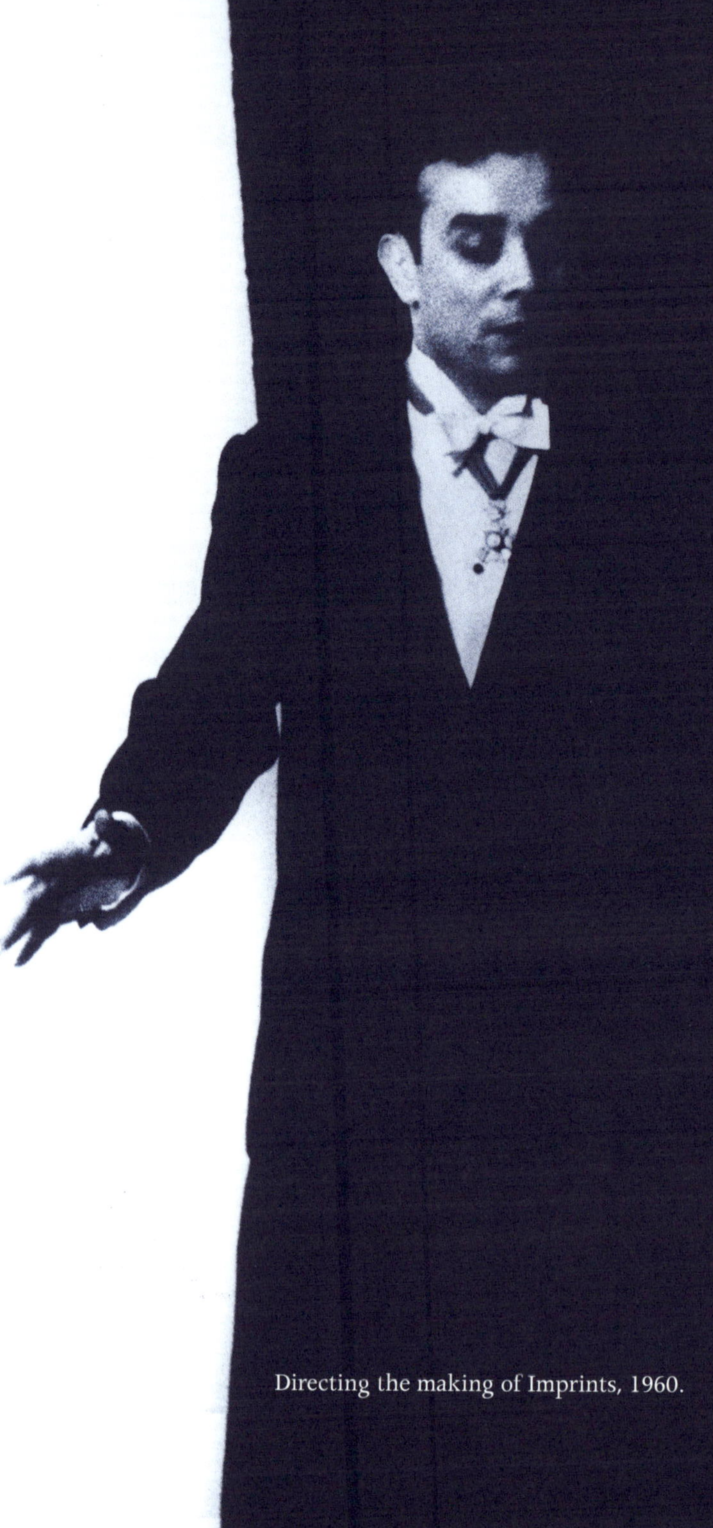

Directing the making of Imprints, 1960.

made this suggestion. But ultimately it seems that Heindel, for whom blue was the color of Spirit, was the crux of Yves' decision—though others, by their suggestions, may unwittingly have pointed him toward this element of Heindel's system. The same confusion can be seen in Takis' belief that Yves borrowed from him the idea of gravity-free or aerostatic sculpture.[†]

Such claims cannot be rejected as without basis, but they are only a part of the story. Clearly Yves was a "grabber." But he grabbed only what he felt already belonged to him due to his privileged relationship to Rosicrucian prophecy. The deeply imbibed Rosicrucian structures, overlaid with Bachelardian "poetics," formed a net held out to his environment; when something caught in the net, he used it, but he used *only* what caught. When an idea (like the blue monochrome, the sponge sculpture, the aerostatic sculpture, or the architecture of the air) obviously fit into his system, he seems to have felt that it belonged to him by right. Though another person might articulate the idea first, that person still did not have real priority, because Yves' system, containing the idea latently, had been there still earlier. (Such is the irrationality of a prophet.) For Yves, who had picked art theory and phenomenology "out of the air," it was clear that, as Georges Poulet wrote, "ideas belong to no one. They pass from mind to mind as coins pass from hand to hand."[108] In a sense, of course, the "origin" of the ideas is irrelevant. It was Yves who molded the varied elements into a distinctive and consistent body of work, each part of which bears his personal touch.

Yves spoke openly about his "system" and the "prophetic" basis of his art to few people—in fact, only to those of whose sympathy he was certain. In the late fifties, for example, he stopped

---

† It is worth noting that the idea is actually very ancient; it had occurred in the context of the Greco-Egyptian mystery religions which lie at some remove in the background of Rosicrucianism. Pliny the Elder wrote (XXXIV.xlii [148]):

> *The architect Timochares had begun to use lodestone [magnetic oxide of iron] for constructing the vaulting in the Temple of Arsinoe at Alexandria, so that the iron statue contained in it might have the appearance of being suspended in mid-air; but the project was interrupted by his own death and that of King Ptolemaus who had ordered the work to be done in honor of his sister.*

Klein and Takis also planned to use magnets.

talking to Arman about Rosicrucianism, because Arman would no longer take it seriously (or the pilgrimages to Cascia!). To Robert Godet he told it, and, more briefly, to Tinguely. ("He is a messenger," Tinguely wrote, "of the future age").[109] Unaware of his "system," and seeing his apparently random forays into various media, one might easily regard him as an opportunist and a Dada. It was precisely this opinion, widely held by people around him, that caused him such pain and frustration. ("The word Dada was used as an insult," says Tinguely, who heard it as much as Yves.)

After 1958 he tried to establish himself as a Bachelardian. But while Yves understood Heindel well enough, he did not really understand Bachelard's phenomenological side, which he misinterpreted in terms of Heindel. This was made painfully clear to him by Bachelard himself when Yves visited him in 1961. Yves began to explain that Bachelard was a kind of crypto-Rosicrucian, and Bachelard threw him out at once. The saintly elder thought Yves was "a crazy man," Arman recalls.

There was also a persistent problem in Yves' understanding of Heindel. The plans for altering and reclimatizing the environment were based ultimately on the *Cosmogonie*, in which Yves had read at age eighteen about the coming age of Space, levitation, and telepathy. But a crucial point which Yves did not understand (or accept) is that Heindel did not predict the dawning of that age until several more centuries had passed. Yves, like an ancient priest performing rites to reconstitute the universe at the New Year, was trying to force it to happen now. ("May the impossible arrive and establish its kingdom *quickly!*")

22

All my desires are born of my dreams. To what fantastic creatures
have I entrusted myself, in what dolorous and ravishing world has
my imagination enclosed me?

PAUL ELUARD

WHEN BERNADETTE ALLAIN PASSED OUT OF YVES' CIRCLE OF intimates, he needed a new "hand" to make his drawings and engineer his maquettes. It was at this juncture that he met the architect Claude Parent.

"What interested me about Yves," says Parent, "was a kind of generosity, and a power of positive scandal.... The liberty with which he lived radiated out of him; everyone felt it, in his actions, his character, his way of being with people. He was extremely spontaneous.... He was an extraordinary comrade and always full of ideas.... Whatever you did with him was an adventure.

"It was very difficult at first, in drawing for Yves, to find out what he wanted. Then suddenly I realized that the more romantic it was, the more dynamically the sky was drawn, the more he liked it. It was a type of drawing that was completely out of style at the time.

"I didn't make him pay for my work. It was a matter between friends. Then one day he wanted to give me something. He said, 'What would you like, from my works?' I said, 'A sponge relief.' He replied, 'No. Those are not really me. You should have a monochrome. That is me.'"

In June 1959, Iris Clert arranged lectures at the Sorbonne for Yves and Ruhnau on "The Evolution of Art toward the Immaterial." For Yves, who still read Tintin and Mandrake the Magician (*"I have no diploma"*), it was a special triumph, a kind of confirmation (as if, now, any more were needed) of his special role as Highest Initiate, as favorite of Saint Rita, as lost cause of all lost causes. Tinguely and Claude Parent both were present at the Amphithéâtre Turgot, where Yves outlined his plans for a World Center of Sensibility, talked of reforming the world economic system, and spoke of making an art work which would consist of reclimatizing all of France—later the world. ("The alchemist is a dreamer...who magnifies himself by 'wishing big.'")

"Lectures at the Sorbonne," says Claude Parent, "were usually very cold and intellectual—a monstrous bore, but irreproachable. But Yves emanated charm. He absolutely seduced the audience. Everyone saw it. It was a genteel seduction of the entire audience." The newspapers covered the event as grand Dada. The only people who took it very seriously were some members of the activist left, who interpreted Yves' plans not as a Dada gesture, nor as the fantasies of a solitary alchemist, but as the beginning of a Fascist movement. His visits to Japan and Spain, his interest in the martial arts, and his evident desire to launch movements contributed to this impression.

But Yves was of course not political in any ordinary sense of the word—the repeal of the law of gravity was his program! Matters of practical policy never entered his head, any more than they would a child's. He organized movements in Paris as once ("the little Captain") he had organized children's games in Cagnes-sur-Mer. As Tinguely says, "He was neither left nor right. He was nothing at all. He was above all that. He was a true poet, who was living a trance of total dream."

23

*"Ha! ha! ha! You see, Captain! On the moon gravity is
actually six times less than on the Earth!"*

TINTIN, in *Explorers on the Moon*

STATIONS/LABORS/CARTOONS: 1960—YVES PUSHES ON THROUGH the spectrum of nature, pursuing his symbolic alchemy to its conclusion.

He exhibits the first Monogold, symbolic of the completion of the Great Work, at the Musee des Arts Decoratifs, in the show *Antagonismes*.

He appears in blue formal dress before a seated audience in the Galerie Internationale d'Art Contemporain and gestures to the orchestra; the musicians begin to play the *Monotone Symphony*. He gestures again. Three naked girls appear, smear their bodies with blue paint, and press themselves against sheets of paper under his guidance.

Writing about this event, Yves stresses his separateness, his voyeurism if you will, as he controls but does not touch:

> *I could continue to maintain a precise distance from my creation
> and still dominate its execution. In this way I stayed clean. I no
> longer dirtied myself with color, not even the tips of my fingers.*

(Now even color is profane before the sanctity of the immaterial!)

*The work finished itself there in front of me with the complete
collaboration of the model, And I could salute its birth into the
tangible world in a fitting manner, in evening dress.*[110]

He extends the magico-artistic function of "supporting birth
into the tangible world," seeking the birth of nature revealed in
the "trace of the immediate," where realms meet, by allowing
the elements to state their projects directly upon the material:
he straps a canvas to the roof of his car and drives from Paris to
Nice and back. As citizen of infinity, he inspects the processes
of the finite:

> *I bound outside and down to the river. Among the rushes and reeds
> I dust color over everything I see there, and the wind making the
> long stems bow, sets them with delicacy and precision against the
> canvas I present to trembling nature; I obtain a mark of plant
> life....It begins to rain; a fine spring shower. I hold out my canvas
> to the rain and it is done! I have the mark of the rain, of the stir-
> ring of the atmosphere.*†

Unfortunately, the Imprints involved him in increasing tension and strained some of his closest relationships. The first
performance had been at Godet's apartment in 1958 (the result
an all-blue canvas, not a silhouette). But it was unclear who had
originated the idea. Iris Clert felt that Yves had borrowed it from
her, Arman that it had been borrowed from him. Yves replied that
at age eighteen, in first "projecting my mark outside myself," he
had imprinted his hands and feet upon his clothing.‡

---

† "Truth Becomes Reality." The "Cosmogonies" are another case of convergence
of Heindel and Bachelard. The basis in Heindel is discussed in the essay "Yves
Klein and Rosicrucianism." In Bachelard (*Poetics of Space*, p. 15) Klein read of
"the images of the four material elements, the four principles of the intuitive
cosmogonies."

‡ Shinichi Segi (interviewed in Tokyo by Jean-Yves Mock in August 1980) recalls
an interesting conversation with Klein in Japan in 1953. They were talking about
the Japanese tradition of inking a fish and applying it to paper to obtain an
imprint of the scale pattern. The word for this process, when transliterated into
the Latin alphabet, is *gyotaku*; Klein, as a Frenchman, pronounced it *jyotalcu*, and
Segi replied that that pronunciation changed the meaning: it was now a woman,
not a fish who was being inked and printed.

Still the outside world increased its invasions of his domain, and he sprang to the defense, at times hysterically. According to Iris Clert, he sued the film director Claude Chabrol for the film *Les Godelureaux*, in which Chabrol portrayed an artist making body prints as an example of the degeneracy of art. Yves' lawyer compared him to Giotto for the profundity of his blue—and lost the case. Hearing that Iris Clert had imprints by another artist in her gallery, he called the police on her and threatened to sue.

His domain had grown too large to defend effectively. His closest friends wrangled with him over priority. He was in constant need of money and wrote Aunt Rose frequent appeals, which she usually responded to. When money arrived he would spend it in one night with a crowd of friends in Montparnasse. When it did not, he would tear up the offending letter and pound his fists into the wall, as he might have done when he was three. In fact, he was growing increasingly rebellious toward the female deities. When in Nice, he stayed not at his aunt's home, but at Arman's.

Meanwhile, his relationship with Rotraut was destabilized by his abrupt changes in mood and role, which she had difficulty following: when he was authoritarian, she was submissive, sent to her room like a child if Iris came round on business; when he was the libertine, she was the procuress, helping him find girls in the bars; when he was the voyeur, she was the performer, dancing erotically at parties. More than once she left him, and returned.

The problem of debt was aggravated when Yves stopped giving judo lessons in 1959, and so were all the other problems. "It was when he abandoned judo," says Bernadette Allain, "that he lost the ability to adjust himself inside, to keep the physical balance necessary to live as intensely as he did. He did not even seem physically solid anymore." A German *judoka* of lesser rank threw him three times easily in what was to have been a collaboration.[111] His friends began to experience him as paranoid and hypermotivated. "He was so restless that he could not even sleep," says Tinguely. "He was the most restless man I have ever known. At night he had to write to avoid being torn apart by despair. He wrote, and he invented other methods to avoid sinking into a nightmare." "He lived," says Iris Clert, "as if his days were numbered."[112]

It was at this time, in this situation, that Yves decided to put his myth "at the very *top*"—to make his Leap into the Void. ("That whole world of young artists who gravitated around him—little by little I developed a real aversion to them, because they were killing the man. That's what it came to, obliging him to go farther each time because it was necessary to be avant-garde, it was necessary to go 'beyond' the others. One was forced, you might say, to throw oneself into the void," says Bernadette Allain.)

24

THE DREAM OF FLIGHT WAS VERY OLD WITH YVES. IT HAD DOMI-nated his spiritual ambitions at least since his liberating first reading of Heindel under Cadeaux's guidance in 1948. The sky as transcendence meant both fulfillment and escape to one who was basically discontented with the things of this world. He had flown in imagination to the far side of the sky from the beach in Nice, and, while meditating on Arman's rooftop, had visualized intensely, for hours, the act of rising and flying through the moon.

Like the monochrome painting, which seems to have entered his consciousness at the same time and with related associations, magical flight remained a constant which went with him everywhere. This was more than an icon, more than an image to define oneself; it was a belief. As Rotraut says: "He was sure he could fly. He used to tell me that at one time monks knew how to levitate, and that he would get there too. It was an obsession. Like a little child he really was convinced that he could do it. He even talked about a machine in which to train people to fly."

This of course was a central part of Yves' role as Highest Initiate and Messenger of the Age of Levitation. Within the terms of that myth, it was not only his destiny, but even his duty, to be the

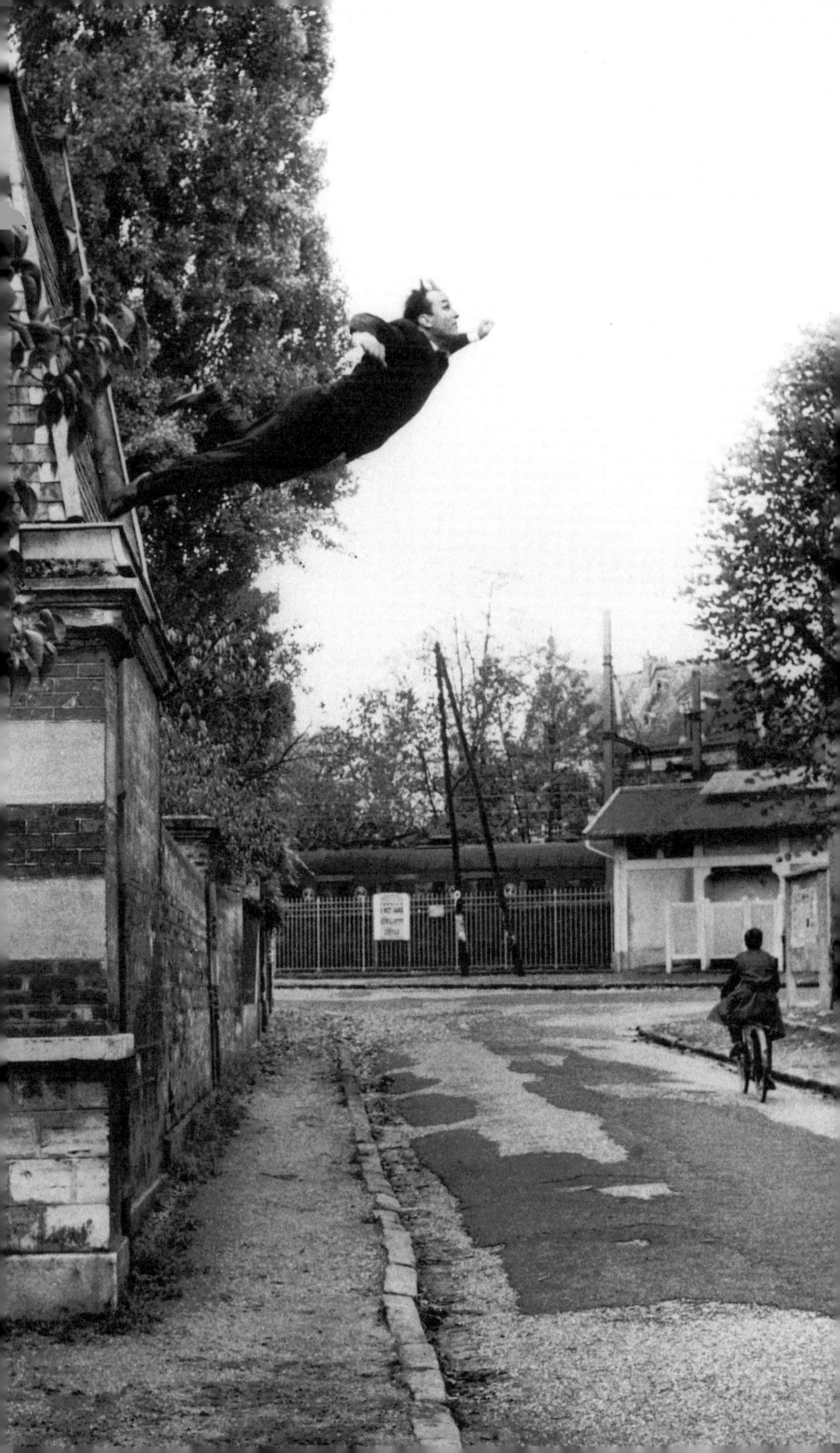

first to demonstrate flight and to teach others to fly until everyone could do it. From 1957 on, the myth seemed really to be unfolding, and the dream of flying once again seemed near. He talked about it obsessively, not only to Rotraut but to everyone.

It is also true that flying and dematerialization—the alternate climaxes of his myth—were both associated in his mind with death, and that the act of flying away to the sky seemed a form of magical sacrifice. A common element in the myth of the Messenger or Savior is that his own sacrificial death is necessary to cement the new age in place. As Yves' state of mind grew increasingly tragic and doomed, he spoke more often both of flying and of death, usually together.

"He would talk about his death," says Claude Parent. "It was passionately interesting to him... What was it he used to say? He would tell me that he would leap, that he would make a famous leap...."

And Tinguely: "He always talked about two things: he talked about levitation, and he talked about just vanishing."

Station: it is autumn, 1960. The King of the Sky pulls back the curtain for another act of his Monodrama. Yves, in a business suit and necktie, gives a demonstration of flying. He stands on a second-story ledge and gazes down at the street, then up at the sky, his home. When the photographers are ready, he tenses his judo-trained muscles and dives out and up in splendid freedom. Gazing intently above (glowing eyes) without thought of the hard street below, he hangs for a moment at the top of his leap (cameras clicking), then rises gracefully over the roofs of Paris, is lost among clouds for a while, and vanishes into his true home, beyond the sky.

This magnificent photograph is a numinous object around which rumors and controversy have clustered as around the miracles claimed for a candidate for sainthood who is suspected of fraud. It has been pointed out that Yves himself, in the first publication of the photograph (in *Dimanche*, November 27, 1960), raised the question of whether the leap was made "with or without a net," and that the subsequent publication history, controlled by Yves, may have been designed to increase ambiguity on this point.[113] Specifically, the bicyclist in the lower right hand corner of the photograph in *Dimanche* (the ploughman who did not see Icarus fall from the sky—a motif which Breughel had adapted from Ovid) is omitted in a later publication. Today various people, including the photographers, claim to know the inside story, then proceed to give wildly conflicting accounts. Even more striking, Yves' own reports were as conflicting as those of the eyewitnesses. To Arman, who was not an eyewitness, "he said, right out, no problem, that it was a montage....But then he insisted that he *could* do it anyway." And Claude Parent: "He swore to me that he levitated. He would not let me alone about it." So skillfully disguised are the plain facts of the event, so effectively has the image been cleansed of historical origin, that protective clouds still cling around it. One thing is certain about the photograph in *Dimanche*; magnification of a print made directly from the negative shows with absolute clarity a montage line running from right to left along the ledge beneath Yves' feet and in a zigzag path through the foliage behind that ledge.

But this photograph by no means tells the whole story. As we will see, the question of the net was not in fact *first* raised by Yves; the question preceded the photographed event and had been forced upon him by circumstances, so that he could not avoid it. First of all, a minimum of three leaps, witnessed by different people and made under different circumstances, must be sorted out from one another. It is probable that no single individual except Yves himself was aware of the series as a whole.

Pierre Restany provides a date and framework for the first leap. "With Yves," he says, "many things happened as a result of fixation, of a sort of intense insistence.... One day he told me he was going to do something very important. He said, 'I'm going to give a practical demonstration of levitation.'" Restany was asked to come to Yves' apartment on the rue Campagne Premiere, to go with him to the leap site, and to witness the "demonstration." Unfortunately, detained by other business, Restany arrived at Yves' apartment late, just as Yves was returning from the event. "When I got there," Restany says, "Yves was tremendously excited; he was in a kind of mystical ecstasy. He truly seemed to have just accomplished some prodigious physical feat. He said to me, 'You have just missed one of the most important events of your life.' He was limping slightly from a twisted ankle. I tell you, if I hadn't gone there and seen the state he was in, I would always have believed that it was a photomontage."

Two crucial points must be made. First, Restany's appointment book for 1960 indicates that this "practical demonstration of levitation" took place on January 12; but a bill for work done for Yves by the photographers Harry Shunk and John Kender shows two dates for a *saut* (leap): October 19 and 25, 1960.[114] The Shunk-Kender dates pinpoint the leap publicized in *Dimanche*; the event referred to by Restany took place ten months earlier. They were separate events. Secondly, Restany's recollection that Yves was limping from a twisted ankle agrees precisely with the recollection of Bernadette Allain, and with no one else's; it is highly probable that the leap missed by Restany was the same which she attended.

Bernadette Allain, who has not previously made a public statement on the question, asserts that she was present at a leap, and that it occurred at Colette Allendy's house on the rue de l'Assomption. She describes it as follows: "For a *judoka* who knew how to fall it was not extraordinary.... It would be expected of someone at his level of training to know how to recover and fall. He did it as a challenge or act of defiance, to prove that he was capable of leaping into the void—that is, not leaping out of a window, but leaping *toward the sky*. He wanted this known... He had nothing underneath him but the pavement—nothing! There was no faking.... I was not amazed because I had seen him do far more extraordinary things on the judo mats.... He knew that he could do it, too. It was only the public who were amazed.... But as soon as he became a celebrity, everyone in the world claimed to have been there and told stories and more stories."

Subsequent events were directly influenced by the fact that Restany had not managed to attend this leap. When they met afterward at the apartment, Yves said, "I am terribly disappointed that you were not there, because *you are my witness*." It is easy to appreciate Yves' dilemma and the courses of action which it led to. He had in fact leapt without a net, and wished to publish the fact; but his official witness, who would be widely believed in the art world, could not guarantee the fact.

It is worth asking why Yves went ahead with the leap on January 12 when he saw that his official witness was not present. First, Yves had repeatedly told his judo companion Marcel Boulois that he was frightened of the leap. On January 12 the stage was set, his nerve was up, and rather than try to prepare himself again on another day, he went ahead with the event. Second, there is the strange poetic-symbolic connection between Yves' obsession with flight-and-death and that of his friend Robert Godet. Pierre Restany's appointment book for January 12, the day of the leap, indicates that later in the afternoon he and Yves went together to Godet's apartment (Yves was limping along the way). The occasion was special. "This," says Restany, "was the day of Godet's departure on that journey from which he would never return." Godet's fiery plunge out of the sky in the Himalayas, which Yves was to consider as a foreshadowing of his own death, was itself shadowed forth by Yves' fanatical leap from Colette Allendy's wall. To Yves himself such synchronicity might have suggested a mythic force.

For some time after January 12 Yves boasted of his leap, and found that no one believed him. The second and third leaps must be seen not as separate events in their own right but as attempts to generate credibility for the unwitnessed first leap. These attempts were not, however, successful. "When he talked about the leap," says Arman, "everyone said it was impossible. They laughed at him. There was a stairway at the Rive Droite Gallery, and Yves wanted to prove that he could leap from some height. He jumped from the stairway and hurt his shoulder badly. It was hurt for two or three months. He had to have it bandaged and everything." Both Jean Larcade and Rotraut recall this leap being made not from a staircase but over a table. In any case, it did nothing to help Yves' credibility.

It was at this point, brooding on the series of events while his shoulder mended, that Yves decided to falsify the event, over a net, in front of photographers. (Why risk a broken leg or dislocated shoulder again, when in fact the feat itself was already accomplished?) This leap was not to be the important, the magical event, as the first one was, but a mere complement or completion of that earlier event, providing the documentation which the real leap, through unhappy chance, had lacked. Therefore it became necessary to obscure the time and place of the photographed leap so that the fiction could be grafted onto the reality of the earlier event.

Shunk and Kender were engaged to record the leap on October 19 and to create the illusion by photomontage. A new leap site was chosen, in Fontenay-aux-Roses, both because Colette Allendy had died in the meantime (on February 22) and because there was a judo club across the street from the new site; Yves knew all the *judokas* in Paris and could count on them to help. Kender recalls that a dozen or so of the *judokas* were enlisted as catchers.[115] Extant photographs show these catchers in place. When Yves leapt, they caught him in a tarpaulin. The leap was made repeatedly to get the facial expression just right. The *judokas* and the tarpaulin were photomontaged out.

Rotraut (not Bernadette Allain) was present at this event and recalls it as follows: "Do you really want to know the truth?... It's idiotic to hide it. He really leapt, but first he went to the judo club to get the *judokas*, and they held a sort of tarpaulin.... He leapt three, four, maybe five times....[Then] he was getting ready to leap without anything underneath him. It was terrible. I became completely unnerved. At one moment I was furious....I thought, *He's going to kill himself.* He was extremely fascinated by that."

Dissuaded by Rotraut, he did not make that final leap which, if successful, would have established his credibility before acceptable witnesses. Instead, knowing that such a leap had in fact been made ten months earlier, he swore Rotraut, Shunk, and Kender to secrecy about the presence of the net, and proceeded to publish the photograph with no date or specification of site. (The second Shunk-Kender date October 25—may represent darkroom work, perhaps the inclusion of the street view with the bicyclist.)

Finally, of course, the history of the icon is not the most important point: it is a time-canceling image, an image of escape from the bonds of history and conditionality, and its message does not hang upon the details of its manufacture. The intensity of the image itself, and the richness of its meaning, are its validation. At one level it is an unbearably poignant image of impatient longing for paradise, a desperate attempt to make paradise disclose itself now, before it is too late. If the Messenger of the New Age has already appeared, has already trumpeted forth from the rooftops his symbolic announcement, can the age itself be far behind?

Viewed not as magic but as art, the Leap is perhaps the most startling and arresting formulation of Yves' "invitation to a voyage." It is a classic icon of the urge to transcendence and of its dire consequences for body and ego.

25

This king flies away from you, ye mortals,
He is not of the earth, he is of the sky.
This king flies as a cloud to the sky.
He goes to the sky! He goes to the sky!
On the wind! On the wind!

EGYPTIAN PYRAMID TEXTS

"SPACE TAKES ON QUITE A DIFFERENT ASPECT IN THE COUNTLESS myths, tales, and legends concerning human or superhuman beings who fly away into Heaven and travel freely between Earth and Heaven, whether they do so with the aid of birds' feathers or by any other means. It is not the speed with which they fly, nor the dramatic intensity of the aerial voyage that characterises this complex of myth and folk-lore; it is the fact that weight is abolished, that an ontological mutation has occurred in the human being himself.... The motif is of universal distribution, and is integral to a whole group of myths concerned both with the celestial origin of the first human beings and with the paradisiac situation during the primordial *illud tempus*....

"Now, if we consider the 'flight' and all the related symbolisms as a whole, their significance is at once apparent: they all express a break with the universe of everyday experience; and a dual purposiveness is evident in this rupture: both transcendence and, at the same time, freedom are to be obtained through the 'flight'.... The creation, repeated to infinity, of these countless imaginary universes in which space is transcended and weight is abolished, speaks volumes about the true nature of the human being. The

longing to break the ties that hold him in bondage to the earth
is not a result of cosmic pressures or of economic insecurity—it
is constitutive of man, in that he is a being who enjoys a mode
of existence unique in the world. Such a desire to free himself
from his limitations, which he feels to be a kind of degradation,
and to regain spontaneity and freedom—the desire expressed, in
the example here discussed, by symbols of the 'flight'—must be
ranked among the specific marks of man.

"The breaking of the plane effected by the 'flight' signifies…an
act of transcending,…[a] longing to go beyond and 'above' the
human condition, to transmute it by an excess of 'spiritualisa-
tion.' For one can only interpret all the myths, rites, and legends
to which we have been referring by a longing to see the human
body behaving like a 'spirit,' to transmute the corporeal modality
of man into a spiritual modality."—Mircea Eliade[116]

26

I breathe the elusive smoke I shall become
And to my incandescent soul the sky
Sings alteration in the restless shores.

PAUL VALERY

YVES' CAREER WAS A LONG PROCESS OF APPROPRIATING THE
entire universe—element by element, stratum by stratum—into
his myth, of symbolically enforcing his concept of essence on all
being. In one sense this activity is metaphysics ("Isn't the meta-
physician," asks Bachelard, "the alchemist with ideas too big to
be realized?"),[117] but in another sense it is cosmic theater—the
imaginary installation of oneself as "director" of the universal
drama.

Yves was, of course, as Tinguely says, "a super-dramatic case,"
and in one sense it was the ever present theatrical implications
which unified his oeuvre. Insofar as he was acting out the myth
of the hero's quest for transcendence, his whole life was theater.
His various immaterial events (*Le Vide*, the Relinquishments) and
the performances of Anthropometries were a kind of theater. In

fact, most of his art objects (the sponge works, IKB sculptures, Cosmogonies, Imprints) announce the processes of their making, thus positing a time axis and implying a form of theater. Georges Mathieu had made the theatrical implications of action painting explicit in 1956, when he painted a large canvas before an audience in the Théâtre Sarah Bernhardt. That event may have influenced Yves, who seems deliberately to have gone beyond it in the performances of Anthropometries (the first of which, ironically, was attended by Mathieu).

But Yves always had other sources than the contemporary art world. As he knew, Japanese painters traditionally painted before audiences works "which must be executed…without hesitation" in order to embody "that indefinable something" without which "the painting…must be considered a failure."[118] Yves echoed this Zen tradition in his term "indefinable" and when he wrote:

> When everything goes well, when I am in form, my best paintings are executed very quickly, without hesitation, directly, and I am pleased with them.[†]

In 1960 Yves' thoughts turned directly to the theater, and his gestures of appropriation reached to the very limits of the universe, in what may be his most brilliant work: *Dimanche, the Newspaper of a Single Day*. This four-page imitation newspaper— Yves' contribution to the Festival d'Art Avant-garde—reproduced the format of a Parisian daily and was distributed to newsstands one Sunday morning (creating amusing theater over many a breakfast table). The text is an astonishing tour de force, Yves Klein pursued by Yves Klein through a maze of imaginary theaters and disguises, simultaneously asserting and exposing the myth of his own omnipotence. If indeed he wrote these pieces on sleepless nights, to avoid "being torn apart by despair" or "sinking into a

---

† "The Monochrome Adventure." Also, the influence of the Japanese *gassaku*, "an impromptu picture in which several artists will in turn participate" (*On the Laws of Japanese Painting*, p. 13), may be seen in the collective imprint of New Realists (shroud anthropometry 11) and the "blind poem" made collectively, on a long scroll, by Klein, Arman, Claude Pascal, and Restany (shroud anthropometry 15), in which the mixture of poetry and visual image is also in the Sino-Japanese tradition. In fact, all the Imprints and some Cosmogonies show Japanese influence. See below, "Yves Klein and Rosicrucianism."

nightmare," then one must again be struck with admiration by his alchemical ability to transmute inner tension into creative force.

Yves begins, in the dateline, as God himself: "Yves Klein presents Sunday, November 27, 1960." (*Fiat lux!*) Beneath it: "The Blue Revolution Continues." "THEATER OF THE VOID," declares the headline, beside it the numinous photograph—Yves' upward gaze, his flying hair—"The Painter of Space Hurls Himself into the Void." The lead story proclaims an ultimate, godlike omnipotence—the appropriation of all space and all beings within it:

> *The theater which I propose is not only the city of Paris, but is also*
> *the countryside, the desert, the mountain, even the sky, in fact, the*
> *whole universe. Why not?*

For one day every person in the world was cast by Yves Klein as actor-spectator upon his universal stage. It was "an historic day for the theater," which for the first time expanded to include all "being itself." This universal theater is a piece of Conceptual Art which, by declaring our everyday actions to be dramatic performances, distances us from them, as in Shklovsky's definition of art as "a defamiliarization, a making strange…a renewal of perception."[119]

Within this macrocosmic theater various microcosmic theaters are nested, some carrying to the limit the gestures of Meyerhold, Brecht, and Dada (for example, handcuffing the members of the audience to their seats), others approaching the Void through metaphysical reductionism and the reification of absences. A "Monotheater" is proposed with "no actors, no audience, no decor, no scene," expressing the unity and mystery of what is happening everywhere all the time. For a fee, an empty seat with your name on it would sit forever beside other empty seats facing an empty stage in a hall whose doors are closed and locked:

> *This constant arepresentation, in this hall which no one enters*
> *after the installation, must have some moments more intense than*
> *others, indicated to the subscribers at the beginning by a program…*
> *At these particular moments…the theater must be brilliantly il-*
> *luminated so that the light can be seen from outside.*
>
> *The director of such a theater should seek,…in long journeys*
> *made for this purpose only, actors who will…constantly renew the*
> *troupe…The new actor so chosen will have nothing to do except*

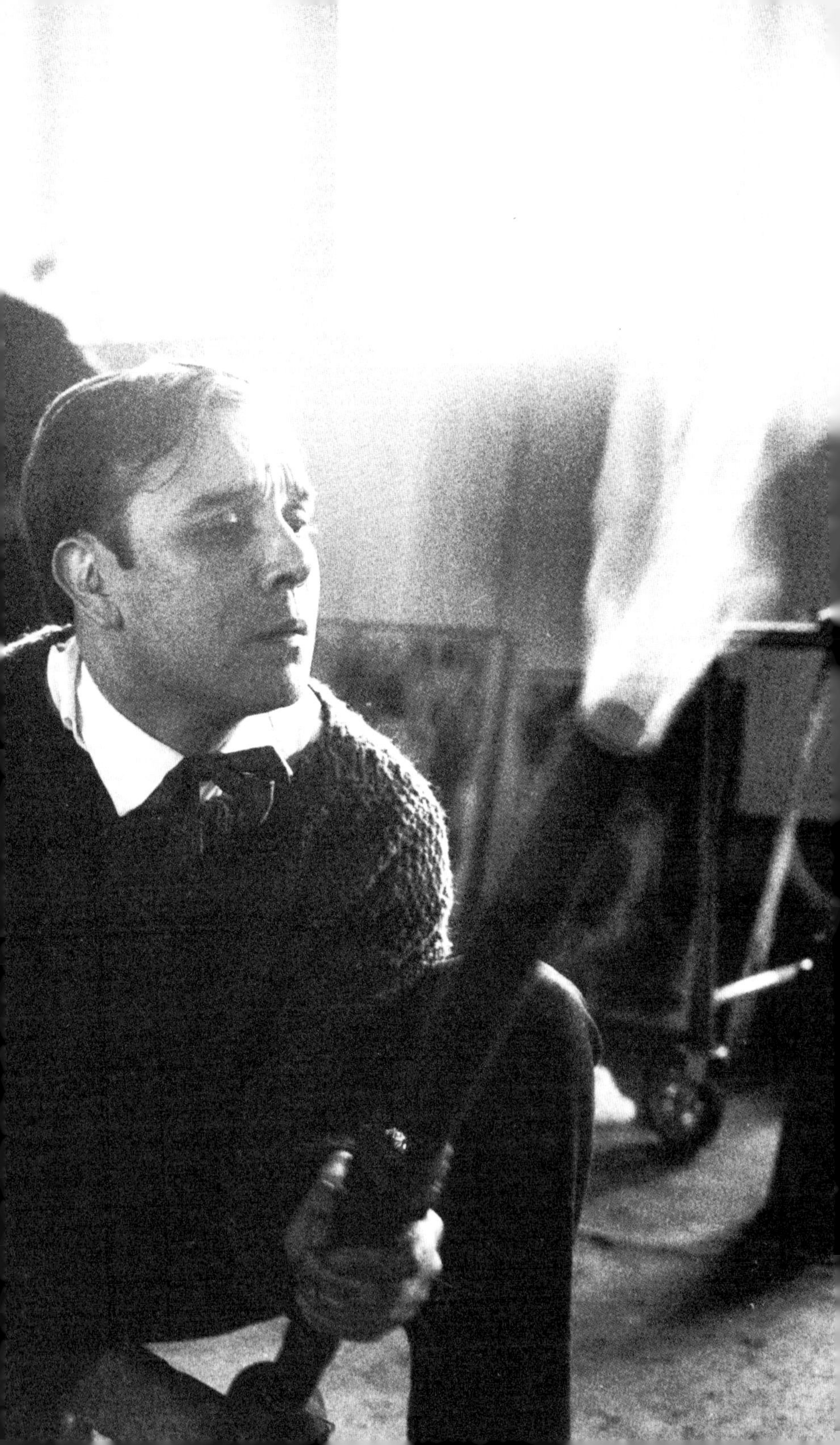

> *know that he is an actor…and be aware of the "moments of hy-*
> *perintensity" indicated to the subscribers in the program. After an*
> *engagement, the actor will be charged with his new solemn respon-*
> *sibility of being an actor and will disappear into the crowd, into*
> *society, to become finally a serious visitor in the gigantic museum*
> *of the past.*

There is a nest of theaters and metatheaters here, interlocking in circular infinities. And at the center, as at the periphery enclosing them, is the theater of Yves' personal myth as self-appointed representative of the Void. On the front page, Yves flies off into space; beneath him a reproduction of one of his own monochromes is captioned "Space Itself" (i.e., he Leaps into his own painting!). Inside, he explains the significance of his upward flight for others:

> *To tell the truth, all this is only one step in the long expedition to*
> *really capture the void, which will happen after my final disappear-*
> *ance…This capture of the void will be realized by those who have*
> *understood this idea, or rather this principle, and who will live it*
> *as a pure ecstatic activity in a manner at last altogether natural.*

This of course, is sheer messianism: not "my death," but "my final disappearance"! (Cf. Zalmoxis, Mithra, Quetzalcoatl, Christ.) He is the Redeemer, who, when he ascends to the sky, will open the way to others after him.

But this is only one glance into the kaleidoscope. In the next, the "final disappearance" is recast as an anima fantasy shot through with romantic longing; and here we encounter what must be considered Yves' most explicit "invitation to a voyage":

> *When I think of you*
> *The same dream always comes back*
> *We are walking hand in hand*
> *On the wild path of our holidays*
> *When little by little*
> *Everything seems to disappear around us*
> *The trees, the flowers, the sea*
> *On one side of the path,*
> *Suddenly there is no longer anything at all*
> *We are at the end of the world*
> *And then…do we turn back?*
> *No…I know that you say no*
> *Come with me into the void!*

> *If you return someday*
> *You who dream also*
> *Of this marvelous void*
> *Of this absolute love*
> *I know that together*
> *Without saying a word*
> *We will leap*
> *Into the reality of that void*
> *Which awaits our love*
> *As I wait for you each day:*
> *Come with me into the void!*

There is a cry of loneliness in that song which echoes the fantasies found by Jung in the works of "solitary alchemists." A psychiatrist once remarked that Yves' ideas were remarkably similar to a delusion system. Yet unlike the truly deluded individual, Yves was able to bracket his private reality as myth, art, and theater. Within these privileged arenas, like a monk in a monastery, he was able to live out his myth as "pure" action which did not refer outside the brackets at all.

Still, the separate reality which the mythophile carries around with him, though it may not threaten society, does threaten to engulf his own ordinary humanity and leave him only the shadowy life of a monument, artifact, or symbol. On the last page of Yves' newspaper there is a strange little essay, "The Statue," which shows that he did at times find his myth burdensome and ossifying, that he sometimes wished to escape from its brackets and, like Odysseus in Plato's *Laws*, lay down the hero's burden and become a plain citizen of the world again:

> When I will finally become like a statue by the practice of exasperating my ego (*l'exasperation de mon moi*), which will have led me to this ultimate rigidity....Then, then alone, I will be able to set this statue in its place and go off by myself into the crowd, to go and see the world at last. No one will notice, because they will all be looking at the statue, and I will be able to walk away, free at last.[†]

[†] This passage suggests that Klein had read some alchemical literature other than the Rosicrucian texts. Jung has found many passages where "the statue evidently denotes the end-product of the process, the Lapis Philosophorum or its equivalent." In the Book of Komarios, for example:

27

*Good luck, I cried, and I saw a sea of flames
and smoke in the sky.*

ARTHUR RIMBAUD

THE LAST YEARS OF YVES' LIFE WERE ENORMOUSLY PRODUCTIVE. His energy was at its peak, and his use of time, while studiedly casual, was fiendishly efficient. Wember's catalogue lists 1,077 pieces made between 1956 and 1962.[120] One does not produce such a body of work by mere publicity-seeking. It may or may not be the case that Yves used work to avoid some inner nightmare; but it is certainly the case that he worked hard and constantly. ("It was as relentless as an army mobilizing," Arman says, "when he decided to do something.")

Early in 1961 Yves received the ultimate mark of success for a young artist, a major retrospective of his works, at the Museum Haus Lange in Krefeld. It was at a time when his program of artistic alchemy, the art of fire, earth, air, water, prime matter, and gold, was nearing completion. The series of Monogolds (1959-61) symbolically completed nature's Great Work of perfecting matter. ("Gold is the sun; to make gold is to be god," says an alchemical text). The great triptych *Monoblue, Monopink, Monogold* (1960) crowned, with its Rosicrucian associations, the mysticism of color and brought it to an end. The theme of the unity of the absolute beginning and the absolute end was rendered into Egyptian form in the three obelisks, blue, rose, and gold, of the following year. This path leads no further, except to dissolve again what it has begun.‡

It is this dissolution, this evanishment of forms through the inner combustion of the overheated spirit, which is shadowed forth in the Fire pieces of 1961. The theme of man as a perfected

---

The body clothed itself in the light of divinity, and darkness departed from it, and all were united in love, body, soul, and spirit, and all became one, and the house was sealed and the statue was erected, filled with light and divinity.

See C. C. Jung, *Mysterium Conjunctionis*, 2d ed. (Princeton, N.J.: Princeton University Press, 1970), pp. 391 ff.

part of nature, at home in any of the elements, has appeared in the architecture of the air as a symbol of freedom and ascension; now, in the architecture of fire at Krefeld, it took on the more aggressive overtones of destruction.

Station: Yves becomes Prometheus in a vested suit and tie, taming fire into fountains, walls, paintings. At Krefeld in January he exhibits the Fire Walls and Fire Fountains of a city beyond the need for nourishment. Back in Paris, at the Centre d'Essais du Gaz de France, he makes the first Fire-Color paintings, burning composition board with a huge flamethrower, adding color selectively,

The Fire pieces (mostly 1961-62), while beautiful in themselves and an appropriate climax to the alchemical period, nonetheless radiate sinister overtones in terms of Yves' myth. "The last phase of the Opus," says the alchemical tradition, "during which the alchemist contemplates the appearance of fiery Light, is the most dangerous."[121] There is more than the "trace of the immediate" in these works: a sex-and-death thrill, a Promethean aggression, an Empedoclean walk to the very edge of the smoky crater. The Fire Paintings with added color have something of Nietzsche's "voluptuousness of hell." The famous photograph of the *Fire Wall* at Krefeld is a deathlike Station of the Myth: Yves' body is consumed by the fifty flames while his head floats in ghostly isola-

---

‡ The status of this triptych is, however, not altogether unambiguous. The evidence is that the three paintings were made separately by Klein, bought separately by the same buyer, and formed into a triptych either by the original buyer or by the present owner, the Louisiana Museum. It is not known whether Klein's agreement was ever obtained. The amalgamation of the three works into a triptych is not without justification, however. After the show of varicolored monochromes at Colette Allendy's in 1956 Klein denounced the practice of establishing a polychromatic interplay between his monochromes of different colors. In 1960, however, at the show *Yves Klein le monochrome* at Jean Larcade's Galerie Rive Droite, Klein returned to the practice of hanging monochromes of different colors in relation with one another, and specifically monochromes of blue, rose, and gold. These three colors were of special sacredness in Heindel's Rosicrucianism, where they represent the body of God. In his transference of Rosicrucian magic to his worship of Saint Rita, Klein came to associate these three colors with her. The ex-voto piece which he dedicated to her in November 1961 was a triptych of pure pigments in gold, blue, and pink. If the Louisiana Museum triptych is to be criticized, it is for the arrangement of the colors in order of the natural spectrum (red, yellow, blue). The evidence suggests that Klein would have put blue in the center.

tion above them. The *Fire Fountain*, innately awesome, scorches us with Heraclitean law: "All things are exchanged for fire, and fire for all things."

In November 1960, Yves and Rotraut traveled to Cascia (for his fourth and last time), to thank Saint Rita for the success of this "lost cause." Yves left an ex-voto object (pure pigments and gold from the sales of "zones of immateriality") accompanied by a long prayer ending, "May all my enemies become my friends, and if that is impossible, may all their attacks on me be in vain—make me, and all my works totally invulnerable!"[122]

28

"Moon rocket to earth...The air's becoming unbreathable,...the last cylinder from the spacesuits has been used up...The others are already unconscious...I wonder if we can possibly get back alive."

TINTIN, in *Explorers on the Moon*

TINGUELY: "IT WAS HIS PERSONALITY WHICH PREVENTED HIM FROM being taken seriously. He was too alive. An artist cannot be so charming, so powerfully persuasive; an artist can't articulate ideas that well. It was almost inconceivable that an artist could be like Yves Klein. It was a handicap to him, his extraordinary charm, his graciousness, his comradely side. He was too fine—not low enough. You have to be low to be an artist—drunk or sick or have ten children. But he was just simply superb! And that, that is dangerous."

Bernadette Allain: "After the judo period he needed a crowd around him—friends, girls—it was his relaxation. You might say he was indifferent to most of them, and in a sense treated them badly. But, from another point of view, he did accept them; he did let them embark on his adventure with him. They were like his attendants or servants; they waited on him, men and women alike, as if he were a pampered child, an only son whose parents, whose whole family adored him."

Tinguely: "His studio was painted white, but really he wanted to line it entirely with mirrors—floor, ceiling, and walls. So he would see only himself. If he had had the money he would surely have done it. It was not one of those projects you think of vaguely for the future—if he had had a little money he would have done it at once. He had great hopes of being able to do it someday."

Yves Klein: "Saint Rita of Cascia, saint of impossible and desperate causes, thank you for all the powerful, decisive, and marvelous help you have given me to the present day—thank you infinitely."

Fred Klein: "We were one hundred percent companions. He was a real friend. But later, he became a little lost from view."

29

No longer any doubt, they're tugging me from below, loading me with ballast, I'm going down, the weight in me, again the weight, again the ground at my feet, what am I doing on the earth again?

HENRI MICHAUX

EARLY IN 1961, LEO CASTELLI, IN NEW YORK, ANNOUNCED AN exhibition, *Yves Klein the Monochrome*, to open on April 11. It was an invitation (at last!) to extend his domain over the ocean to America—from which, said Heindel, the new humanity of the Age of Space would arise. Yves and Rotraut flew to New York and lived for two months at the Chelsea Hotel,

On April 12, the day after the Castelli opening, Yuri Gagarin made the first manned space flight and reported (to Yves' delight) that from space the earth looked blue! Yves felt confirmed in his conviction that the Blue Age, the age of return to Space, would dawn in his own time. Still, a rocket is not levitation, and science alone (Heindel was explicit on this point) could not fulfill the ancient prophecies. Yves remained true to Heindel, though he could easily have slipped away from him through a relaxed interpretation. Yuri Gagarin was not the Messenger; his flight was a sign—but it was not the event itself. Yves wrote:

> It is not with rockets, Sputniks, and missiles that modern man will achieve the conquest of space… It is by means of the powerful yet pacific force of his sensitivity that man will inhabit space.[123]

Yet despite the more or less propitious omen, the show at Castelli's did not go well. The New York critics ridiculed it. "Have you ever been all blue?" asked the *Herald Tribune*. "I've got the Yves Klein blues," lamented the *New York Times*. *Art News* called him "the latest sugar-Dada to jet in from the Parisian common market," "the George M. Koan of French Neo-Dada" and "a Dali—junior grade." In fact, the show was misconceived, an anachronism; featuring the blue monochromes, as in 1957, it gave little hint of the range and depth that Yves' work had achieved by 1961.

The New York artists' reactions were mixed, as Yves for two months tried to annex them to his kingdom (hadn't the School of New York, after all, been replaced by the School of Nice?). Some (Larry Rivers, Barnett Newman, Marcel Duchamp) welcomed him; others were put off. He met Rothko, who turned away without a word. Reinhardt was pleasant but noncommittal. To all those working in monochrome styles Yves said they could be barons of the monochrome—but he was the king. In much the same spirit he regarded Rothko as a precursor of his own work. This kind of talk did not go over. Most New York artists pointedly boycotted the show. Nothing sold,

It was a disaster, and Yves felt the strain. Here he was not the "only son, adored by all the family." When mocked publicly as a failure, he underwent a rare break ("When the Discord Spirit come, I make me absolutely cold and without any emotion....") and hospitalized his tormentor with judo blows. He smoked constantly and at times drank too much.

Outwardly there was still the challenging smile and the laughter of a "superb companion." But privately, with increasing frequency he told Rotraut, "I feel so old and so lonely," and other remarks not particularly healthy for a very young man. As he felt the myth's sacrificial ending tightening around him, death entered his thoughts more and more.

He was thirty-three years old.

He wrote:

> Only very recently I have become a sort of undertaker... Some of my latest works have been tombs and coffins.[124]

In June, Yves and Rotraut flew to Los Angeles for a show at the Dwan Gallery and quickly found they were in a different and friendlier atmosphere. A group of Los Angeles artists asked him if he had really jumped as on the front page of *Dimanche*, and when he said yes—they simply believed him! Partly it was because Tinguely had prepared the way for him the year before, becoming great friends with Ed Kienholz and others, but partly it was a cultural stance which naturally approved many of the things New York naturally condemned. In the looser, warmer, less intimidating West Coast atmosphere, Yves and Rotraut became vacationers, visiting the Hearst castle, the bullfights in Tijuana, and Disneyland, which (like all children) they greatly enjoyed, bringing home two souvenir booklets.

Still a strange and deadly vibration hung over Yves, who was painfully stung by his failure in New York. He and an associate of the gallery went sharkshooting with 30/30 rifles in the Pacific, watching the blood-maddened sharks devour each other in the water around the boat. Later Yves talked of the experience in a fascinated but loathing way.

One day he and Rotraut went driving with Ed Kienholz and Walter Hopps in a Land Rover, navigating by compass on the Mojave Desert. Yves insisted that he wanted to go to Death Valley to make a Fire Fountain there. He kept asking if they were in Death Valley yet, and even when repeatedly assured that they were not going that far seemed convinced that they were indeed in Death Valley; he was amused and fascinated by the theme of death.

"One afternoon," says the Los Angeles painter Ed Moses, "I took him up to my place in the hills to see my work. I had been told that he would be a supersophisticated operator. But instead he was charming, open, friendly. He looked right at everything, very simple and curious.

"Afterward, he had to get back to the gallery fast. So I gave him a Death Ride down the canyon—a real Death Ride. But that guy didn't flinch a muscle—he was ice cold, just joked, as we tore around the curves, about how he had been making coffins or something…the undertaker artist…." ("Tantine! The car is absolutely sensational!") He rode through the woods on the back of Ed Kienholz's motorcycle, and was once provided a helicopter by the Dwan Gallery, delighting to descend from the sky—and return to it.

30

*I am going to unveil all the mysteries: religious mysteries, or
natural mysteries, death, birth, the future, the past, cosmogony,
nothingness. I am a master of phantasmagoria.*

ARTHUR RIMBAUD

BACK IN PARIS, INSPIRED IN PART BY GAGARIN'S FLIGHT, YVES
began the series of Planetary Reliefs. But he was losing interest in
the usual materials of art and wanted to work with the raw fabric
of life, eliciting its hidden forces and expressions.

> I shall give up the use of color, I think. I shall work with the
> perspiration of the models, mixed with dust, and even, perhaps,
> with their own blood.[125]

The idea was occultly powerful. Heindel had written,

> The blood is…the vehicle of the subconscious memory, and in
> touch with the Memory of Nature, situated in the highest divi-
> sion of the Etheric Region.[126]

Having read in a book on sorcery that menstrual blood was the
most powerful, Yves hired a Montmartre prostitute at the right
time of the month, to make Anthropometries of her own lunar
blood. The girl panicked midway—when the blood had been applied to her, but not to the canvas yet—and became hysterical.
Pierre Restany was called over to calm her down.

Undaunted, Yves revised his strategy. A second attempt was
made with Rotraut—using beef blood this time—and ten blood
imprints of her body were made. Then terrible news came. A
young Japanese artist, inspired in part by Yves' Leap and his
Anthropometries (especially, perhaps, the "Hiroshima" imprint,
ANT79), was reported to have leapt from a high building onto a
canvas in the street, killing himself and willing the canvas to the
Tokyo Museum of Modern Art, which, according to the story,
rejected it.

Yves was deeply shaken. He feared that the blood imprints
had occultly brought about this tragedy. After all, blood is "in
touch with the Memory of Nature," the central switchboard of the

universe, whose circuits were infinite and inscrutable. The blood imprints were "diabolical." Or were they cryptic notices, from the central switchboard, of how closely death was approaching him? Was the event in Japan, in a sense, an invitation? To take the weight of the omen from Rotraut onto himself, Yves signed each of the canvases with a single thumbprint of his own blood, then called Restany over at midnight to witness the burning of the series.

31

I am the lover
I have wings
I will teach you to fly.

MAX JACOB

ON JANUARY 21, 1962, YVES AND ROTRAUT WERE MARRIED IN the church of Saint-Nicolas des Champs, Paris, to the accompaniment of the *Monotone-Silence Symphony*. Yves, lover of ritual and disguise, wore the plumed hat and crusader's cape of a Knight of Saint Sebastian and was attended by a retinue of knights. The wedding was an extraordinary event, a ceremonial pageant, like the ritual mating which preceded the sacrifice in ancient fertility religions.

Rotraut was pregnant with their son, Yves.

There was partying into the night. Old friends who had fallen away returned and were reconciled.

Soon thereafter, the Discord Spirit laid its final marks upon him.

32

*He moves toward a place of quietude and peace where
he can finally stop being wind. But his nightmare
has already lasted a long time.*

HENRI MICHAUX

As soon as the New Realists had been officially formed,
in his apartment in October 1960, Yves had attempted to appropriate the movement into his work, to make his work the matrix
in which the others' hopes for immortality would reside. In November he had gathered the members in his apartment again for
a collective imprint on the theme of the Void.

Now, in 1962, when his own drama was drawing toward its
close, he moved even more emphatically to incorporate the others
into his approaching transfiguration. The perishable Collective
Imprint would be eternalized in a Collective Portrait Relief. Plaster
casts of the New Realists would be made, converted into bronze,
then painted in Yves' heraldic colors (the colors of the Void), and,
rendered timeless like the statues of Egyptian pharaohs, exhibited
together. But the composition of the group was clearly hierarchi-
cal. The other New Realists were to be painted in International
Klein Blue and exhibited against a gold ground; Yves himself, in
the center, would be gold, against a blue ground—supernatural,
otherworldly, in this world but not of it, a ghostly king among his
chevaliers. This project was terminated by the very transfiguration
which it heralded. Only the cast of Arman was finished; those of
Martial Raysse and Claude Pascal remain unpainted plaster. The
others were never cast.[†]

Station: in the company of Jean-Pierre Mirouze (who had
helped Yves at Gelsenkirchen, and with whom Yves planned to
make films), and his oldest friends, Arman and Claude Pascal, the
Monogold Vampire makes his will: as Proprietor of the Void, he

---

[†] The plaster cast of Arman had been painted blue and mounted on a gold
ground before Klein's death. The bronze casting of Arman was made from the
plaster after Klein's death. It is worth mentioning that the genitals of the three
casts are identical, having been cast from a classical statue.

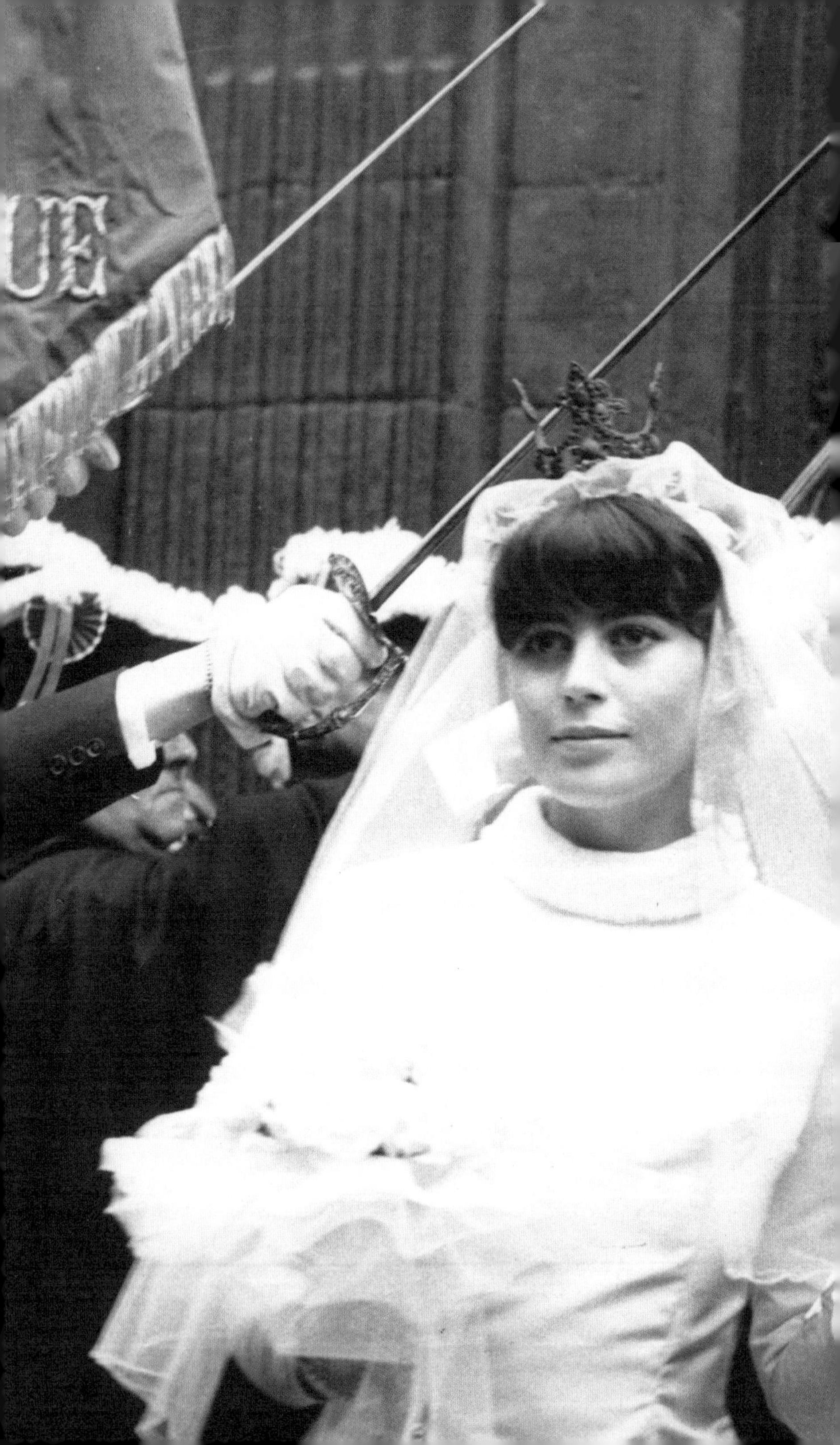

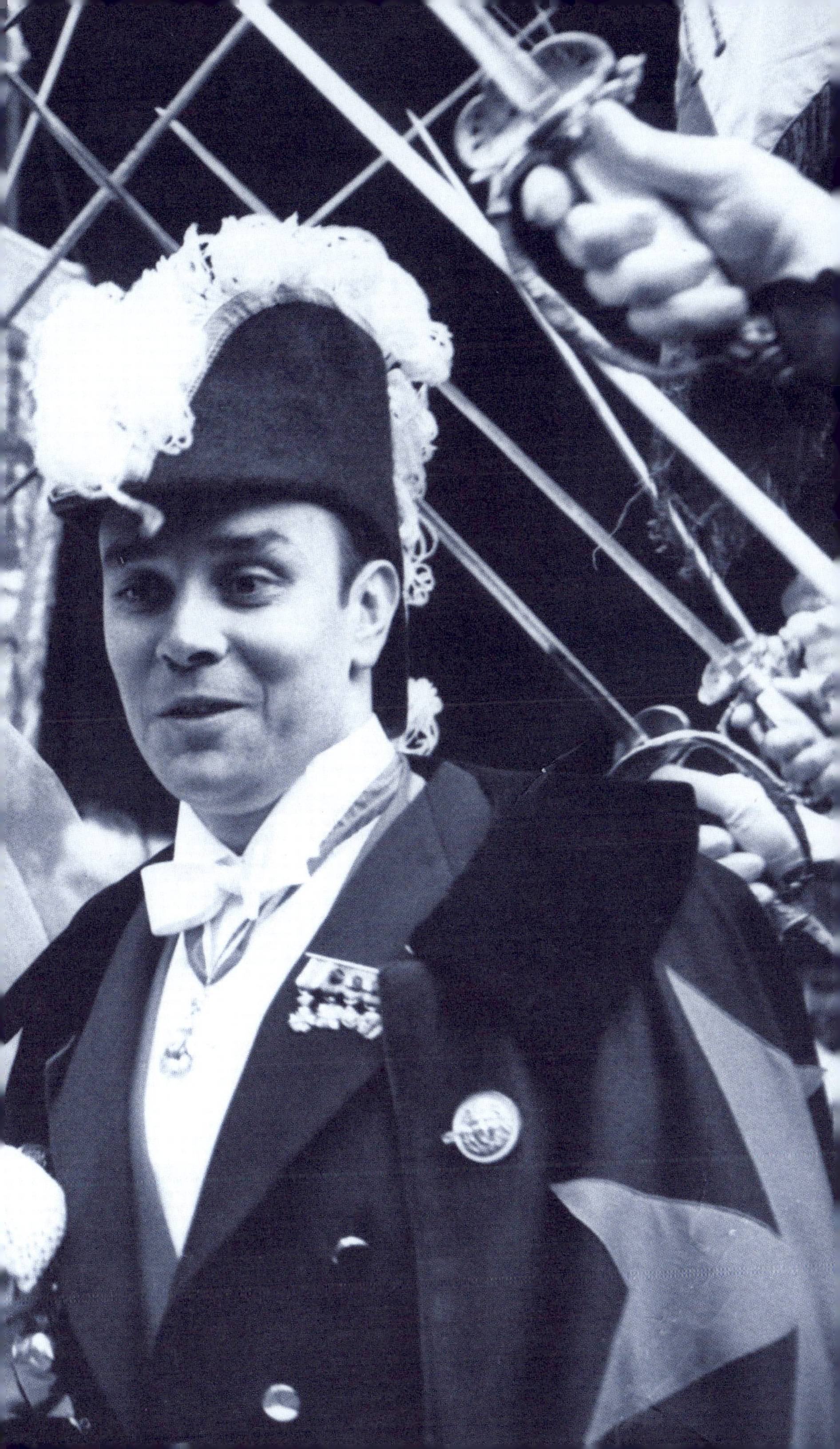

leaves all immaterial space to the others, as well as the right to make monochromes of International Klein Blue and sign them with his name. Sacramentally, he perpetuates his nature in his disciples.

Station: The Citizen of infinity is photographed lying as if dead beneath the gold-leafed "Tomb of Space," safely returned to his home in the absolute.

33

They made you pay for the bread
The sky earth water sleep
And the misery
Of your life.

PAUL ELUARD

IN 1961, GEORGE MARCI, AN ASSOCIATE OF YVES' DEALER, JEAN Larcade, arranged for an Italian director to make a film of Yves and his work—a film which would present performances of Anthropometries in a serious light, repairing the damage done by Chabrol in *Les Godelureaux*. The film was directed by Gualtiero Jacopetti, but Yves was filmed by Paolo Cavara, a cameraman with whom he felt a certain bond of trust. He was paid three thousand francs to cover expenses, and in July 1961 performed Anthropometries (ANT SU 8.1 and 8.2) to the accompaniment of the *Monotone Symphony*, a re-creation of the famous performance of March 1960, which had been parodied by Chabrol. For weeks Yves talked about the film, which he was convinced would put his reputation "at the very top." In fact, his critical sense of the situation was askew.

Back in Italy, unknown to Yves, the footage was mutilated. A brief sequence (only five minutes) was taken out of context, giving it a comical air. The *Monotone Symphony* was removed from the soundtrack and replaced by an insipid American popular song. The passage was edited into the film *Mondo Cane*, a vulgar collection of oddities ridiculed by a contemptuous voice-over narration. Much more negative than Chabrol's film, *Mondo Cane* would also be distributed much more widely.

The film was to preview at Cannes in May 1962. Rotraut, then about six months pregnant, did not attend. Yves flew to Cannes on May 11 or 12 and there met George Marci, with whom, on the evening of the twelfth, he rode to the screening in a taxi. (The legend that he drove down in a blue Rolls Royce and blue tuxedo is not founded on fact, though Yves himself seems to have begun it.) Yves' honest expectation was to witness a film about twenty minutes long entirely about himself.

So there was Yves, caught at last—crushed in the collision between his private myth and the outside world. Sitting in the darkened theater among people he had expected to impress, he watched himself, a Mandrake the Magician cartoon, absurdly overplaying with gestures of eye and hand which the camera made into comedy. It is difficult for one who admires Yves' career to watch this sequence; his self-importance, his apparent lack of ironic distance, make one almost wish to turn away. (How must it have made *him* feel?) And he was not even the centerpiece of this freak show, but just another trivial absurdity among sequences of people eating insects and drinking turtles' blood.

No better trap was ever devised for a hunted animal! Yves with his uncompromising imago, Yves who always had to be first at everything, Yves who would tolerate no resistance, the Master of the Blue Sky, the Proprietor of Color, the Conquistador of the Void! If there was one thing—and there was—which he absolutely could not deal with, it was to be ridiculed. ("His biggest problem—and I think in fact he died of it—was those terrible angers.... It was something that came out from inside of him, and he could not resist it.") ("Softness and softness again... Remember!")

After the showing Yves was "furious and nervous," says George Marci, as he struggled to repress his anger. ("His face would go completely, *completely* white...") Even before the screening he had complained repeatedly that he did not feel well—unusual for Yves, who had once defined art as health. He retired alone to his hotel room to pass a sleepless night fighting his personal nightmares as the Discord Spirit went berserk in his mind. The next morning, when George Marci was to meet him at his hotel, he had disappeared, flying back to Paris alone.

For several days Yves struggled with the Discord Spirit. The sense that his destiny was threatened by ridicule made him increasingly brittle. Unfortunately he had to make a public appearance almost at once, before the Discord Spirit had been exorcised.

Three days after the screening of *Mondo Cane*, Yves was to take part in a public discussion on the relationship of art and industry at the Musée des Arts Décoratifs. Eugène Claudius-Petit, who was presiding, could not have known how delicate Yves' mental and physical condition was.

Not long before, François Mathey of the Musée des Arts Décoratifs had arranged a meeting for Yves, Restany, and Tinguely with an industrialist involved in compressed-air products, to discuss the practical possibilities of the architecture of the air. The businessman had treated them "like fools," remembers Restany—especially Yves, who was the spokesman.

Now, in the debate on art and industry, the memory of this event took Yves in its grip, and he launched a furious diatribe on the stupidity of businessmen. Turning on Restany and Tinguely, who were also members of the discussion panel, he shouted, "You did nothing, you said nothing, you did not come to my aid at all." Claudius-Petit, perceiving him as a child in a tantrum, silenced him peremptorily. "Yves went white as a sheet," says François Mathey. For a Knight of the Grail, with his "strange need of royalty," to be dismissed in mid-sentence in the midst of his own court was an unbearable humiliation.

After the debate Yves walked with Restany and Rotraut to the opening of the show *Donner à voir* at the Galerie Creuze, where Restany had arranged a New Realist room, including the Portrait Relief of Arman. Yves was silent, strained, and pale. He may already have been in an infarction. At one point he said that he had to sit down, and stopped for a cognac. At the gallery an unfamiliar pain gradually suffused his chest and shoulders; by the end of the opening it was intolerable. He could not walk properly. He was taken to a doctor. There was no ambiguity: his heart was "breaking." Even for one who had tried to eternalize himself, time had become impossible to ignore.[†]

Two days later, sitting "very quietly" on the floor of his almost-empty apartment, he told Claude Pascal that he had nearly died. His eyes had a new expression, solemn, sober, no longer playing a game.

His doctor laid down strict conditions for the continuance of his life—conditions which the Conquistador of the Void could hardly accept. One night as Jean Laffont, manager of La Coupole and long a close friend, walked him to the door after dinner, Yves' frustration burst out. "Everything is going wrong," Yves said. "The doctor says that I've got to stay home. I'm hardly allowed to move. When I was in Japan I started taking stimulants. It helped me in judo, but look where I am now. You know me. For me to stay lying down is out of the question. It's just impossible."

34

Had I not once a lovely youth, heroic, fabulous, to be written on sheets of gold, good luck and to spare!

ARTHUR RIMBAUD

THE END WAS APPROPRIATELY MYTHIC, AND MARKED BY OMENS. Death seemed to draw nearer to him, and he seemed to know it. On May 13 Franz Kline died, and Joan Miro, thinking that it was Yves, sent Rotraut a letter of condolence. Yves carried the letter in his pocket, showing it to friends for amusement. On June 2 he wrote to Miró: "Just a little note to show you that l am really alive."

---

† The legend that *Mondo Cane* "killed" Klein is very strong in the oral tradition. George Marci, however, denies emphatically that Klein had a heart attack at Cannes, and Klein himself seems to agree, since various references in his letters and conversations indicate that he thought his first heart attack took place at the opening at the Galerie Creuze.

In fact, neither George Marci's nor Klein's opinion can be taken as medical authority. A heart attack (understood as the moment when a major part of the heart tissue dies) may either precede or follow, by several days or even weeks, the pain which is its outer sign; it may be accompanied at onset only by the sort of mild discomfort of which Klein complained at Cannes, or by no immediate discomfort at all. All that can be said about the date of Klein's first heart attack is that it seems to have occurred sometime in the period including both the Cannes screening and the opening at the Galerie Creuze.

In considering the actual "cause" of the heart attacks, whether prolonged use of stimulants, inhalation of synthetic resins, or his "celebrated temper tantrums," it is well to remember that Klein seems to fit rather closely what medical doctors call the "cardiac profile" or "cardiac personality."

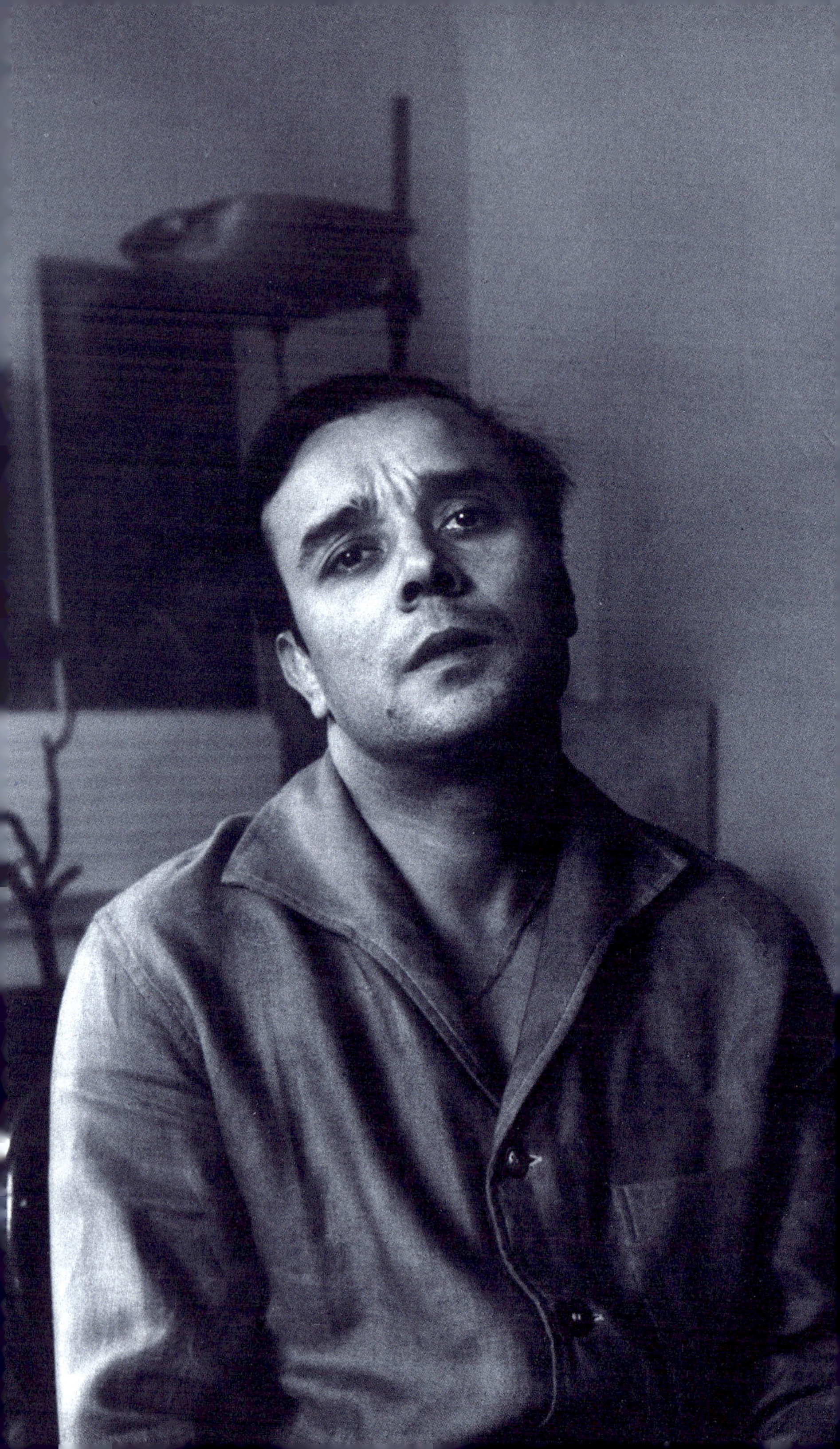

Yet at the same time he seemed to feel that Miro had been prophetically, if not factually, correct: that his time was in fact up. On May 26 he wrote to Larry Rivers, saying, "I have had a heart attack just ten days ago, and I am going to have another one." Death seemed easier to accept than an invalid's life. "It's funny," says Rotraut, "that he had finished everything, just like someone who is getting ready to go on a trip—or to die. He answered all his letters and made sure there was money for me, fixed the name of his son in advance, and designated a godparent [Arman]. Everything was ready." He did not seem frightened or despondent. Death, after all, had always been associated with his deepest and fondest dream, that of flying away from the world, or dematerializing out of it. "He always thought of death as the immaterial," says Rotraut. "It was an obsession with him."

Still, his intention wavered. He believed that his career was at some crucial turning point, but at times was not certain what it was. Was this to be the final performance, death, or merely another turning point along the way? Late in May he broke off with the dealer Larcade, as once he had abruptly left Iris Clert, and on June 4, two days before his death, he dropped by Karl Flinker's gallery unannounced, asking to talk. They made a dinner appointment for June 7.

The next day Yves met Edouard Adam and complained, as he had to others, about the effect of stimulants on his health and the severity of his doctor's advice: "He wants me to relax my efforts; he wants me to paint miniatures, I who wish only to paint space! It is impossible!"

In fact he was deeply depressed by the breakdown of his health and the impossible instructions of his doctor. That night, as he sat in La Coupole with Rotraut, "He had the same dark sad eyes that I had seen when he was about to go to Gelsenkirchen and was telling me that he was going to die [because of *Le Vide*]. He had the same eyes, almost filled with tears. 'Yves,' I said, 'it's strange; you have the same look you had that day'; and then the tears did come out. When we left, I had the sensation that he was being threatened every moment; as we walked back to the apartment I kept turning

---

Left: Klein shortly before his death, 1962.

around as if someone were about to attack him with a knife."

And indeed someone or something seemed to be on Yves' trail that night. "About three or four o'clock in the morning," Rotraut recalls, "there was a knock at the door. Yves said, 'That's strange. Go see who it is.' And it was a German architect or something, no one we knew, who wanted to meet Yves. I didn't let him in." The anonymous predawn summons reverberated like an omen in the nearly empty apartment.

The next morning another unaccustomed visitor arrived. Yves' doctor had phoned Fred Klein to inform him of the gravity of Yves' condition, and Fred made a rare visit to his son's apartment to communicate his concern. He advised Yves to leave at once for a vacation in the south of France. But Yves, of course, had appointments to keep. When his father left he went to lunch with Jean Larcade, and it seemed that a reconciliation between them was approaching. Both excited and confused by his dilemma, Yves ate heavily and drank wine, then said that he had to go home and rest for several hours, as his doctor had advised. At home, finding the elevator broken, he climbed the stairs.

Yet still he did not rest immediately, but fretted for a while over the question of how, considering the state of his health, his career could continue. Rather than make "miniatures," as he contemptuously said, he would concentrate on immaterial works, to relieve himself of the physical labor which his doctor warned him he would not survive. For a moment the idea pleased him, as it rid him at last of the need for a separate studio, which had always been financially out of reach and a source of great frustration. He stood looking at a red monochrome hanging on the wall. "From now on the whole world will be my studio," he said in his last claim to omnipotence, his last appropriation of the universe into his art, "and I will make only immaterial works."

But meanwhile, if he was not allowed to work, he could at least, as his father had suggested, go on a vacation. A friend came by, and Yves asked him to drive his car to Nice while he and Rotraut took a plane, since the doctor had said that driving was too strenuous for him. But even as the arrangement was being made, there was another call to the doctor, who said that he absolutely must not go on a vacation or indeed go anywhere. He was only to "rest." The Conquistador of the Void was to sit like a tame bird and make no further efforts to fly.

When he and Rotraut were alone, he seemed at last ready to "rest." "He was sitting on the bed and now he stretched out. He was lying stretched out on the bed and I blew a kiss to him and said, 'I love you,' as I often did. He said, 'Don't say that; never say that,' which he had never said before… Then in a moment he said, 'Call the doctor; I feel strange.'" When she left the room to phone, the "strange" feeling spread quickly through his entire being. His heart opened up, the "absolute love" of the Void at last rushing in, while something of him, some gold vibration or fiery paradox, rushed out ("free at last!"), to fly weightlessly, in an instant, beyond the sky.

When she returned, his body lay still in a smear of vomit on the bed. It was about six o'clock in the evening, five weeks after Yves' thirty-fourth birthday. Arman, Protector of Animals, arrived minutes later and helped tend to the body.

("When I was told that he had died," says Tinguely, "I was very suspicious. I thought it was one of those extraordinary things he used to put over on us. Because he had always talked about two things: he talked about levitation, and he talked about just vanishing.")

35

Thy mother the sky reaches forth her arms to thee.
Now thou art one with thy mother the sky.

EGYPTIAN HYMN AT THE PHARAOH'S DEATH

STATION: IN THE NEWSPAPER *DIMANCHE*, YVES FORESEES HIS death as brought on by the utter loneliness and isolation of being not an ordinary person but a myth. On a certain day, at a certain hour, every citizen of France goes indoors. Streets, countryside, public squares are absolutely empty. But Yves alone is taken up violently by his fellow men and thrust, against his will, out of doors. Totally alone, unseen by human eyes, he begins to cease to exist as he walks through the empty streets. Soon he has disappeared altogether—and the citizens of France, opening their doors, resume life again.

His constantly shifting approach to the Void, marked by the Stations or Labors, ended in this desolate separation from mankind: Yves the little Captain, walking from the forest, his arms filled with mimosa blossoms; Yves flying from the summer terrace through the moon; Yves signing his name on the far side of the sky; Yves in crusader's costume, the Champion of Color, ready to free us all from the entanglements of line; Yves, his magnetic eyes glowing, shaping pure space in the empty gallery; Yves selling zones of the Void (were they *really* his to sell?), pursuing the Great Work through the four elements toward Prime Matter, leashing destructive fire (how long would it stay tame?), Yves delighting to be the warlock-master of naked young women who groveled in slime at his feet; Yves leaping into the Void, grinning with vampire teeth, lying in the Tomb of Space; Yves fading into thin air as he walks alone through deserted streets, fading…fading…finally, gone.

("From now on I will make *only* immaterial works!")

These gestures still rustle with life in our minds. It is their very smallness which writes them in letters of gold. Compacted into real moments of an individual life, the most fundamental questions gazed out in all honesty. Universals forced their way through his small density and opened spaces in it, zeros of meaning, question marks.

For Yves, art, like spiritual ascesis, meant an attempt to eradicate the self in favor of a higher principle which perhaps could be induced to flow through the gutted channel. It was a path to the blue deep from which all gods and angels arose or descended or were temporarily and apparitionally constituted like clouds. His works were pointers toward the "innermost," icons of the abyss within oneself and each thing, whereby one might plummet through to infinity.

Obviously his works contributed greatly toward giving direction to the art of the sixties and after—monochrome painting, environmental sculpture, nonstatic art, Conceptual Art, Minimal Art, new media, mixed-media—but it is the radical purity of his endeavor, granting all its problems and imperfections, that is most impressive. He gave both a body and a voice to absolutist art, and as if that were not enough, he gave it a myth too. His attempts to absorb universal meaning into his public image through symbolic acts must be seen as heroic if, like much heroism, fatal.

Edward Lucie-Smith, among critics, seems to have fairly appraised his career:

> I do believe that Klein was perfectly sincere and serious in what he did, and I do believe, in addition, that what he did was pointful rather than pointless. Klein also wanted to cleanse the temple; he wanted to rob art of the materialism (which he equated with materiality) which seemed to him to corrupt it, to weight it down.... Heroes are commonly thought of as men whose actions make some kind of statement, stress a moral value. By this definition, Klein was certainly a hero of sorts.

And these lines of Mallarmé (whose blank page gobbled Yves up) may stand as his epitaph:

> *Gilt by the chaste dawn of the Infinite,*
> *I admire myself, see me as angel! I die, I adore*
> *—may the glass be art, may it be mysticity—*
> *to be reborn, with my dreams a crown for me,*
> *in the anterior sky where beauty flowers.*
> *But, alas, Here-below is master, his intimacy*
> *sickens me sometimes in this certain shelter,*
> *and the dirty vomit of Stupidity*
> *makes me hold my nose before the azure.*
> *Are there ways, O self who know asperity,*
> *to break the crystal outraged by this monster*
> *and to escape, on these wings without feathers*
> *—at the risk of falling throughout eternity?*[127]

36

*Let us contemplate undazed
the extent of my innocence.*

ARTHUR RIMBAUD

Language is never innocent.

ROLAND BARTHES

THE FUNCTION OF WRITING," SAYS ROLAND BARTHES, "IS TO maintain a clear conscience."[128] The author's "self" is validated by the imposition upon it, as a kind of mask, of a literary sign to which the writer entrusts his claims of identity. It is an attempt to create oneself anew through a style of words.

Yves Klein was unusually open or direct (or naïve) in the act of entrusting himself, for definition, to a literary sign. For various reasons less naïve and more cunning, he defused his primary sign—that of the occult initiate—by interpenetrating it with the sign of the ironist, which in turn he defused by leading it back into the first, as the laugh of the master who is above it all. This system of reciprocally confirming and canceling signs, designed to give space in which to operate as an unashamed self, seems to have provided little real freedom. There are various views about what Yves would have done if he had lived longer. Restany suggested that he would have pursued the immaterial architecture and related technological prophecies; Arman, that he would have gone into politics; Rotraut, the theater; to George Marci he declared his intention to "paint" with a movie camera. Perhaps his unrelentingly contradictory and creative character would have produced some hitherto undefined occupation involving these activities and more. But in any case it seems certain that he would have had to escape from his myth somehow, "to live it down," to dissociate himself from the literary sign system which, designed as a solution, became a cul-de-sac. The belief that an artist can fashion himself in a form of human perfection as he can fashion an inanimate art material seems ill-founded. He is already fashioned. The marks of early experience cannot be gessoed over. Under pressure of frustration the rigorous requirements of the claim of personal perfection drift into the zone of *sprezzatura*.[129]

Various reductionist models—mostly involving overcompensation for deficiencies of early experience—are available for Yves' motivation in undertaking his mythic project. On top of this is a certain false expectation arising from the tradition of grace—of Saul's instant and permanent transformation into Paul—which implies that peak experiences are permanent. Yves had the misfortune not merely to regard his own early peak experiences as signs of permanent transformation, but even to advertise them as such.

But, questions of personal motivation aside, one must acknowledge his accomplishment. There is no doubt that he created a myth—a variant, an instantiation, of a basic mythic structure—and that his myth must be regarded as an art work. The famous photographs—the Champion of Color, the Leap into the Void—present to us a mythological character ritually garbed in the vestments of art as he performs his mythological Labors. The work overall is finished, subtle, humorous, daring, and powerful.

Disraeli aptly described dandies as "princes of a fantasy world,"[130] and the peculiarly French combination of romanticism, mysticism, and dandyism offers a tradition for Yves. Balzac, Barbey d'Aurevilly, Baudelaire, and Sartre cumulatively described dandyism as a type of transcendental spirituality;[131] Barbey in particular identified the dandy as the foremost of artists, *because his life is his art*. Indeed, insofar as the dandy creates himself, he reflects the activity of an absolute; he abrogates time and causality and transcends their conditions. Dandyism at all levels involves "perpetual contradiction and ambiguity" as one of its constants.[132]

Yves' love of costumes and public posturing, his fastidiousness, his pretense of complete self-control, his constant advertisement of himself as an art work or a perfect being, his desire to incorporate into his character the most enormous contradictions, are all traits related to the transcendental dandyism of which Barbey, Baudelaire, and Sartre wrote. But Yves expanded this tradition into even more difficult realms and claims by his incorporation of the Japanese posturing of the samurai (to avoid the association of dandyism with homosexuality?), by his marriage and procreation (both rigorously excluded from pure dandyism), and above all by the incorporation of a full-scale hero myth which he feigned to act out and pretended to want others to take seriously. The difficulty of this multifaceted undertaking, combined with the production of a major body of external art works, can hardly be overestimated.

Schelling, spokesman for the romantic transcendentalist aesthetic, defined art as "the resolution of an infinite contradiction in a finite product."[133] Yves, whose view of art was similar, attempted to make *himself* the finite object within which infinite forces strain to annihilate one another, to bring them directly into his own body and mind in an attempt at perfection which resembles religious self-sacrifice.

The minor adjustments of the outer record which were necessary to fulfill this program are trivial. They are a small price for the remarkable image which he offered up, as a free gift, with such simplicity and curiosity. The maintenance of so elaborate and excessive a pose was a kind of ravaging ascesis. There is some merit to the view, enunciated occasionally, that for Yves early death was a solution.

In Yves' body of work as a whole, the myth may be viewed either as one artifact among many, underscoring the astonishing diversity of materials and genres he worked in, or as a matrix within which the other works exist and by which they are given a supererogatory thematic coherence. More than a single mythologem is involved. Restany has compared Yves to both Prometheus and Achilles.[134] The latter exemplum is the less accurate (except for the famous childishness of the perpetually eighteen-year-old hero); the former is of limited relevance.

The essential structure of Yves' myth is magical flight, or ascension, or, in its mentalist (Platonic) version, magical vision, seeing into the realm of Forms. In terms of art, the artist becomes a hierophant, opening the vision of Reality to all; as Schelling said, "When a great painting comes into being, it is as though the invisible curtain that separates the real from the ideal world is raised."[135] Whether by flight, by vision, or by expansion into oneness with space, the hero of such a myth establishes in his own person a symbolic link between above and below, suggesting a fructifying exchange of sacred power.

Yves' myth, energized by the antitheses material/immaterial, earth/sky, line/color, and by the mediating structures of magical flight and dematerialization, is as ancient as the "Bird-Man" of Lascaux. It refracts into many aspects hinted at by Yves' rich and contradictory nature, which contains micro-cosmically the strata of human history. A shamanic level is intimated by the concrete imagery of flying to the sky, and by the interest in taboo materials such as blood; the Neolithic spirituality of the Dying God is disclosed in Yves' sacramental theory of painting; in his love of royalty and flight, the Bronze Age king who returns to the far sky, as in Egyptian afterlife myth the pharaoh presides over the court of Re-Osiris among the circumpolar stars. But Yves' myth is most closely paralleled in the Orphic structure of descent from the sky and hope to reascend there through ascetic and magical means. In Persian messianism and Christianity, the being from beyond the sky descends in order to lead others after him in his reascent. This motif is echoed in the alchemical pattern of sublimation and precipitation, and is clearly stated by Yves in *Dimanche*.

In terms of literary genre-criticism Yves' myth has various associations, not least the inevitable resonance with Aristotle's definition of the tragic flaw. "The great majority of tragic heroes," says Northrop Frye, "do posses hubris, a proud, passionate, obsessed or soaring mind which brings about a morally intelligible downfall.... The tragic hero usually belongs...to the *alazon* group, an imposter in the sense that he is self-deceived, or made dizzy by hubris."[136]

When Yves' life-myth is regarded as a series of symbolic tableaux, it shows affinities to the medieval procession or pageant and the related miracle and passion plays. When viewed from the hostile point of view of those who awaited his downfall, he swaggers like the *miles gloriosus*.

It is remarkable that the literary genres to which Yves' life bears the least resemblance are the most realistic ones, the novel and the history. His quick and sensitive mind picked up and resonated to every motif in the zone of the quest and the ascent, while attempting to edit out all that was soiled with history and origins.

To quote Tinguely once more: "It was a dream he was living. And he lived it altogether truly. He was a true poet."

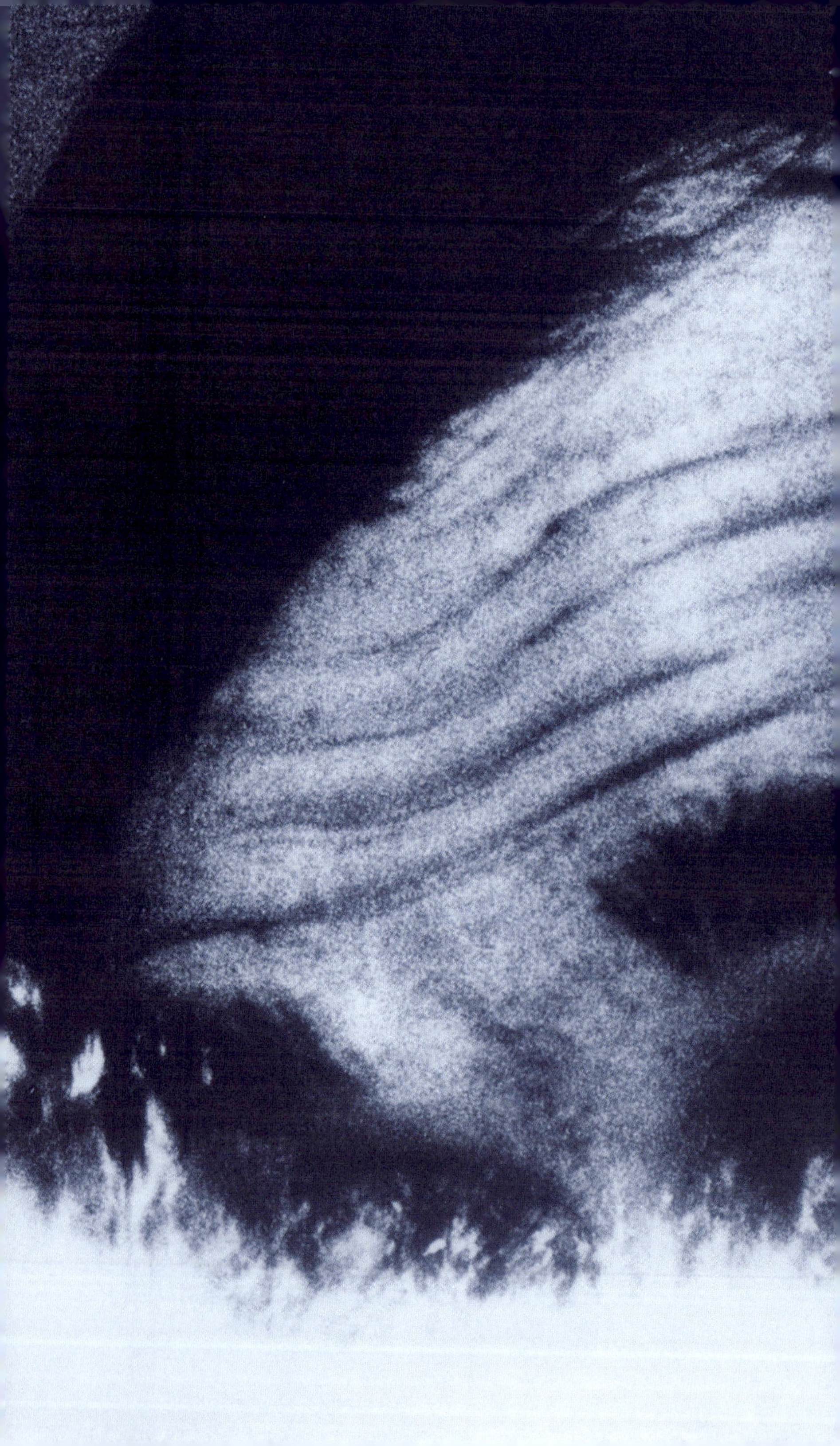

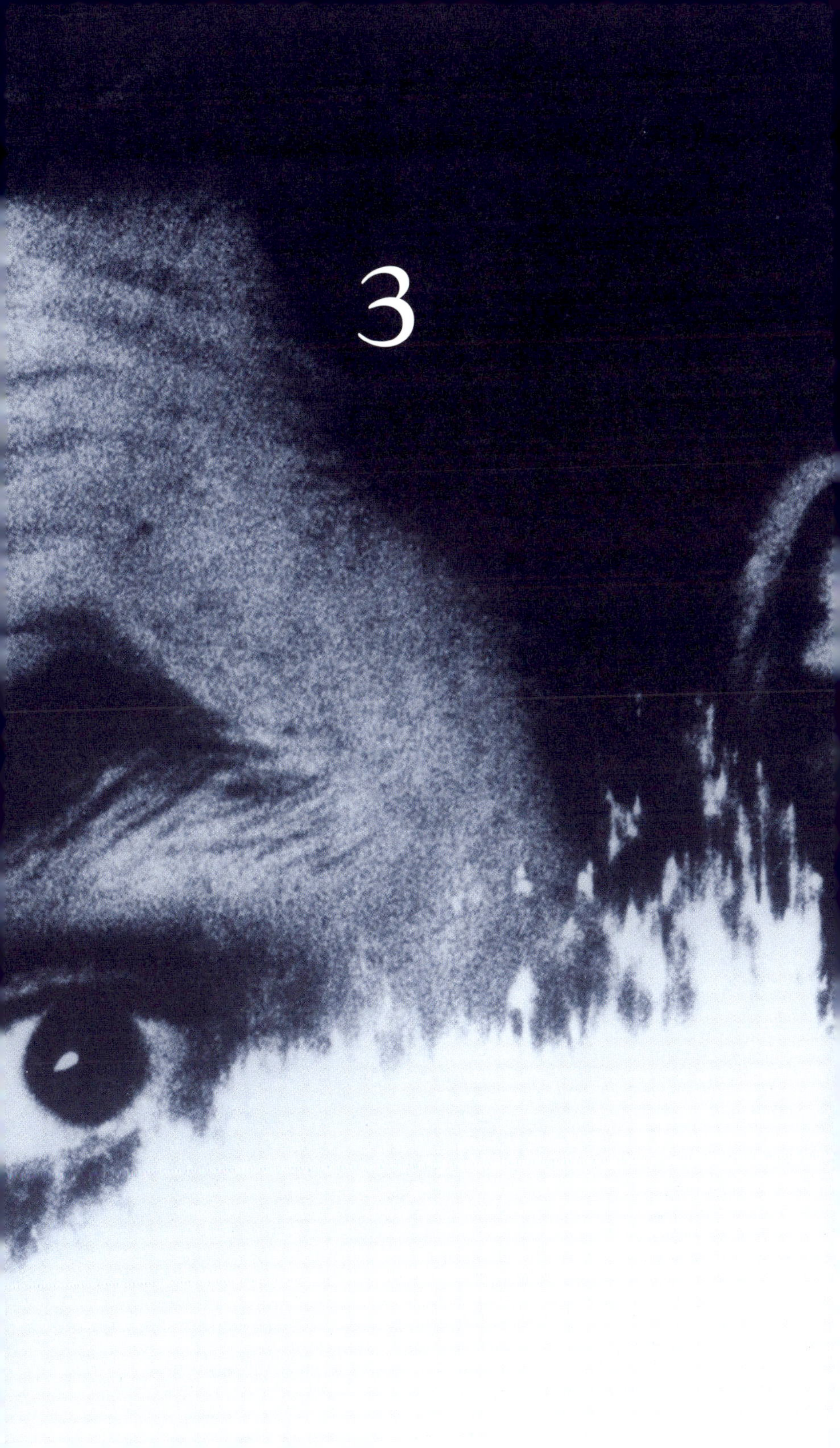
3

Yves Klein and Rosicrucianism

Advance information about...an artist's concepts is necessary to
the appreciation and understanding of contemporary art.

JOSEPH KOSUTH[1]

The artist's own comments about what is said in one or another
of his works may certainly be of interest.... But the language of
art means the excess of meaning that is present in the work itself.
The inexhaustibility that distinguishes the language of art from all
translations into concepts rests on the excess of meaning.

HANS-GEORG GADAMER[2]

The relation of language to painting is an infinite relation. . . .
Neither can be reduced to the other's terms: it is in vain that we
say what we see; what we see never resides in what we say.

MICHEL FOUCAULT[3]

IN CONCLUDING HIS ESSAY ON THE MYTH of Isis and Osiris,
Plutarch denies that any of the dozen or so interpretations
he has reviewed is true by itself and affirms that all of them together (despite their contradictions) constitute a kind of truth.
His intuition that hermeneutics must remain sufficiently open to
embrace not only complementary but even contradictory readings
foreshadows both the multi-model approach generated by modern
positivism and the phenomenological insistence that a myth (or an
art work) transcends any single horizon of subjectivity.

[195]

Basic philological work on Yves Klein's extensive oeuvre has hardly begun. It may eventually result in an integrated layering of readings which, like Plutarch's stratified approach to myth, can be held to constitute a meaning. But initially philology must proceed by isolating partial models, which may ultimately be merged in a synthesis.

It is well known that Klein's work has a remarkable inner consistency or logic. What is not widely understood is that this consistency reflects the faithfulness with which he translated into visual and art historical terms an idea system whose native context was not art, namely, the Rosicrucianism of Max Heindel. Philological analysis of the relationship between Klein's writings and Heindel's is necessary groundwork from which a more synthetic approach to Klein's art may develop. The task is undertaken here without any claim that this model can exhaust the meaning of Klein's works. On the contrary, it is not so much an interpretation of his works which is offered here as a reconstruction of his sources and intentions, which are of interest in themselves.

Around the end of 1947 or the beginning of 1948, when Klein was nineteen, he obtained a copy of Max Heindel's *La Cosmogonie des Rose-croix*, the "manual" of the Rosicrucian Society of Oceanside, California.[4] At once he began practicing the Rosicrucian teachings intensively, in the company of his close friends Claude Pascal and Armand Fernandez (later Arman), under the guidance of an older Rosicrucian, Louis Cadeaux. In June 1948 Klein officially joined the Rosicrucians. For more than three years he received monthly lessons (written, like the *Cosmogonie*, by Max Heindel) and faithfully sent his worksheets to Oceanside for review. For another year and a half (until mid-1953) he received the lessons but did not send back his worksheets. In mid-1953 his official membership lapsed.[5] He continued to read in the *Cosmogonie* for several more years; until about 1958 it was the central book of his life.

Between 1955 and 1962 Klein produced both a variegated body of art works and an interesting body of writings on the theory of art, his own art especially.[6] Through these writings a kind of luminous pattern seems to shine without entirely revealing itself. Much of that pattern can be clarified by a study of Klein's usually unacknowledged allusions to Heindel's works, especially the *Cosmogonie*. I will first summarize Klein's theory of art, then Heindel's Rosicrucian system, and then will explicate the detailed correspondences between them.

The central theme of Klein's essays is a mystical conception of space, conceived as free energy, in contrast to form, or bound energy. Space is identified with alchemical Prime Matter, containing a universal "memory" of past, present, and future, and functioning as the source of the world of form. Psychologically, pure space equates with the free (enlightened) mind, form with the bound (neurotic) mind. In terms of painting, this fertile space is called "pure pictorial sensibility." The artist whose mind is free like space can crystallize this pictorial energy into any object by mental concentration; the higher sensibility which has been locked into the object by the artist can be regained from it by the viewer, who can, in fact, be awakened to cosmic consciousness by the experience.

The metaphysical dichotomy between space and form appears in painting as the Battle between Line and Color. Line divides and obstructs the pure space of cosmic sensibility, while color asserts the freedom and fullness of space and tends to make the artist one with it (to "return him to Eden"). In fact, pure color is not merely an analogue of this cosmic space/sensibility, it is an actual materialization of it—especially blue, the color of sea and sky, the two most abstract and illimitable natural entities. The artist who has realized the sensibility of pure space will express himself in pure color; the artist who lacks this cosmic openness of mind will express himself through the neurotic entanglements of line and form.

But the artist can express the sensibility of space in other ways, too. The "trace of the immediate" shows prime matter just beginning to crystallize into bound space. Above all, the "art of the immaterial" is the truest expression of this sensibility and will be the typical mode of future art in the technological Eden of aerial men. The artist makes immaterial art by leaving the aura of his sensibility in an apparently empty space, from which it can be regained by the sensitive observer at any time. The artist may also "specialize" his sensibility into specific, but invisible, forms, which are also works of immaterial art, or he may project it over long distances.

In a not very distant future, Klein wrote, all men will evolve into this sensibility and will become more or less one with space, able to levitate their physical bodies or to operate immaterially, out of their bodies altogether. At that time human societies will be reconstituted, through a union of science, art, and religion, in an Edenic state; the surface of the earth will be reclimatized to accommodate the new immaterial mode of living and, consonant with his new identity with space, man will live in houses of compressed-air currents. We are nearly in that age now, Klein held, as is shown by his own prophetic works and by the flight of the Russian spacecraft Vostok 1 (during which Yuri Gagarin said that the earth, from outer space, looks blue).

This theory, and to a degree the works which express it, are based primarily on the Rosicrucian thought of Max Heindel, with a smattering of Buddhism and glances at Gaston Bachelard thrown in. The central idea of Heindel's *Rosicrucian Cosmoconception* is the polarity, and ultimate synthesis, of Life and Form.[7] Life is pure spirit, equated with apparently empty space; Form, on the other hand, is bound spirit, and equates with physical matter. These conditions alternate through long stages of human evolution. At the beginning is the stage of Life, in which there is no illusion of ego separation but awareness of Oneness-with-the-All. In ensuing periods, the principle of Form gradually gains dominance over Life, and the illusion of ego separation smothers awareness of Oneness-with-the-All. Finally, awareness of separate existence will somehow combine with awareness of Oneness-with-the-All, at the triumphant culmination of human evolution.

> At present we are nearing the end of the age of Form, and in the next Epoch we will begin to open up again to awareness of Life. When this happens we will no longer be bound to the gross physical body, the ultimate product of the age of Form, but will gain control, successively, of a series of higher vehicles which are now obscured from our awareness by our bondage to Form. The first sign of this upward trend toward Life will be control of the Desire Body (the grossest of six "immaterial" vehicles); at that point we will gain the ability to levitate, to read the memory of nature, and

> to manipulate the order of things through mental activity alone.
> In each new age the dominant vehicle remakes the environment
> to suit itself—as at present the gross physical body has created for
> itself an environment of solid matter. In the next Epoch, when the
> Desire Body needs an environment less bound to Form and more
> open to Life, the environment will be remade by science, which
> will become an arm of religion and will turn human life back in
> the direction of empty space, where alone Life and freedom are
> to be found.

Klein's career was an expression of this belief system; he regarded himself as the instrument of evolution, presaging and hastening the dawn of the new age.

The leading ideas of both Heindel's and Klein's thought were Space and Evolution. For Heindel, Space is equated with all six invisible realms higher than the physical and is accessible only to the initiate who has performed certain inner transformative works. Space is not dead emptiness, but invisible fullness:

> In our present materialistic period we have unfortunately lost the
> idea of all that lies behind that word Space. We are so accustomed
> to speaking of "empty" space, of the "great void" of space, that
> we have entirely lost the grand and holy significance of the word,
> and are thus incapable of feeling the reverence that this idea of
> Space and Chaos should inspire in our breasts.
>
> To the Rosicrucians, as to any occult school, there is no such
> thing as empty or void space. To them, space is Spirit in its attenu-
> ated form; while matter is crystallized space or Spirit.[8]

Heindel's equation of Space with Ovidian chaos, or with the undifferentiated Prime Matter of the alchemists, is transposed by Klein into painterly terms in his definition of space as "unlimited pictorial sensibility." In a passage which Klein underlined in his copy of the *Cosmogonie*, Heindel wrote:

> Chaos is the seed-ground of the Cosmos....We shall no longer won-
> der how "something can come out of nothing," because Space is
> not synonymous with "nothing." It holds within itself the germs
> of all that exists during a physical manifestation.[9]

All of Klein's art relates in some way to this central concept of featureless etheric fullness. As he wrote:

The void has always been my essential preoccupation.[10]

In rejecting nothingness I found the void. The meaning of immaterial pictorial zones issued from the depths of the void.[11]

I seek above all...to create in my realization this transparency, this void immeasurable, in which lives the Spirit permanent and absolute, freed from all dimensions.[12]

The absolute void...is entirely naturally the true pictorial space.[13]

It is Evolution which is carrying us toward the void. According to Heindel, we have reached the farthest extension into matter, and the next stage calls for our reawakening to Pure Spirit and simultaneously our expansion beyond the physical realm into space:

During the remaining half of this Period and the entire three remaining Periods, man must expand his consciousness so as to include all of the six Worlds above this Physical World.[14]

[Man's] next step in progress will be towards an expansion in consciousness that will include the Etheric Region, then the Desire World, etc.[15]

This transition will be marked by both mental and physical changes in the human vehicle and the human culture which is its expression and its matrix. One of these changes which was already visible in Klein's time was the exploration of outer space. Says Heindel:

[Modern science] does not recognize the... fact insisted upon by occult science... that the whole atmosphere around us, the space between the worlds, is Spirit.[16]

The Etheric Region extends beyond the atmosphere of our dense earth.... the Desire World extends further into interplanetary Space than either of the others.[17]

Thus travel into outer space is travel toward Pure Spirit and away from matter. Klein viewed the flight of Yuri Gagarin as confirmation that we are now on the verge of this great turning point in human history.

According to Heindel, humanity, in the next Epoch, will gain control of the Desire Body, and thereafter movement will be through levitation; truly spiritualized human beings will be able to separate themselves from the gross body at will, and will no longer need physical spacecraft:

> In the Physical World, matter is subject to gravity. In the Desire World,...forms levitate as easily as they gravitate. Distance and time are also governing factors of existence in the Physical World, but are almost nonexistent in the Desire World.[18]

Klein underlined in his copy of the *Cosmogonie* mostly passages describing the Desire World, and wrote "Transfiguration" large in the margin next to the description of levitation. His own desire to levitate was an anticipation of this stage of evolution, as were his *Leap into the Void*, the "Anthropometry" entitled *People Begin to Fly*, and the Düsseldorf speech announcing that

> we will all become aerial men, we will know the upward force of attraction toward space, toward nothing and everything at once: earthly gravity having been overcome, we will literally levitate in a total physical and spiritual freedom.[19]

In fact, it seems that Klein viewed his own career as one of the announcements or signs of the impending transformation of humanity, using terminology to describe it which clearly derives from Heindel's theory of Evolution. Heindel uses the term "Period" for a vast cosmic phase (we are now, for example, in the "Earth Period"), and the terms "Revolution" or "Epoch" for smaller phases within Periods. Klein's announcement in 1957 of the "Blue Revolution" ushering in the "Blue Epoch" referred not merely to the displacement of one artistic style or school by another, but to this imminent spiritualization of all mankind.

Heindel, like writers in various Eastern traditions, specifically associated the void of Pure Spirit with the color blue, saying, "Blue shows the highest type of spirituality," that is, the spirituality which has become one with Space/Spirit.[20] Klein followed him in associating the Void, or Pure Spirit, with the color blue.[21] The Blue Epoch, then, is to be nothing less than the Epoch of return to Space/Spirit. President Eisenhower was the first head of state who was honored with a notice of this Revolution, perhaps because of Heindel's statements:

> From the people of the United States will descend the last of all
> the Races in this scheme of evolution.[22]

> From the United States will the next "chosen people"…be chiefly
> derived.[23]

Similarly, the Blue Revolution's plans to alter the surface of the earth spring from Heindel's assertion that

> before a new Epoch is ushered in…there must be "a new heaven
> and a new earth"; the physical features of the Earth will be changed
> and its density decreased.[24]

Klein's "architecture of the air" is a means to decrease the density of the environment, and his reclimatization schemes connect with Heindel's statement that

> climate, flora and fauna are altered by man under the direction of
> higher beings.[25]

Heindel and the Rosicrucian tradition in general describe the next Epoch (the return to Space) as a return to Eden, a term which recurs continually in Klein's writings.[26] For the individual, the return to Eden means escape from the body, reimmersion in Space/Chaos, and consequent realization of Oneness-with-the-All. For the community, it means the union of technology, religion, and art to create a milieu in which the transition to the Desire Body will be hastened and facilitated. Klein's attempt to synthesize Rosicrucianism, technology, and art was a response to Heindel's insistence that in order to make the transition to the Desire World,

> Religion, Science and Art must re-unite in a higher expression of
> the Good, the True and the Beautiful.[27]

His deliberate attempts to fulfill Heindel's prophecies suggest that Klein believed, or hoped, that he might be the transition figure announced by Heindel:

> At the end of our present Epoch the highest initiate will appear
> publicly when a sufficient number of ordinary humanity desire
> and will voluntarily subject themselves to such a leader.… After
> that time races and nations will cease to exist. Humanity will form
> one spiritual fellowship.[28]

Klein's announcement to President Eisenhower of the end of

the French national government certainly sounds as if he is taking this mantle on himself, as do his statements that Space itself acknowledges him as its "Conquistador" and makes him the "Proprietor of COLOR."[29]

As Conquistador of Space it is the initiate's duty to champion the advancement of others on the path of Evolution, and as the Proprietor of Pure Color it is in his power to do so. Klein's announcement of the Battle between Line and Color, and of himself (in Knight of Saint Sebastian costume) as the Champion of Color, shows him at the forward edge of Evolution, championing the incoming age against the reactionary attraction of the old. The distinction is not only based on Heindel but was explicitly laid out by Heindel when he said:

> The Physical World is the world of Form. The Desire World... is particularly the world of Color.[30]

The physical world is tied to Form (in Klein's terms, line) because it is centered in Ego; the Desire World expresses itself as Pure Color because it is Spirit, which knows no internal divisions. As Klein wrote:

> Pure color [is] the universal soul in which the human soul bathes in the state of earthly paradise.... This universal color soul...is life itself.[31]

The art of Pure Color, then, is equivalent to immersion in uninterrupted Space and constitutes a return to the Eden of Life-without-Ego. Klein expresses this in perfectly Heindelian terms:

> By saturating myself with the eternal limitless sensitivity of space I return to Eden...and that is why, in my work, I refuse more and more emphatically the illusion of personality, the transient psychology of the linear, the formal, the structural. Evidently the subject I am traveling toward is space, pure Spirit.[32]

Line, which must express itself by dividing, separating, and making limits, entangles and imprisons the openness of color and thus destroys paradise:

> Paradise is lost [when] the entanglement of lines becomes the bars of a prison.[33]

Human history is the long drama of line invading color (Heindel's "Age of Form") and color struggling to free itself (for the "Age of Spirit"):

> Line, jealous of color, the true inhabitant of space, tries to free itself from the condition of tourist in space; it breaks itself up and invades the picture surface....
> Color, humiliated, defeated, prepares its revenge over long years.[34]

The Edenic age of unity at the beginning of time was the age of color; it was followed by a long degeneration into multiplicity, as line invaded and broke up the picture surface. Color began to reassert itself with the works of Delacroix and Van Gogh, and now, in Klein's work, stands ready to regain

> the field and usher in a new age of unity. The goal of art (as of life) is to regain that ineffable peace in nature and man before the intrusion of line into color.[35]

In terms of Evolution, then, art based on Line and Form is regressive; it is a remnant of the Epoch of the gross body, which is now ending. Art based on pure color with no internal division is prophetic of the incoming age. Thus Klein's announcement of the Battle between Line and Color is the announcement, in artistic terms, of the end of one age of human evolution and the beginning of another. When he writes,

> the whole immense evolution across the ages aims at the discovery of the mystery of color,[36]

he is evidently referring to Heindel's doctrine of our long evolution toward the Desire World, the realm of color.

This same Heindelian dichotomy—between Space as free Spirit and Form as bound Spirit—is the basis of Klein's theory of the monochrome, which is perhaps the cornerstone of his writings. A key passage from "The Monochrome Adventure" (Klein's most ambitious essay) deserves to be quoted in full:

> Through color I experience a feeling of complete identification with space. I am truly free. If a color is no longer pure, the drama may take on disquieting overtones. As soon as there are two colors in a painting combat begins; the permanent spectacle of this battle of two colors may give the onlooker a subtle psychological and

> emotional pleasure, that is nonetheless morbid from a purely hu-
> man, philosophical point of view…. Lines, bars of a psychological
> prison,…are our chains, they are the concretization of our mortality,
> our sentimentality, our intellect, even our spiritual domain. They
> are our heredity, our education, our framework, our vices, our aspi-
> rations, our qualities, our wiles. In short, our whole psychological
> world, with all its subtlest recesses.
>
> Color on the other hand, both in nature and in man, is that
> which is most immersed in cosmic sensibility. That sensibility
> has no recesses but is like humidity in the air. For me, color is
> sensibility "materialized." …Color is free, it is instantly dissolved
> in space…. The line goes toward infinity, but color has its being
> right in infinity. Colors are the true inhabitants of space. The line
> only travels across space.

Clearly he is thinking of Heindel's "The Desire World…is particularly the world of Color" when he writes, "Color has its being
right in infinity…. Colors are the true inhabitants of space."
Underlying the passage is Heindel's distinction between Life/
Spirit/Open Space/Color and Ego/Matter/Closed Space/Form. In
many passages Klein makes this quite explicit by using the term
"Life" (or "LIFE") in ways which cannot really be understood
without knowing the Rosicrucian usage:

> Life itself does not belong to us; it is through sensibility that we
> can achieve it.[37]

> [Art work] should be like an open channel for penetration by
> impregnation in the sensibility of the immaterial space of LIFE
> itself.[38]

> I propose to artists that they pass by art itself and work individually
> to return to the real life in which a man no longer thinks he is the
> center of the universe, but the universe is the center of the man.[39]

> I love in myself everything that does not belong to me, that is, my
> life, and I detest everything that belongs to me: my education, my
> psychological and optical inheritance,…my vices, my defects, my
> qualities, my manias.[40]

But it is probable that there is more than Rosicrucian influence
here. Klein read several books on Buddhism during his formative
Rosicrucian period, both in France and in Japan, and although his
sources in Buddhist literature cannot be specifically identified,[41]
it seems that in the passages just quoted and others like them

he was synthesizing Zen and Rosicrucianism and expressing the synthesis in art historical terms.

In Buddhist literature, the enlightened mind is often likened to empty space or the open sky with no internal divisions. As Milarepa, a Tibetan Buddhist sage, put it:

> *A wise man knows how to practice*
> *The space-like meditation.*
> *In all he does by day*
> *He attaches himself to nothing.*[42]

Klein's art is space-like in its monochromy and immateriality; in its rejection of form it "attaches itself to nothing." He entitled himself "the Painter of Space,"[43] hostile to the birds and clouds which limit the openness of the sky by drawing lines across infinity,[44] and Buddhist authors also speak this way, for example Milarepa:

> *[The awareness of voidness] is like the feeling of staring into a*
> *   vast and empty sky...*
> *Thinking of the magnitude of the sky*
> *Meditate on the vastness with no center and no edge...*
> *It was fine when I contemplated the sky! But I felt uneasy when I*
> *   thought of the clouds...*[45]

The art of the empty sky is the blue monochrome, portrait of Space and of the mind which is clear like Space.

According to Buddhist psychology, the origin of neurosis is a tendency to solidify energy so that it ceases to fill space completely and be one with it (as pure color does), and becomes a barrier (a line) dividing space into subject and object, ego and other. The arising of this first mental barrier is called "primary dualistic fixation," and it equates with the one line Klein refused to add to a monochrome in 1955 to get it into a show. Once this first barrier is in place, others are produced from it by a kind of mechanical momentum. Finally, space—the mind like the open sky, which formerly was open and free—becomes clogged and obstructed by unnecessary barriers which force one's energy to flow in certain channels. The overall pattern of these channels comprises the individual personality, the "education,...inheritance,...vices,...defects, [and] qualities" which the painter of space rejects. The cure consists in erasing these barriers through meditation until the mental space is open again.[46]

And in painterly terms all this, as Klein saw, points toward the monochrome, toward erasing the cloudlike forms from the pure skylike ground. Buddhist authors at times even express this process in terms of eliminating figure from ground; the Zen image is wiping the dust from the mirror. The monochrome is an analogue of the experience of emptiness (shunyata):

> Attention can be directed either to the concrete, limited forms or to the field in which these forms are situated. In the shunyata experience, the attention is on the field rather than on its contents.[47]

We may compare the words of a developmental psychologist on the ego-discovering and ego-transcending stages of life:

> It is necessary that the ego discover itself by a figure-ground relationship to this material universe, but it is also necessary to transcend this relationship.[48]

In a similar spirit Klein said that the monochrome is the only physical way of painting which permits attaining the spiritual absolute.[49] Heindel's system points to the same conclusion for the painter: Life pervades Space and is negated by Form, which divides and obstructs Space. Hence the painter who heralds the end of the age of Form and Ego and the beginning of the age of Space and Life must, like the Buddhist meditator, erase internal barriers and restore Space to its wholeness. This means abolishing figure (which represents Form and Ego) from the ground (which represents Space and Life). The art of Form is evolutionarily outdated, just as is the physical eye which perceives it; art must now move directly toward the Void:

> For me painting is no longer a function of the eye; it is a function of the only thing which does not belong to us: our LIFE.[50]

> I am against line and all its consequences: contours, forms, compositions. All paintings of that type, whether figurative or abstract, seem to me to be windows of a prison of which the lines themselves are the bars. Far away, where color dominates, is freedom! The viewer of a painting with lines, forms, and composition remains the prisoner of his five senses.[51]

In the next age, when the immaterial Desire Body arises, we will not only be freed from our senses, but will live naturally in the realm "where color dominates," the Desire Realm. The artist of that new age will produce works that are one with the infinite, that is, with Life:

> Life, Life itself..., is the absolute art.[52]

But this new art cannot be made authentically without a corresponding inner erasure of barriers from the artist's mind, restoring it, like the ground of the painting, to the state before "primary dualistic fixation" set in.[53] The artist's "education, inheritance, vices," and so forth are affronts to the infinity of primal mind, as lines and figures are affronts to the infinite ground of the painting, which is the seed-bed of art as Chaos is the "seed-ground of the Cosmos," holding all things in a state of "pure pictorial sensibility."

When in 1957 Klein adopted the title "Yves the Monochrome," he was announcing, or claiming, that he had erased dualistic fixation from his own mind as he had erased figure from his paintings; that he had, in other words, entered the Desire World, the realm of color. Other artists, he believed, would follow if he beckoned on the way. At this evolutionary turning point the artist must realize his true kinship with Space and disentangle himself from the deathlike art of Ego and Form, which negates Life:

> [Artists who] wish to save their personality at any cost will kill their spiritual self and lose their LIFE.[54]

> [Monochromism is] a sort of modern-day alchemy, practiced by painters, born of the tension of experiencing...a bath in space vaster than infinity.[55]

> The artist who creates should no longer do so for the sake of signing his work, but, as an honest citizen of the immeasurable space of sensitivity, should create always from his awareness that he exists in a state of profound illumination, as does all the universe but which we neither see nor feel, enclosed in the psychological world of our inherited optics.[56]

> The true painter of the future will be a mute poet who will write nothing, but recount, without detail and in silence, an immense picture without limit.[57]

> My monochrome paintings are landscapes of freedom.[58]

By painting Space, Klein was painting the All and acting out in his own person the condition of return to the All, to the mind like open sky. It is this awareness that comprises the "monochrome spirit," which Klein insisted was the essence of his painting and which he said was lacking in, for example, the white monochromes painted by Rauschenberg around 1950.[59]

After 1957 Klein made monochromes only of what he called "rose, gold, and blue," but mostly of blue (a near-ultramarine patented in 1960 as International Klein Blue—the name suggesting the new age which these paintings inaugurate, an age beyond distinctions of race or nation). Rose, gold, and blue are in effect red, yellow, and blue, the three primaries, and Heindel gives special importance to these colors, which, he says, "are God and make up the triune godhead," and which "correspond to the three aspects of God."[60] By working with these colors Klein was reconstituting Space in the likeness of God. But it was especially blue which for both Heindel and Klein represented the absolute, or Life. This symbolism was, in a sense, confirmed for Klein when Gaston Bachelard (in a tradition going back to Mallarme's azur) identified blue with the absolute.[61] Blue for Klein is above all the color of dimensionless Space:

> Blue has no dimensions. It is beyond dimensions while the other colors are not.[62]

> The blood of the body of sensibility is Blue.[63]

> I have consecrated myself to finding the most perfect expression of Blue."[64] *(Note the Heindelian capitalization.)*

Thus when Klein painted various objects (from a miniature Nike of Samothrace to a globe of the world) with International Klein Blue, he was expressing the idea that Life or Spirit permeates ("impregnates") all things, even when they seem bound to the rack of Form. As Klein himself said in a passage which paraphrases many Heindelian statements:

> *It was an impregnation which went beyond dimensions, which traversed everything, which impregnated itself into everything, in matter as well as in the atmosphere or in the void.*[65]

This "impregnation" of matter by Spirit is perhaps best exemplified by the blue sponge works, which, like the blue monochromes, were first exhibited in 1957, the year of the Blue Revolution. The first sponge sculpture was exhibited at the multifaceted show at Colette Allendy's, in conjunction with the exhibition of blue monochromes at Iris Clert's. It was followed in later years by more sponge sculptures (sponges painted blue and mounted on blue pedestals) and the sponge reliefs (sponges painted blue and mounted in groups on blue-painted wood), of which those at Gelsenkirchen are the most impressive examples.

Art historically the sponge works relate both to the found object and to the development of new media. In Heindelian terms they, like the Nike painted in IKB, represent the permeation of all things with the Life of the "blue deep" of Space. Klein's own statements on the sponge works clearly direct us to this interpretation:

> I had this experience in 1956 while painting my monochromes with sponges; after the sponges had dried, they were impregnated with blue. And I said to myself, that is beautiful in itself, and even more it is remarkable because it is the portrait of someone who saw how I was making my monochromes. It [the sponge] was there. It was a presence. It was impregnated with blue. It is the phenomenon of impregnation that is important.[66]

> While working on my paintings in my studio, I sometimes would use sponges. They became blue very fast, of course. One day I saw the beauty of the blue in the sponge; this instrument of work had become prime matter.... [They were] portraits of viewers of my monochromes who, after having seen them, after having voyaged into the blue of my paintings, come back totally impregnated in sensibility, like the sponges.[67]

In fact, Klein's interpretation of these works seems to be directly based on passages in Heindel's *Cosmogonie*: the sponge is the only image Heindel uses (and he uses it repeatedly) to illustrate the permeation of the material realm by Spirit.

> Let us take a spherical sponge to represent the dense earth.... Imagine that sand permeates every part of the sponge and also forms a layer outside the sponge. Let the sand represent the Etheric Region, which in a similar manner permeates the dense earth and extends beyond its atmosphere.[68]

We may regard the solar systems as separate sponges, swimming in a World of Divine Spirit.[69]

But the blue works were not the ultimate expressions of Space art. They remained the material signs of an immaterial essence. Kiein was able to deny that Rauschenberg's monochromes were really monochromes on the grounds that the essence of any work of art is immaterial:

> The pictorial quality of each painting [is] perceptible by something other than its material physical appearance.[70]

In fact, in order to be real, a painting must be invisible.[71] The physical painting is only a remnant of the passing age of the Physical World:

> The physical painting has a right to exist only because people believe only in the physical, even while they feel obscurely the essential presence of the other thing.[72]

Of two paintings physically identical, one may be a real work of art, the other not.[73] What matters is the condition of the artist's mind. If he has developed higher sensibilities which relate to Life rather than to Ego, then Life will be present in his work at the etheric level and can be picked up by the etheric sensors of the viewer. Thus a specially trained sensibility is necessary to experience art; only special viewers, those "gifted with a body or vehicle of sensibility," will be able to carry away the immaterial essence of what they see.[74]

Klein definitely felt that his own works were rich in this higher-dimensional essence, so much so that a really receptive viewer, standing before one of the IKB monochromes, becomes, through receiving the immaterial essence of the painting, "extra-dimensional in sensibility, all in all, impregnated [like the sponges] with the sensibility of the universe."[75]

From this denial that the power of an art work resides in its physical form, it is a small step to the actual elimination of the physical object altogether. As Heindel had asserted,

> Life may exist independently of Concrete Form; may have Forms not perceptible to our present limited senses, and amenable to none of the laws which apply to this present concrete state of matter.[76]

In 1958 Klein took this step, declaring that "the sensibility of color, still very material, must be reduced to an airier, more immaterial sensibility."[77]

> The Blue Epoch's sequel would be the presentation to the public of pictorial sensitivity. . . unconcentrated and uncontracted.[78]

The decision to eliminate the art object altogether became a program which dominated the remainder of his life. "Painting is a mode of existence," he wrote; "it is indecent and obscene to materialize."[79] The artist of the future will simply stabilize his sensibility in a certain space and leave it there to be picked up by the higher vehicles of his viewers.[80] This will be true immaterial art.

This theory, again, seems based on Heindel. In the coming Epoch, according to Heindel, man will reside primarily in the nonphysical Desire World, and art will necessarily be immaterial. In a sense the IKB monochromes are the last paintings of the gross physical Epoch; the immaterial works are the first works of the new or dawning Epoch, the first works not bound to a physical vehicle at all.

Klein devoted at least seven years to Rosicrucian work, and his art of the immaterial seems to constitute a claim to adepthood. According to Heindel, the first higher ability that is gained is the ability to read, from the etheric realm, the memory of nature, on which future art will be based. Klein definitely is expressing this view when he writes:

> Human sensibility can be all-powerful on the immaterial level. His sensibility can read the memory of nature, past, present, future.[81]

Next comes mastery of the Desire Body, which is, says Heindel,

> a vehicle of transcendent qualities, marvelously adaptable and so responsive to the slightest wish of the indwelling spirit that in our present limitations, it is beyond our utmost comprehension.[82]

With this vehicle the artist will create through mental concentration alone works of art which are much more splendid than any which the physical body can experience:

> The painter [who attains to the Desire World]…soon learns that
> his thought blends and shapes these colors at will. His creations
> glow and scintillate with a life impossible of attainment to one who
> works with the dull pigments of Earth.[83]

In more distant future Epochs, the artist's power will grow even
more awesome. In fact, Heindel provides us with a preview of art
history for the next few Epochs: in the dawning Epoch the artist
will create, through concentration projected onto the Prime Matter, "forms which will live and grow like plants." In the next, "he
can create living, growing and feeling things"; finally, "creatures
that will live, grow, feel and think."[84]

Klein's first immaterial work, the room left empty in the Colette
Allendy exhibition in 1957, went unnoticed by the visitors. The
next year saw a more direct and ambitious foray into the immaterial in the classic exhibition Le Vide, in which the Galerie Iris Clert
was emptied entirely of furnishings, painted white by the artist's
own hand, and exhibited with various associated Blue Revolution
motifs to thousands of avant-garde enthusiasts. The event was art
historically apposite to an extraordinary degree and in a distinctly
French tradition. Consider a philosopher's remarks on the many
attempts to respond to Mallarme's seminal avant-gardism:

> The production [by Mallarme] of the blank sheet of paper as the
> poem on which he was engaged would find its parallel in the area of
> the fine arts not in the production of a blank canvas, but in some-
> thing like the gesturing toward the content of an empty studio.[85]

But this is by no means all that Klein meant by the exhibition,
which expressed his Rosicrucianism quite as much as his sense of
the art historical moment—in fact, it is Klein's great brilliance to
combine the two approaches so smoothly that either may seem a
complete account of his intention. In this case Klein was exhibiting more than an empty space with transcendental implications.
Something of his intention is hinted at in Albert Camus' famous
comment in the guest book of the opening: "With the void, full
powers." In Klein's own words he was "manipulating the powers
of the void."

Starting in 1947 in Nice, in the company of Claude Pascal and
Armand Fernandez,[86] and continuing until the end of his life,[87]

Klein had practiced meditation on the lines set forth by Heindel, who instructs the aspirant to still his mind and visualize some object:

> At first the pictures which the aspirant builds will be but shadowy and poor likenesses, but in the end he can, by concentrating, conjure up an image more real and alive than things in the Physical World. When the aspirant has become able to form such pictures and has succeeded in holding his mind upon the picture thus created, he may try to drop the picture suddenly and, holding his mind steady without any thought, wait to see what comes into the vacuum.
>
> For a long time nothing may appear and the aspirant must carefully guard against making visions for himself, but if he keeps on faithfully and patiently every morning, there will come a time when, the moment he has let the imaged picture drop, in a flash the surrounding Desire World will open up to his inner eye. At first it may be but a mere glimpse, but it is an earnest of what will later come at will.[88]

In time, one who has mastered this technique will not merely behold the Desire World, he will be able to "mold the ever-changing matter of the Desire World into innumerable and differing forms of more or less durability."[89] At this stage,

> the painter has endless delights in the ever-changing color combinations.... He is, as it were, painting with living glowing materials and able to execute his designs with a facility which fills his soul with delight.[90]

Both Arman and Claude Pascal, who were still Klein's constant friends at the time of the exhibition Le Vide, testify that, prior to the opening, Klein spent forty-eight hours alone in the gallery practicing visualization exercises on the Heindel method, leaving the apparently empty gallery space filled with the "glowing and scintillating" forms of the Desire World molded by his concentration. He was not exhibiting merely the idea of emptiness or minimal-ness, but the actual presence of Prime Matter (Life) activated into a certain "more or less durable" configuration by his concentration. The full title of the exhibition, written by Klein, read,

> The specialization of sensibility from the state of prime matter to the state of stabilized pictorial sensibility.[91]

The Prime Matter, or Spirit, which was diffused through that room as through all space, was specialized by the artist into a certain form by concentration, then stabilized by him in that form long enough for the exhibition to take place.[92]

As Klein himself said, it was a gallery of paintings, although

> it was empty; I presented the atmosphere of painting in a picture gallery and not only the walls, as many have believed.[93]

The visitors, whether they realized it or not, were walking among specialized forms of the "living glowing material" of the Desire World. Accordingly, something more than art education was going on in them. The extra-dimensional faculties of the viewers were being shaped invisibly by Klein's immaterial works; far from merely seeing an exhibition, the viewers were being hastened on the evolutionary path toward the new age. Klein later estimated that about forty percent of the visitors had been successfully "impregnated" with the new level of sensibility.[94]

It seems that the artist took the occult level of this event quite seriously. Sometime later he confided to his wife-to-be that he had done something "very dangerous" that night, for which he feared he might have to die.[95] Again, the source of this anxiety may be found in Rosicrucian teachings. According to Heindel, in order to manipulate the invisible worlds, the "vital body" must be separated from the physical body and enter temporary union with bodies from the planes being visited:

> When a medium allows his or her vital body to be used by entities from the Desire World who wish to materialize, the vital body generally oozes from the left side... .Then the vital forces cannot flow into the body as they do normally, [and] the medium becomes very exhausted....The danger of contracting disease is much greater.[96]

If the vital body separates from the physical body too long or too completely, death may result.

In 1959, Klein began selling "zones of immaterial pictorial sensibility" for a quantity of gold leaf (a different quantity for each series!), which would then be thrown into a river or other natural body of water while the buyer burned his receipt, thereby finalizing the "transfer." The ritual, like the adoption of the name "Yves the Monochrome," was an announcement of Klein's claim to mastery of the Void and hence to proprietorship of it. The alchemical associations of gold make it a proper coin for such transcendent wares, and by throwing it away the artist demonstrates that his art, like the sky, is "attached to nothing."

In the same year Klein "participated immaterially" in a group exhibition in Antwerp, standing briefly in his space in the Hessenhuis gallery and leaving it impregnated with his sensibility, indicated thereafter only by a sign which read,

> At first, nothing; then a deep nothingness; then a blue depth. (After G. Bachelard.)[97]

On the one hand this event might be called Conceptual Art, and as such it shows Klein's usual keen awareness of the art historical moment. On the other hand, it is a display of yogic, indeed almost godlike, prowess. The artist, through the technique of impregnating space with his sensibility, reproduces the basic creative method of the universe as described by Heindel:

> When God desires to create, He seeks out an appropriate place in space, which He fills with His aura, permeating every atom of the cosmic Root-substance of that particular portion of space with His Life.[98]

Well might Klein boast, "I have created paintings in immaterial states.... I have manipulated the forces of the void."[99] It is not known what further immaterial works he was planning, but clearly the art of the immaterial had come to the forefront of his career. Minutes before his sudden death he expressed the intention of making, thenceforth, *only* immaterial works.[100]

Klein's monochrome paintings and art of the immaterial were the center of his career and mark its two stages. But they were accompanied by other works, perhaps secondary, which function as elaborations and underscorings of his Rosicrucian ideas. They will be discussed more briefly.

At some time after reading Heindel's *Cosmogonie* Klein conceived the famous *Monotone Symphony*: a group of singers and instrumentalists produce a single chord (basically a D-major triad in second inversion—D, F-sharp, A, with emphasis on the A),[101] for a specific number of minutes (varying from performance to performance), and then keep silent for a specified time.

Like the monochrome paintings, this work has a Rosicrucian meaning, based on Heindel's *Cosmogonie*. In fact, in this case alone do we have Klein's specific acknowledgment of Heindel's influence:

> At "Judo" (1947), a Rosicrucian cosmogony (a jazz interpretation of Max Heindel, Oceanside, California), I played the piano and dreamed of having a great orchestra, of composing, with music of a single tone, a "monochrome" symphony (not necessarily like jazz in spirit or rhythm), a single musical mass saturated with space, a melody melted into one note throughout.[102]

According to the *Cosmogonie*, sound is metaphysically prior to color; it resides at a higher level of the universe:

> The Physical World is the world of Form.
> The Desire World is particularly the world of Color; but the World of Thought…is the sphere of Tone.[103]

The World of Thought lies beyond the Desire World and is the second of the six higher realms through which Evolution will lead us. At this level sound and color are inextricably mixed, though sound is more primal. Heindel explains:

> When a certain note is struck, a certain color appears simultaneously… Color and sound are both present, but the Tone is the originator of the color…, it is this tone which builds all forms in the Physical World.[104]

Heindel gives specific attention to single prolonged tones and their effects:

> If one note or chord after another be sounded upon a musical instrument…a tone will finally be reached which will cause the hearer to feel a distinct vibration in the back of the lower part of his head… That note is the "key-note" of the person whom it so affects. If it is struck slowly and soothingly it will build and rest the body, tone the nerves and restore health. If, on the other hand, it be sounded in a dominant way, loud and long enough, it will kill as surely as a bullet from a pistol.[105]

Sound, then, is metaphysically prior to bodies and wields creative or destructive power over them.

A potential highest initiate could hardly ignore this power, especially when Heindel advertised it so temptingly, saying:

> None ranks so high as the musician…. His is the highest mission,
> because as a mode of expression for soul life, music reigns supreme.
> …music is different from and higher than all the other arts.[106]

The *Monotone Symphony* seems an attempt to wield the power of the "key-note" as a creative, alchemical instrument, actually strengthening the bodies of the listeners and building them for their transfiguration into higher vehicles. In fact, the keynote theory applies to entities larger than human, and may even enable the initiate to wield cosmic power and exert an effect on the entire earth:

> The musician can hear certain tones in different parts of nature…
> These combined tones make a whole which is the key-note of the
> Earth—its "Tone."[107]

There is no mistaking where the title of Klein's "Cosmogonies" came from. Their substance also may be largely based on Heindel. Klein wished to show the direct mark (the "trace of the immediate") of the traditional four elements: water (the traces of rain on a prepared canvas), air (powdered pigment blown by the wind against a prepared canvas), fire (the "Fire Paintings"), and earth (the "Planetary Reliefs"). This program shows the influence of Heindel in several ways. First, the artist working with the four elements just at the point where they rise from or return into Prime Matter duplicates the process of alchemy whereby, Heindel said, Spiritual Evolution is advanced.[108] Secondly, not only does the title "Cosmogonies" recall Heindel's title, but the works themselves epitomize Heindel's theory of Evolution, which holds that at the beginning of each great cosmic Period one of the four elements came into existence: in the Saturn Period there was only fire; in the Sun Period air was added; in the Moon Period, water; and in the Earth Period, earth.[109] Each element, in other words, symbolizes the inception of a new phase of Evolution up to and including our present Period. Thirdly, the invitation to the elements to express themselves directly and "randomly" on the empty surface relates to Heindel's description of how forces from the Void reach through into the Physical World. These forces penetrate into our world along apparently random lines of force, such as "the lines of force along which ice crystals form in water," which are in fact reflections of lines of force in the higher, invisible realms. Thus the rain "Cosmogonies," "Fire Paintings," air "Cosmogonies," and "Imprints" are crystallizations of energy patterns from higher worlds, beckoning on the path of Evolution. This intimate connection of realms Klein called "the immediate" and associated with the pole of Life:

> My goal is to extract and obtain the trace of the immediate in natural objects.
> This manifestation is always distinct from form, and it is the essence of the immediate, the trace of the immediate.[110]

This concern with "the immediate" relates also to Klein's Zen experience, and it is worth noting that the air-and-plant "Cosmogonies" (especially numbers 17-20 and 31)[111] look very much like Japanese grass paintings.

The "Fire Paintings" have, in addition to their place in the alchemical scheme, the special significance which Heindel attributes to gas, describing it as "not far removed from Chaos" and quoting Commenius, "Ad huc spiritum incognitum Gas voco" ("This unknown spirit I call Gas").[112] The fact that gas flame is blue seemed additionally significant to Klein, who denied that red and yellow were true colors of fire: fire, like all things close to the infinite, must first of all be Blue.

In addition to their functioning as the earth element in Klein's artistic alchemy, the "Planetary Reliefs" relate to Heindel's emphasis on the differentiation of the planets from the sun as signs of Evolutionary Periods[113] and to his doctrine of the Planetary Spirits (occult cosmic masters residing in the different planets and guiding the Evolution of our solar system),[114] as well as to the imminent prospect of actual interplanetary travel after Vostok I.

The "Anthropometries" have art historical, Zen, and Rosicrucian content. Art historically they relate to Paleolithic cave art (the hand prints), and it is probably not accidental that most of them are female imprints which look very much like ancient elementary goddesses. Many of them deal with the theme of levitation and thus with Rosicrucian evolutionary theory, especially ANT 96, *People Begin to Fly*, and ANT 102, *Architecture of the Air*, of which

Klein specifically spoke as prophecies of the coming age of aerial men. In addition it seems very likely that they had Zen associations for Klein. He spent two years in Japan and specifically refers to the work of Hokusai, about whom there is a famous anecdote which is supposed to express something of the essence of Zen art. Hokusai was ordered to produce works on a certain day for the shogun's amusement:

> The day came and Hokusai, not in the least awed, entered the august presence carrying a basket. He stretched out a long roll of paper on the floor, drew a few dark-blue lines along it with a brush, then took a chicken from the basket. As those present watched with bated breath he coated the chicken's feet in vermillion ink of the kind used for seals, and turned it loose on the paper. The chicken ran away over the paper, leaving a trail of brilliant footprints as it went. Hokusai prostrated himself before the Shogun. "Autumn Maple Leaves Drifting on the Tatsuta River," he announced, and with one more obeisance withdrew.[115]

Hokusai's type of Zen art was called *ukiyo-e*, "floating-world prints,"[116] of which Klein's phrase "trace of the immediate" may be a slightly loose translation. In the description of Hokusai preparing the chicken's feet while the audience watched "with bated breath" one may dimly hear the source of those performances (such as the one in *Mondo Cane*) in which Klein prepared his girls and "let them loose" on the canvas in front of an attentive audience.

The architecture of the air never got beyond the drawing-board stage, but it is easy enough to see where it fits into Klein's scheme. It, like the "Anthropometry" *People Begin to Fly*, prophesies that "technological Eden" in which a whole society will be living in the condition of free space. As Klein conceived this age, "spaced-out" humans will not only live in invisible dwellings and travel by levitation, but also communicate through telepathy: they will have the ability "to dream reciprocally each others' dreams" and to perceive the "thoughts which fly through the air."[117]

These "thoughts which fly through the air" are surely parts of Heindel's "memory of nature," which is everywhere moving around us at the etheric level, and which at the beginning of the new Epoch human beings will gain the ability to read. Once this ability develops, Heindel noted, it will be used for telepathic conversation and will make spoken language more or less obsolete as a mode of communication

In 1960 Klein published a photograph in which he seems to make a swan dive from a second-floor ledge. From the art historical point of view the leap is an immediate prototype for Happenings, Conceptual Art in which a documentary record replaces the art object, and body art. From a Rosicrucian point of view it represents the ascent from the Physical World into the Desire World and is yet another prophecy of the incoming age of levitation by its first artistic explicator. The headline, "A Man in Space," identifies the picture as in part a parody of the incipient Soviet and American space programs, stressing Heindel and Klein's belief that soon we will not need external vehicles to enter space:

> Today anyone who paints space must actually go into space to paint, but he must go there without any faking, and neither in an airplane, a parachute, nor a rocket: he must go there by his own means, by an autonomous, individual force: in a word, he must be capable of levitating.[118]

> Not missiles, rockets, or Sputniks will make man the "conquistador" of space.... He could not truly conquer space...until he has realized the impregnation of space by its own sensibility.[119]

But the subtitle, "The Painter of Space Throws Himself into the Void," has another intention. At the second publication of the photograph, in the Krefeld catalogue of 1961, Klein captioned it "The Leap into the Void." The phrase "Leap into the Void," as Klein knew from his long sojourn in Japan and his study and practice of meditation, is a technical term in Zen meditation manuals, signifying the moment when, being very advanced in concentration, the meditator lets go the last vestiges of self and becomes free like open Space.[120] It is worth noting that Klein, always a Westerner, translated into an image of physical derring-do what in its native tradition was an inward mental event.

The foregoing analysis of the sources of Klein's thought has not mentioned Gaston Bachelard very prominently, and it is well to explain why. Past writers on Klein[121] seem to exaggerate his debt to Bachelard. Klein encountered Bachelard's writings first in April 1958,[122] a full ten years after Klein's thought had been shaped by the sage of Oceanside, California. Clearly he felt sympathy with Bachelard's assertions that "by changing space, by leaving the space of one's usual sensibilities, one enters into communication with a space that is physically innovating," and that "every new cosmos is open to us when we have freed ourselves from the tie of a former sensitivity."[123] But Bachelard did not provide the rigorous system of Klein's thought; that came from Heindel, while Bachelard, ten years later, provided welcome confirmation from a compatriot. In addition, Klein found Bachelard convenient as, in effect, a "cover" for his own Rosicrucianism. Bachelard's writings on the poetic imagination provide a kind of vague mood study or reverie on ideas very similar to Heindel's but not enunciated with Heindel's old-fashioned dogmatic precision; Klein found that when he presented himself as inspired by Bachelard he was taken more seriously than he was as a Heindelian disciple.[124] By that time Klein himself had come to see the label "Rosicrucian" as an embarrassing one to bear. He was happy to bring his ideas, based on Heindel though they were, into the wider cultural arena where Bachelard's writings (or at least his name) circulated. And, in case this sounds like an (at least nominal) apostasy, Heindel himself had advised:

> [An initiate] does not call himself a Rosicrucian; no true Brother does so publicly.... Not even the most intimate friends or relatives know of a man's connection with the order.[125]

In reading Klein's writings it is well to be aware that his apparent allusions to Bachelard are in fact often disguised allusions to Heindel. Bachelard, for example, uses the term "imagination" a great deal, and Heindel does not. Klein picked it up from Bachelard's works, but the meaning which he privately assigned to it is purely Heindelian. "Imagination" is in fact a synonym for "immaterial sensibility," which in turn signifies the mind which has become open like Space. As Klein wrote:

> This imagination of which I am speaking is not a perception, a trace of a perception, a memory, a familiar thing, a habit of colors and forms.... It has nothing which can be perceived with the five senses, with the domain of sentimentality, or even of pure and fundamental emotion.[126]

In conclusion, there seems little doubt that Klein's brilliant theory of art and his multifaceted work involved the conscious and deliberate translation of the Rosicrucian system of Heindel into mid-twentieth-century art historical terms. Though other models may be useful also, it would be unwise for any interpreter to disregard this aspect of his career, which is unmistakably indicated by the biographical evidence, the testimony of his closest friends, and the documentary evidence in the Klein archive.

Although it seems both clear-cut and pervasive, Heindel's influence does not in the least detract from the originality of Klein's career—it makes it, in fact, more impressive. Many abstract artists have felt that their work was an expression of some traditional body of ideas, but none has arrived at so strong and solid a connection between the art historical context and the traditional ideas as has Klein. Malevich's "Ouspenskyism," Mondrian's Theosophy, Newman's Cabalism, Reinhardt's Zen are correspondences less clearly and fully articulated than Klein's Rosicrucianism. In short, Klein's career is a paradigmatic expression of the fact that abstract art may have both a philosophical content and a spiritual direction.

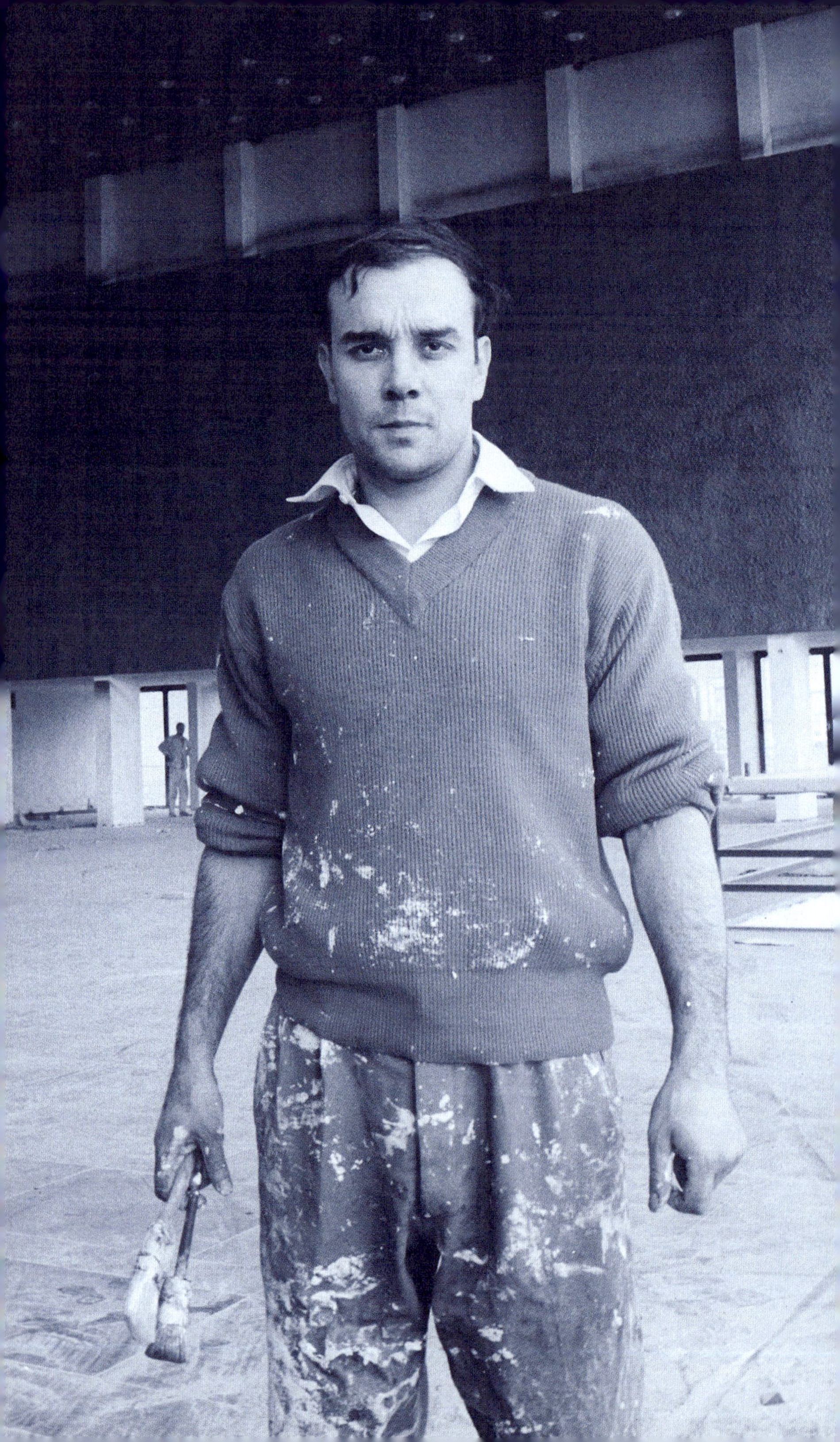

Chronology

1928

Yves Marie Klein is born to Fred Klein and Marie Raymond on April 28 at 7:15 a.m., in the home of his maternal grandparents, rue Verdi, Nice, France. He is baptized in the Roman Catholic rite and dedicated to Saint Rita d'Cascia. Fred Klein, born in 1898, is a painter whose works will be first exhibited in Holland in 1930. Marie Raymond, born in 1908, is a painting student who will begin to exhibit her works in Paris in 1945.
After several months his parents go to Paris, leaving him in the care of his maternal aunt, Rose Raymond, in his grandparents' house.

Kasimir Malevich writes, "The painter is no longer bound to the canvas, but can transfer his composition to space."

1929

Remains in Nice.

Albert Einstein publishes the Universal Field Theory.
The American stock market crashes;
worldwide depression deepens.
The Museum of Modern Art founded in New York City.

Left: Klein working on the Gelsenkirchen murals, 1959.

1930

Spring: Taken to Paris to live with his parents.
Autumn: Has a serious illness which endangers his life.

France begins building the Maginot Line.
Art Concret founded in Paris;
includes Hélion and Van Doesburg.
Publication of Civilization and Its Discontents,
by Sigmund Freud.

1931

Pierre Laval elected premier of France.

1932

Economic pressure forces the Kiein family to return to the home of
Marie's parents in Nice. After several months his parents return
to Paris; he remains in Nice.

Franklin Roosevelt elected U.S. president.
Surrealism introduced to the U.S. through an exhibition
organized by Julien Levy at his gallery in New York City
(previewed in 1931 at the Wadsworth Atheneum, Hart-
ford, under the title Newer Super-Realism).

1932–1939

Living in his grandparents' house, in his aunt's care, in Nice. His
parents spend several summers with him in Cagnes-sur-Mer.

1933

Adolph Hitler appointed chancellor of Germany.
Wassily Kandinsky leaves Germany for France.

1934

Publication of Art as Experience *by John Dewey.*

1935

Autumn: Enters the Ecole Masséna in Nice, where he remains

until 1938; not generally successful in his schoolwork there.

*Widespread government support of art begins in the U.S.
as part of the New Deal economic recovery program.
Malevich dies in the U.S.S.R.*

1936

*Leon Blum elected premier of France.
Hitler and Mussolini proclaim
the German-Italian Axis.
Exhibitions, Fantastic Art, Dada, and Surrealism and
Cubism and Abstract Art, Museum of Modern Art,
New York City.*

1937

May 27: Makes his private first communion in Nice. Summer: Artists' festival in Cagnes-sur-Mer; his parents participate.

Guernica bombed in the course of the Spanish Civil War.

1938

Autumn: Enrolled in private school on the rue Dante in Nice; his academic performance improves.

Early careers of such American artists as Barnett Newman, Jackson Pollock, Ad Reinhardt, Mark Rothko, and Clyfford Still under way.

1939

Returns to Paris early in the year to live with his parents. May 25: Makes his public first communion at Notre-Dame-des-Champs, Paris. Summer: In Cagnes-sur-Mer with his parents. Surprised by the declaration of war and unable to leave, they remain there until 1943. Autumn: Enters school in Cagnes-sur-Mer.

*France and Great Britain declare war on Germany.
Einstein takes a secret letter to President Roosevelt explaining the nature of atomic power and urging that the
U.S. harness it before Germany does.*

*First arrivals of vanguard artists in New York City
from war-torn Europe.
Founding of the Museum of Non-Objective Art (now the
Solomon R. Guggenheim Museum), New York City.*

1940

*France falls to Germany. Marshal Pétain
heads the French government.
Charles de Gaulle establishes a Free French
government in exile.
Japan joins the German-Italian Axis.
Piet Mondrian leaves France for New York City to stay.
Kandinsky paints* Sky Blue *in Paris.
Japan bombs Pearl Harbor.
The U.S. enters World War II.
The Manhattan Project to build an atomic bomb
begins in secret in the U.S.
Germany invades the U.S.S.R.*

1942

*World War II rages in Europe, Africa, and Asia.
Peggy Guggenheim opens a gallery, Art of This Century,
in New York City, exhibiting European moderns
and younger, advanced American artists.
Clyfford Still paints* Untitled (PH-613), *revealing a vast,
post-cubist space, in Oakland, California.
Marcel Duchamp arrives in New York City to stay.*

1943

Returns to Paris with his parents; lives at 116 rue d'Assas. Plays
the piano and generally neglects his schoolwork.

*The French Resistance takes shape.
Roosevelt, Churchill, and Stalin meet in Teheran to discuss the future partition of Europe.
Publication of* Being and Nothingness,
*by Jean-Paul Sartre.
Jackson Pollock paints* Guardians of the Secret *and has
his first one-man exhibition at Art of This Century.*

*Clyfford Still retrospective, San Francisco
Museum of Art, California.*

1944

June: Goes on a Boy Scout camping trip to Normandy, returning to Paris just before the Allied landing. Is sent to the village of Milhars in the Tarn until late August.

*Liberation of Paris by the Allies.
Jean Dubuffet has his first exhibition in Paris.
Deaths of Kandinsky in Paris and Mondrian
in New York City.*

1945

Autumn: Enters the Ecole du Genie Civil, 52 avenue des Wagrams, 75017 Paris, a private school that prepared students to take the Merchant Marine examination after the baccalaureate. Marie Raymond exhibits paintings in the Salon des Surindependents, her first showing in Paris.

*Surrender of Germany.
Death of Roosevelt.
The first atomic bomb is tested in New Mexico, then
dropped on Hiroshima and Nagasaki. Japan surrenders.
De Gaulle elected president of the French
provisional government.
Execution of Mussolini. Suicide of Hitler.*

1946

Spring: Attempts the first baccalaureate exam and fails, thus becoming ineligible for the Merchant Marine Academy. Is never again formally enrolled in an academic institution. Marie Raymond participates in a group show at the Galerie Denise René, Paris; Fred Klein has a show at the Centre Anglo-Français, London. Summer: Goes to London with his parents.

*Back in Paris, Marie Raymond begins her Monday
night salons, which continue until 1954.
Works in a bookstore, the Librairie des Champs-Elysées.*

The United Nations founded.
Barnett Newman paints The Beginning
and Euclidian Abyss.
Ad Reinhardt's first exhibition,
Betty Parsons Gallery, New York City.

1947

August: Returns to Nice when his parents go to Holland for a show of Fred Klein's works. In Nice, begins painting scarves, some abstract, some figurative, a practice he continues off and on for several years.

September: Rose Raymond sets up a bookshop for him in her Philips appliance store, 39 rue de l'Hotel des Postes, Nice. (He works in the shop until October 1948.) Enrolls in judo classes at police headquarters in Nice; there meets Claude Pascal and Armand Fernandez. September 2: Becomes white belt in judo, that is, his formal instruction begins. December 19: Becomes yellow belt in judo.

Around the end of 1947 or the beginning of 1948, discovers Max Heindel's *La Cosmogonie des Rose-Croix*.

The U.S. program for European economic recovery
(Marshall Plan) developed.
Manned supersonic flight achieved in California.
Publication of Psychologie de l'art, *including "Le Musée*
imaginaire," by André Malraux.
Jean Dubuffet exhibits in New York City.
Jackson Pollock paints Galaxy *and* Alchemy.
Pollock, Rothko, and Still each has his first exhibition at
Betty Parsons Gallery, New York City.

1948

January: Begins the systematic practice of Rosicrucianism with Claude Pascal and Armand Fernandez.

May: Klein, Claude Pascal, and Armand Fernandez meet Louis Cadeaux, who instructs them in Rosicrucianism and puts them in touch with the Rosicrucian Society of Oceanside, California.

May 4: Becomes orange belt in judo.

June 18: Klein and Pascal become members of the Rosicrucian
Society. Attaches a small blue monochrome disc to his Rosicrucian
notebook. The three friends divide the universe among them-
selves and alter their names: Yves Klein becomes Yves, Armand
Fernandez becomes Arman, Claude Pascal becomes Pascal Claude.
They become vegetarians and practice meditation daily, creating
a "temple" in the cellar of Arman's parents' house; Klein
paints one wall of the "temple" blue.
Imprints hands, feet, and question marks on his shirt.
Speaks (according to Arman's recollection in 1960) of "covering
judokas with blue to obtain sharp, violent imprints."
September: Hitchhikes through Italy (Genoa, Portofino, Rapallo,
Pisa, Rome, Capri, Ischia, Naples, Pompeii, Messina, Venice,
Genoa, Nice).
September 24: Becomes green belt in judo.
November 16: Enters military service and is stationed
in Germany, on Lake Constance.

Harry Truman elected U.S. president.
The Cold War intensifies. U.S.S.R.'s blockade of Berlin.

1949

October 27: Discharged from the army.
November: Goes to England with Claude Pascal; they live first
on Hollywood Street, then at 69 Cromwell Road, SW7. Works at
Robert Savage's frame shop on Old Brompton Road. Takes English
lessons, attends Rosicrucian meetings and judo classes. Attempts
to sell his parents' paintings at various galleries.
Conceives the idea of one-note or one-chord music as the
visual corollary of one-color painting.
In late 1949 or early 1950, executes small rectangular monochromes of pastel on paper or cardboard; exhibits them privately
to friends in his room.

The People's Republic proclaimed in China
under Mao Tse-Tung.
The German Federal Republic established.
The U.S.S.R. tests its first atomic bomb.
The U.S. test-launches guided missiles.
Publication of Essays in Zen Buddhism, *by D. T. Suzuki;*

it is translated into many languages.
Jackson Pollock paints Number 10; *Mark Rothko paints*
Violet, Black, Orange, Yellow on White and Red;
Clyfford Still paints 1949-C (PH-110).
Robert Rauschenberg creates
Female Figure (Blueprint).
Lucio Fontana creates Black Environment *and his first*
perforated monochrome canvases.

1950

April: Klein and Claude Pascal hitchhike to Ireland and work at
Jockey Hall, an equestrian club. Pascal mentions in his journal
that Klein is drawing and painting.
April 4–26: Marie Raymond participates in a group show at Co-
lette Allendy's gallery, Paris.
May: Tries with no success to sell his parents' paintings
in Dublin galleries.
May 21: Writes a long reflection on painting in his journal.
July: Completes the Rosicrucian Society's intermediate
course in philosophy.
August 25: Goes to London and resumes working
in the frame shop. Claude Pascal arrives soon thereafter.
Autumn: Sends a postcard from London to Arman in Nice, one
side monochrome pink, the other bearing a text by Claude Pascal:
"The year 1951 will be pink Massacre." Returns to Nice, stopping
at Rosicrucian headquarters in Paris.
December 27: Completes the Rosicrucian Society's
third course in philosophy.
December 31: Visits the Matisse chapel at Vence with
his grandparents and aunt.

The Korean War begins.
Tachiste painting in Paris and Abstract Expressionism
in New York and San Francisco at full tide.
Pollock paints Autumn Rhythm *and* Lavender Mist;
Newman paints The Name I! *and* Vir Heroicus Subli-
mis; *Rothko paints* Green, Red on Orange.
Newman's first one-man exhibition, Betty Parsons Gal-
lery, New York City.
Sam Francis (one of a wave of younger American artists)

*settles in Paris and begins large "all-over"
near-monochromatic paintings.
Nicolas de Staël's first one-man show in New York City.
Young Painters in New York and France organized by Leo
Castelli at the Sidney Janis Gallery, New York City.*

1951

January: Takes Spanish lessons.
February 4: Goes to Madrid, lives at 5 Calle de Puebla,
and trains at two judo schools.
Makes journal references to (1) "ideas capable of revolution-
izing the world"; (2) presentation of monochrome paintings with
appropriate musical accompaniment; (3) an allegory of colors.
Conceives the idea of fountains of fire and water
(according to his statement in 1958).
March: Begins to teach in two judo schools and
makes a strong impression in both.
June: Travels in Spain with his parents, grandmother, and aunt,
then returns to France with them.
August 30: Becomes brown belt in judo.
September: Tours Italy with his aunt, Rose Raymond.
Autumn: Lives in Paris near his parents, attending his mother's
salons and auditing a course in Japanese at the École des Langues
Orientales. Writes a letter of inquiry to the
Institut Franco-Japonais of Tokyo.

John Cage and Robert Rauschenberg make Automobile
Tire Print, *and Rauschenberg creates
his series of White Paintings.
Barnett Newman paints* Cathedra.
*Ellsworth Kelly's first one-man show in Paris.
Publication of* Abstract Painting: Background
and American Phase *by Thomas Hess.*

1952

February: Writes in his journal that he should spend
four hours a day on Heindel's *Cosmogonie.*
July: His maternal grandmother (and godmother) dies in Nice.
August 22 or 23: Embarks for Japan at Marseilles, stopping at

Crete, Suez, Djibouti, Colombo, Singapore, Saigon,
and Hong Kong.
September 23: Arrives in Yokohama.
October: Engaged as a teacher at the Institut Franco-Japonais,
Tokyo. Enrolls in the Kodokan Judo Institute, starting over again
with the white belt and progressing quickly through brown.

Dwight D. Eisenhower elected U.S. president.
Ellsworth Kelly paints Painting for a White Wall *and*
Red, Yellow, Blue, and White.
John Cage, with Rauschenberg, Merce Cunningham,
David Tudor, and Charles Olsen, creates the first proto-
happenings at Black Mountain College, North Carolina.
Jackson Pollock exhibition, Galerie Fachetti, Paris.
Georges Mathieu exhibition, Stable Gallery, NYC.
Harold Rosenberg's essay "The American Action
Painters" published in Art News.

1953

January: Awarded the first *dan* black belt at
the Kodokan Institute, Tokyo.
July: Second *dan*.
December: Obtains the diploma of fourth *dan*.
Invites a group of Japanese friends to his home to see small
monochrome paintings in primary colors on paper or cardboard.
Arranges shows of his parents' works at the Institut Franco-
Japonais, the Bridgestone Gallery, and
the Museum of Modern Art, Tokyo.

Death of Stalin.
End of the Korean War.
Publication in English of The Voices of Silence, *includ-*
ing "Museum without Walls," by André Malraux.
Jean Tinguely begins making Meta-Machines
in France.
Un Art autre (A Different Art) exhibition organized by
Michel Tapié in France.
Clement Greenberg asserts the superiority of the new
American painting over the French in a symposium titled
"Is the French Avant-garde Overrated?"

Jasper Johns creates his first important abstract work,
Untitled, *a green painting.*

1954

February: Arrives in Paris after a month's travel. The French
Federation of Judo rejects his Kodokan diploma.
April: Signs a contract with Bernard Grasset, Paris, for publication
of his book, *Les Fondements du Judo,*
which appears in November.
May: Goes to Madrid, with Claude Pascal, as "technical director"
of the Spanish Federation of Judo and is actively involved in
teaching judo. Klein hangs monochrome paintings of unknown
colors and sizes in the judo hall.
Publishes the booklets *Yves Peintures* and *Haguenault Peintures.*
November: Rose Raymond visits him in Madrid,
and he returns to France with her.
December: Attends the European judo championships
in Brussels as a spectator.
A drawing possibly of this period, signed "Gi 1954" and dedicated to Klein, is titled *Project for a Machine to Capture Pictorial
Sensibility*; draftsman unknown (Klein archive, Centre Georges
Pompidou, Paris).

The first hydrogen bomb exploded in a test
in the South Pacific,
End of the French Indo-China War.
Beginning of the war in Algeria.
Ad Reinhardt exhibits yellow and blue near-monochrome
paintings in New York City.
César and Jean Tinguely have their first exhibitions
in Paris.
Death of Henri Matisse.

1955

January 11: Dines with his mother at Hans Hartung's house,
where Sam Francis' work is described to him. Refers to the plates
in *Yves Peintures* as "unicolor."
February: Begins teaching judo at the American Center, and
continues to teach there until 1959. Spring: Submits an orange

painting to the Salon des Realités Nouvelles;
the painting is rejected on July 5.
Meets Jean Tinguely.
Meets Bernadette Allain, a young architect.
August 5: Uses the term "monochrome" in a letter and writes
of it as "an idea of absolute unity in perfect serenity."
September: Opens a judo school at 104 boulevard de Clichy,
Montmartre; in the judo hall he hangs several seven- or eight-
meter-long monochromes in various colors, including blue, white,
and pink, before which he sits to meditate.
October 15: First public exhibition, *Yves: Peintures*, Editions
Lacoste—Club des Solitaires, 121 avenue de Villiers, 75017 Paris:
shows monochromes of various colors.
October 24: Phones Pierre Restany, whom he has not met, and
asks his help in arranging an exhibition at Colette Allendy's
gallery. The next day Restany goes to Colette Allendy's
and broaches the subject.
December 1: Meets Restany.
Meets Heinz Mack, who visits his studio in the foyer
of the judo school.
Meets Iris Clert.

Death of Albert Einstein.
Jasper Johns paints Green Target
and Large White Flag.
Robert Ryman makes his first white painting.
The Gutai Art Association, Osaka, presents art and per-
formances by advanced Japanese artists. Kazuo Shiraga
creates Making a Work with His Own Body
on a Slab of Wet Clay.
Death of Nicolas de Stael.

1956

February 21–March 7: Exhibition, *Yves: Propositions mono-*
chromes, Galerie Colette Allendy, 67 rue de l'Assomption, 75016
Paris; the catalogue's preface, "La Minute de Vérité," is written by
Pierre Restany. At the gallery, meets Marcel Barillon de Murat, a
Knight of Saint Sebastian, who invites him to join the order.
March 11: Dubbed a Knight of Saint Sebastian in the church of
Saint-Nicolas-des-Champs

Summer: Closes his judo school in Montmartre because of
financial difficulties. The monochromes which
had hung there are destroyed.
October 25: Appeals to the French Federation of Judo
to recognize his Kodokan diploma.

Fidel Castro begins the revolution in Cuba.
Georges Mathieu creates "Paintings in Performance" be-
fore an audience at the Théâtre Sarah Bernhardt, Paris.
Sam Francis and Ellsworth Kelly have their
first American exhibitions.
Arman's first one-man exhibition, Paris.
John Cage tours the U.S., lecturing.
Michel Tapié tours the U.S., lecturing on art informel.
Death of Jackson Pollock. Pollock retrospective,
Museum of Modern Art, New York City.

1957

January 2–12: Exhibition, *Yves Klein: Proposte Monocrome,
Epoca Blu*, Galleria Apollinaire, Milan. Eleven identical blue
monochromes hang in one room, several monochromes of differ-
ent colors in another. A red monochrome is bought by
Count Panza de Biumo, a blue by Lucio Fontana.
May: Double exhibition: May 10–25, *Yves le monochrome*, Galerie
Iris Clert; May 14–23, *Pigments purs*, Galerie Colette Allendy. At
the Iris Clert opening, 1,001 blue balloons are released and the
Monotone Symphony is played in a version
recorded by Pierre Henry.
Records the "Blue Cries" soundtrack for a short film he makes
about his Paris Blue Period exhibitions.
May 31–June 23: Exhibition, *Yves: Propositions monochromes*,
Galerie Schmela, Düsseldorf.
June 24–July 13: Exhibition, *Monochrome Propositions of Yves
Klein*, Gallery One, London.
Group shows: April, *Micro Salon d'avril*, Galerie Iris Clert, Paris;
summer, *Ouverture sur le futur*, Galerie Kramer, Paris; August,
Internationaler Bericht der Gesellschaft der Freunde Jonger Kunst,
Kunsthalle, Düsseldorf; October 12–30, *Arte Nucleare*, Milan.

The European Common Market created.

The U.S.S.R. launches the first earth satellites
(Sputniks I and II).
Piero Manzoni creates his first "achromes."
Founding of the Zero Group, Cologne.
The Gutai Group presents Art on Stage *in Osaka, includ-*
ing voices and sounds from an empty stage
and an archery performance.
Imaginary Spaces *exhibition organized by*
Pierre Restany, Paris.

1958

January: Commissioned to decorate the foyer of the new city theater in Gelsenkirchen, Germany. Spring: Moves to 14 rue Campagne Premiere, Paris, where he lives till the end of his life. April: Makes his first pilgrimage to the shrine of Saint Rita in Cascia, Italy, leaving a prayer that "the blue may be accepted everywhere." Writes Iris Clert from Assisi about "entirely blue monochrome panels" by Giotto, and declares Giotto his predecessor.

April 28: Opening of the exhibition *La Spécialisation de la sensibilité a l'état matiére premiere en sensibilite picturale stabilisée (The Specialization of Sensibility from the State of Prime Matter to the State of Stabilized Pictorial Sensibility)*—also known as *Le Vide (The Void)*—at Iris Clert's gallery in Paris. Attempts to sell immaterial paintings in the gallery space. For his thirtieth birthday, his mother gives him Gaston Bachelard's *L'Air et les songes*.

May 20: Writes to President Eisenhower declaring the termination of the French national government by the Blue Revolution. A related letter from the same period, to the president of the International Conference on the Detection of Atomic Explosions, proposes that all future nuclear explosions be colored blue.

June 5: First "living brush" work, at Robert Godet's apartment on the Ile Saint-Louis (the term "Anthropometry" will be coined by Pierre Restany in 1960).

August: Meets Rotraut Uecker in Nice.

September: Goes to Cascia with his aunt, Rose Raymond, to leave a small blue monochrome for Saint Rita.

October: In Gelsenkirchen, meets with Werner Ruhnau; they carry out experiments which fail to produce an "air roof."

November 17: Opening of a joint exhibition with Tinguely, *Vi-*

tesse pure et stabilité monochrome (*Pure Speed and Monochrome Stability*), at the Galerie Iris Clert. The exhibition includes blue discs turning at 300 kilometers per hour.
Indicates in sketches and notes various projects never realized: (1) an "air roof" for a ruined German church; (2) the blue illumination of all paintings in the Salon des Realités Nouvelles; (3) a blue monochrome Stations of the Cross for the chapel of Saint Martin, Pontoise; (4) a "pneumatic rocket"; (5) an exhibition of chemically prepared paintings on the theme "Evil and War Disappearing before John XXIII," some of which were to change color, others to disintegrate into powder within thirty minutes of being exposed to air.

*Charles de Gaulle elected president of the
Fifth French Republic.
Publication of Zero I in Düsseldorf.
Rothko begins his Four Seasons project, a unified series
of near-monochromatic murals.*

1959

January: Speaks at the opening of Tinguely's exhibition at the Galerie Schmela in Düsseldorf.
March 17: Shows an immaterial piece at a group show, *Vision in Motion*, at the Hessenhuis, Antwerp; offers it for sale for one kilogram of gold.
Spring: Begins working with Claude Parent on drawings for the "architecture of the air."
Draws up a proposal for aeromagnetic sculpture, asserting his priority in the idea over Takis.
June 3 and 5: Lectures at the Sorbonne on "The Evolution of Art toward the Immaterial" and "Architecture of the Air."
June 15–30: Exhibition, *Yves Klein: Bas-reliefs dans une forêt d'éponges*, Galerie Iris Clert, Paris.
July 7: Breaks with Iris Clert.
October 12: Writes to architect Philip Johnson requesting that he and Ruhnau be invited to the United States to lecture on the "architecture of the air."
November 18: First sale of a Zone of Immaterial Pictorial Sensibility, to Peppino Palazzoli. In December he sells three more zones.
December 15: Attends the opening of the city theater in

Gelsenkirchen. Stops teaching judo.
Publication of *Le Dépassement de la problématique de l'art.*
A film by Jean-Pierre Mirouze, *L'École de Nice,*
includes sequences of Klein.
Group shows: May 29, *Artistes et architectes de Gelsenkirchen*, Galerie Iris Clert, Paris; July 3, *Junge Maler der Gegenwart*, Kunstlerhaus, Vienna; September 4, *Sélection pour le XI Primio Lissone*, Galleria l'Attico, Rome; October 2, *Première Biennale des Jeunes de Paris*; October 7, Leo Castelli Gallery, New York; November 8, *Kunstsammler am Rhein und Ruhr, Malerei 1900-1959*, Städtisches Museum, Leverkusen; *Dynamo 1*, Galerie Renate Boukes, Wiesbaden.

Fidel Castro becomes premier of Cuba.
Publication of Marcel Duchamp, *by Robert Lebel,*
in Paris and New York City: first comprehensive
discussion of Duchamp's work.
The New American Painting, *Alfred Barr's major exhibition including Newman, Pollock, Rothko, and Still,*
opens in Paris as part of its European tour.
Takis exhibits "telemagnetic" sculptures in Paris.
Manzoni exhibits Air Bodies *(balloon works) and his*
canned excrement, each work offered for sale
at the price of its weight in gold.
Allan Kaprow presents Eighteen Happenings
in Six Parts *in New York City.*
Frank Stella paints his first series of
black abstract paintings.
Robert Irwin paints his first near-monochrome
"line paintings."

1960

January 12: Leaps from the ledge of Colette Allendy's house, 67 rue de l'Assomption, in the presence of Bernadette Allain.
March 9: Performance, *Yves Klein: Anthropométries de l'epoque bleue*, Galerie Internationale d'Art Contemporain, Paris.
April 23: At La Coupole, founds ADAM, the Association pour le Dépassement de l'Art Moderne (Association for the Bypassing of Modern Art); the association has no further meetings.
May: Obtains a patent on a paint formula under the title International Klein Blue.

With Restany, Mirouze, Pascal, and Arman, founds the International Klein Bureau, empowering the others to make IKB monochromes and sign them with his name.

Summer: Makes the first Cosmogonies.

October 11–November 13: Exhibition, *Yves Klein le monochrome*, Galerie Rive Droite, Paris.

Leap photographed at 3 rue Centil Bernard, at the corner of Maréchal Galileri in the suburb of Fontenay-aux-Roses, Paris.

October 27: Les Nouveaux Réalistes founded by Restany in Klein's apartment; signers of the group's first manifesto, written by Restany, are Arman, François Dufrêne, Raymond Hains, Martial Raysse, Daniel Spoerri, Jean Tinguely, and Jacques de Ia Villeglé. A quarrel that erupts at this first meeting leads to the verbal dissolution of the group, which however remains precariously intact for some time.

November 10: Makes a "Collective Anthropometry" of New Realists Arman, Hains, Restany, Tinguely, and himself.

November 27: *Dimanche, le journal d'un seul jour* goes on sale. Considers undertaking two lawsuits: one against Iris Clert for selling "false anthropometries," the other against filmmaker Claude Chabrol for a fictional portrayal of the making of Anthropometries in the film *Les Godelureaux*.

Group shows: February, *Antagonismes*, Musée des Arts Decoratifs, Paris; March 18, *Monochrome Malerei*, Stâdtisches Museum, Leverkusen; April, *Les Nouveaux Réalistes*, Galleria Apollinaire, Milan; November 18, second Festival d'Art d'Avant-garde, Paris.

John F. Kennedy elected U.S. president.
Ad Reinhardt devotes the rest of his life to making
60-inch-square black paintings of almost imperceptibly
trisected space. His black paintings are exhibited at
the Galerie Iris Clert, Paris.
Jean Tinguely creates Homage to New York *at the Museum of Modern Art and visits southern California.*
Arman exhibits Le Plein *(the gallery filled with garbage),*
Galerie Iris Clert, Paris.
A Zero Group exhibition in Düsseldorf includes inflated
forms illuminated in the night sky by searchlights.
Edward Kienholz conceives "Concept Tableaux" (written
propositions such as The World*) in Los Angeles.*
La Monte Young performs his Butterfly Sonata *in Berke-*

*ley, California. The composition is silent: the composer
sits at a piano, releases a butterfly from a jar, and leaves
the stage when the butterfly has vanished from sight.*

1961

January 14–February 26: Exhibition, *Yves Klein: Monochrome und
Feuer*, Museum Haus Lange, Krefeld, Germany.
April: Travels to New York with Rotraut Uecker and stays
at the Chelsea Hotel.
April 11–29: Exhibition, *Yves Klein le monochrome*, Leo Castelli
Gallery, New York City.
April 25: Accredited by the French Federation of Judo,
long after he has stopped teaching judo.
Various journal entries attest to extreme financial difficulties.
May: Travels to Los Angeles with Rotraut Uecker.
May 17–June 10: In a group show, *A 40° au-dessus de Dada*,
Galerie J, Paris, organized by Restany. In connection with this
exhibition Restany writes a second manifesto, declaring the New
Realists to be descendants of Dada; Klein writes from the United
States objecting violently, and only Restany signs the manifesto.
On October 8, Klein, Raysse, and Hains declare the New Realists
dissolved because of the manifesto.
May 29–June 24: Exhibition, *Yves Klein le monochrome*,
Dwan Gallery, Los Angeles.
June: Exhibition, *Yves Klein*, Galleria La Salita, Rome.
July 17-18: Back in Paris, performs, for cameraman Paolo Cavara,
sequences of Anthropometries which will appear in
Gualtiero Jacopetti's film *Mondo Cane* the following year.
July 18-19: Makes thirty Fire Paintings at the Centre d'Essais du
Gaz de France, Paris. The presence of a naked woman for the Fire
Anthropometries on the second day causes the center's director
to withdraw permission for further sessions. (Klein had
worked at the center several days earlier in the year.)
August 17: Writes to Philip Johnson objecting to Fire Fountains
and Fire Paintings by others planned for the upcoming
New York World's Fair. No known response.
Summer: Makes a film with Sacha Sosnowsky of imprints
of Rotraut Uecker's body in sand.
November: Occupied with making Planetary Reliefs.
November 1: His contract with art dealer Jean Larcade goes into

effect: Klein is to be paid 3,500 francs per month, in return for
which Larcade can buy Klein's works at one-third normal price
and receives a 20 percent commission on sales in Europe
and 5 percent on architectural projects.
Visits Cascia, accompanied by Rotraut Uecker, leaving an
ex-voto with a long prayer. A few weeks later,
makes his last visit to Cascia.
November 21: Exhibition, *Yves Klein le Monochrome: Il
Nuovo Realismo del Colore*, Galleria Apollinaire, Milan.
In collaboration with Claude Parent, plans fountains of fire and
water, *Les Fontaines de Varsovie*, for the Palais de Chaillot,
Paris (never realized).

*First manned space flight: a U.S.S.R. satellite orbits
the earth with Yuri Gagarin, and U.S. astronaut Alan
Shepard mans a rocket into space. The earth is directly
observed as a blue sphere in the black void of space.
Joseph Beuys begins teaching at the
Düsseldorf Art Academy.
Manzoni exhibits* Line 1000 Meters Long, *in response to
Klein's championing of color in the "Battle between Line
and Color." Manzoni also signs and exhibits
living human beings.
Robert Rauschenberg and Frank Stella have
exhibitions in Paris.*
Sixteen Americans *exhibition at the Museum of Mod-
ern Art, New York City, includes works by Kelly, Johns,
Rauschenberg, and Stella.
Publication of* Silence *by John Cage.
Dan Flavin begins making monochrome art works,
which include electric light fixtures.
Mark Rothko retrospective, Museum of Modern Art,
New York City, followed by a European tour,
including Paris.*

1962

January or February: Begins casting Portrait Reliefs of
the New Realists.
January 21: Marries Rotraut Uecker in the church of Saint-Nicolas-des-Champs, Paris. A party is held afterward in Larry Rivers'

studio. Pierre Henry presents Klein with his second recorded version of the Monotone-Silence Symphony.

January 26: Sale of a Zone of Immaterial Pictorial Sensibility to Dino Buzzatti.

February 2: Sale of another zone to Michael Blankfort. (Edward Kienholz has bought a zone as well, but the ritual of transfer is completed only after Klein's death, by Rotraut Klein and Arman.)

March 1: Makes a collaborative "Scroll Poem" on a cloth scroll about fifteen feet long, with Claude Pascal, Arman, and Restany.

March 7: In the group show *Antagonismes 2: L'Objet*, Musée des Arts Décoratifs, Paris, contributing maquette drawings (by Claude Parent) for the "architecture of the air" and related projects, and the "Scroll Poem."

March 30: Photographed lying beneath *The Tomb— Here Lies Space*.

May 11 or 12: Flies to Cannes for the premiere of *Mondo Cane*; suffers shock and humiliation at the manner in which he is portrayed.

May 14: In Paris, breaks off with Jean Larcade by letter, complaining that his monthly salary has not been paid regularly.

May 15: Participates in a panel discussion at the Musée des Arts Décoratifs, at which he becomes agitated and angry. Afterward he goes to the opening of the exhibition *Donner à voir* at the Galerie Creuze, where he experiences severe chest pain later diagnosed as a heart attack.

June 6: Dies of heart failure in his apartment on the rue Campagne Premiere in the presence of Rotraut Klein.

July 23-31: Exhibition, *Rétrospective Yves Klein*, Tokyo Gallery, Tokyo.

August: Rotraut Klein gives birth to Klein's son, Yves, in Paris.

November 5-24: Exhibition, *Yves Klein*, Alexander Iolas Gallery, New York City.

Georges Pompidou forms a government in France.
The U.S. military council established in South Vietnam.
Cuban missile crisis.
Pope John XXIII convenes the Second Vatican Council.
Tinguely stages Study for the End of the World
in the Nevada desert.

Jasper Johns exhibition, Galerie Sonnabend, Paris.
An exhibition at the Janis Gallery, New York City, shows
French New Realists and U.S. and English Pop artists
together for the first time.
Ben Vautier puts himself on sale as a "living, moving
sculpture" and "signs" Yves Klein's death as an art work.

1963

April: Exhibition, *Yves Klein et le langage du feu*, Kaiser Wilhelm
Museum, Krefeld.
April 30–May 20: Exhibition, *Yves Klein le monochrome:
Peintures de feu*, Galerie Tarica, Paris.
May: Exhibition, *Yves Klein*, Svensk-Franska
Konstgalleriet, Stockholm.

John F. Kennedy assassinated. Lyndon B. Johnson
becomes U.S. president.
Hans Haacke begins his water and wind sculptures.
Rauschenberg retrospective, Jewish Museum,
New York City.
Death of Piero Manzoni.
Ben Vautier "signs" Manzoni's death as an art work.

1964

March–April: Exhibition, *Yves Klein, le monochrome: Empreintes*,
Galerie Bonnier, Lausanne.
April 15–May 20: Exhibition, *Peintures de feu*, Galerie
Schmela, Düsseldorf.

The U.S.'s Ranger III takes the first photographs
of the dark side of the moon.
Rauschenberg wins the grand prize at the Venice Biennale.
Brice Marden begins making monochromatic paintings.
Dan Flavin exhibition of fluorescent light, Green Gallery,
New York City.
Robert Mangold's first one-man exhibition, New York City.
Arman exhibition, Stedelijk Museum, Amsterdam.

1965

April 12: Exhibition, *Yves Klein*, Galerie Alexandre Iolas, Paris.
October 22–December 13: Exhibition, *Yves Klein, a Retrospective Exhibition*, Stedelijk Museum, Amsterdam.

De Gaulle re-elected president of France.
Tinguely retrospective, Jewish Museum, New York City.
Joseph Beuys' Twenty-four-Hour Piece, *Düsseldorf.*
Stan Vanderbeek begins developing his Movie Drome,
which relates to some of the projects Klein outlined
in Dimanche.
Günter Brus and Rudolf Schwarzkogler begin their
self-injury pieces in Vienna.
Exhibition, Inner and Outer Space, an Exhibition
Concerning Universal Art, *organized by Pontus Hulten,*
Moderna Museet, Stockholm, includes a major
Yves Klein selection.

1966

March 3–April 3: Exhibition, *Yves Klein*,
Palais des Beaux-Arts, Brussels.
Summer: Exhibition *Yves Klein, peintures de feu*,
Galerie Bonnier, Lausanne.

France leaves NATO.
Major public demonstrations in the U.S.
against the Vietnam War.
Daniel Buren makes identical "paintings"
of stretched red fabric in Paris for two years.
Major early earthworks by Richard Long, Robert Morris,
and Robert Smithson, which relate to Klein's project of
remodeling and reclimatizing the face of the earth.
Bruce Nauman and Vito Acconci begin body works
in the U.S.
James Turrell makes his first Projection Pieces
in southern California.
Ad Reinhardt retrospective,
Jewish Museum, New York City.
Brice Marden one-man exhibition, New York City.
Death of André Breton.

1967

January 25–March 12: Exhibition, *Yves Klein*, Jewish
Museum, New York City.
Exhibition, *Yves Klein*, Galerie Bischofberger, Zurich.

Israeli-Egyptian War in the Middle East.
Robert Ryman's first one-man exhibition,
New York City; he creates the Standard series
(thirteen all-white paintings on steel).
Daniel Buren and others hang paintings in an inaccessible
room and distribute a leaflet describing them in detail.
Claes Oldenburg installs an "invisible sculpture" behind
the Metropolitan Museum of Art, New York City, digging
a grave-size hole and filling it up again.
Hans Haacke creates Sky Line *(a balloon piece),*
Central Park, New York City.
Publication of "Art as Idea as Idea,"
by Joseph Kosuth.
Joseph Beuys founds the German Student Party,
Düsseldorf.
Michael Heizer's first earthworks, Nevada.
Rockne Krebs creates his first laser light structures,
Washington, D.C.
Zero Group dissolved.
Jackson Pollock retrospective, Museum of Modern Art,
New York City.
Death of Ad Reinhardt.

1968

February 17–March 17: Exhibition, *Yves Klein—Louisiana*,
Louisiana Museum, Humlebaek, Denmark.
April 2–May 12: Exhibition, *Yves Klein in Nürnberg*, Institut
fur Moderne Kunst, Kunsthalle, Nuremberg.
June: Exhibition, *Yves Klein*, National Gallery, Prague.
November 7–December 15: Exhibition, *Yves Klein*,
Galerie Michel Couturier, Paris.

Assassinations of Martin Luther King and
Robert Kennedy in the U.S.
Richard M. Nixon elected U.S. president.

Tet offensive in Vietnam.
The U.S.S.R. invades Czechoslovakia.
Worker and student demonstrations in France.
James Lee Byars sends a mile of gold thread into space
on a series of helium balloons, New York City.
Robert Irwin and James Turrell begin perceptual
phenomena research with Dr. Edward Wortz
in southern California.
Death of Lucio Fontana.
Death of Marcel Duchamp.

1969

January 25—March 11: Exhibition, *Yves Klein, 1928–1962,*
Musée des Arts Décoratifs, Paris.
June 30–August 15: Exhibition, *Yves Klein,* Galerie
Lambert-Monet, Geneva.
November: Exhibition, *Le Monochrome,* Galleria Blu, Milan.
November–December: Exhibition, *Yves Klein,*
Galleria d'Arte Martano, Turin.
Exhibition, *Yves Klein,* Musee d'Art Moderne, Grenoble.

American astronaut Neil Armstrong becomes
the first man on the moon.
First Concorde flight, Paris—New York.
De Gaulle resigns as president of France;
Georges Pompidou elected as his successor.
Exhibition of Takis' Magnetic Fields, *Guggenheim*
Museum, New York City.
Jean Tinguely's Kamikaze Monument, *Kanagawa, Japan.*
Christo's Wrapped Coast: One Million Square Feet
performed on the South Australian coast;
photodocumentation by Shunk-Kender.
Exhibition, The Ghost of James Lee Byars
(an apparently empty room), Kunsthalle, Düsseldorf.
Exhibition, Number 7, *organized by Lucy Lippard for*
the Paula Cooper Gallery, New York City: an apparently
empty room contains a magnetic field by Robert Barry,
air currents by Hans Haacke, existing shadows
by Robert Huot, and other works.
Exhibition, Invisible Painting and Sculpture, *organized*

*by Tom Marioni for the Richmond Art Center,
Richmond, California.
Joseph Beuys accepts full responsibility for any snowfall
in Düsseldorf from February 15 through February 20.
James Turrell and Sam Francis make aerial pieces with
planes and clouds over Pasadena, California.
Exhibition,* When Attitude Becomes Form, *including
a major Yves Klein selection, organized
by Harold Szeemann, Berne.*

1970

January 26: Exhibition, *Yves Klein le monochrome,*
Galleria dell'Obelisco, Rome.
November–December: Exhibition, *Klein—Manzoni,*
Studio C Arte Moderna, Brescia.
December 2-31: Exhibition, *Yves Klein,* Galleria
Civica d'Arte Moderna, Turin.

*China launches its first space satellite.
Robert Barry's exhibition of a closed gallery, Los Angeles.
Deaths of Mark Rothko and Barnett Newman.*

1971

February–March: Exhibition, *Yves Klein,*
Museum of Modern Art, Belgrade.
June 9–July 25: Exhibition, *Yves Klein,* Kunstverein, Hanover.
August 4-29: Exhibition, *Yves Klein,* Kunsthalle, Berne.

*Presidents Pompidou and Nixon meet in Paris.
Massive U.S. bombing in Cambodia and North Vietnam.
Tinguely retrospective at the Centre National d'Art
Contemporain, Paris.
Barnett Newman retrospective, Museum of Modern Art,
New York City.
Chris Burden's* Shoot, F Space, Santa Ana, California:
*the artist is shot through the arm with a
.22-caliber rifle bullet.
The Rothko Chapel inaugurated in Houston,
with eight murals by Mark Rothko.*

1972

December 16, 1972–February 17, 1973: Exhibition,
Marie Raymond—Yves Klein, Chateau-Musée, Cagnes-sur-Mer.

*President Nixon visits China, opening diplomatic
and cultural relations.
Daniel Spoerri retrospective at the Centre National d'Art
Contemporain, Paris.
Documenta V exhibition, Kassel, Germany, presents the
largest international survey of advanced and
controversial art forms since World War II.*

1973

February 3–March 14: Exhibition, *Yves Klein*,
Galerie Karl Flinker, Paris.
March 30–May 5: Exhibition, *Yves Klein*,
Gimpel-Hanover Galerie, Zurich.
May 30–June 23: Exhibition, *Yves Klein*, Gimpel Fils, London.
May 27–July 29: Exhibition, *Frühe Gelbe, Schwarze, Weisse,
Orange, Grune: Bilder von Yves Klein*, Kaiser Wilhelm
Museum, Krefeld.

*Eric Orr creates Zero-Mass Space (the first of a series of
dematerializing spaces), Pomona College, California.
Ellsworth Kelly retrospective, Museum of Modern Art,
New York City.
Death of Robert Smithson.*

1974

March 20–April 28: Exhibition, *Yves Klein*, Städtische
Kunstsammlungen, Ludwigshafen, Germany.
March 20–May 15: Exhibition, *Yves Klein, 1928–1962*,
Tate Gallery, London.

*Death of Georges Pompidou.
Richard Nixon resigns as U.S. president.
The world oil shortage and increasing prices disrupt the
international economy.
James Turrell begins the Roden Crater Project in Arizona.*

Arman retrospective, La Jolla Museum of Contemporary Art, California.

1975

*First international manned space flight: U.S. and U.S.S.R. satellites link up in earth orbit.
U.S. troops withdraw from Vietnam.*

1976

June 4–July 12: Exhibition, *Yves Klein*, Nationalgalerie Berlin, Neue Berliner Kunstverein, and July 20–August 28, Städtische Kunsthalle, Düsseldorf.
October 19–November 20: Exhibition, *Yves Klein, Feux*, Galerie Karl Flinker, Paris.

*American scientists land a robot on Mars.
Inauguration of the Musée National d'Art Moderne, Centre Georges Pompidou, Paris.
Gerhardt Richter begins sets of identical Gray Paintings.
Robert Rauschenberg retrospective, Smithsonian Institution, Washington, DC, followed by a U.S. tour.*

1977

March 3–April 2: Exhibition, *Yves Klein*, Sidney Janis Gallery, New York City.

*Launching of the first U.S. space shuttle.
Jasper Johns retrospective, Whitney Museum, NYC.*

1978

*The United Nations opens its conference on disarmament.
Mark Rothko retrospective, Guggenheim Museum, New York City.*

1979

Oct. 19–Nov. 17: Exhibition, *Yves Klein*, Fuji Television Gallery, Tokyo.

Eric Orr's Space as Prime Matter, Gold as Prime Matter,
Fire as Prime Matter *exhibited in Los Angeles.*
Clyfford Still retrospective, Metropolitan Museum
of Art, New York City.

1980

The price of gold reaches a record high on the
international market.

1981

Westkunst exhibition, including a major Yves Klein
selection, organized by Kasper Koenig, Cologne.

1982

February 5– May 2: Exhibition, *Yves Klein, 1928-1962:*
A Retrospective, Institute for the Arts, Houston, and
Rice University, Rice Museum, Houston
June 18–August 29: Exhibition, *Yves Klein, 1928-1962:*
A Retrospective, Museum of Contemporary Art, Chicago
November 18–January 9, 1983: Exhibition,
Yves Klein, 1928-1962: A Retrospective,
The Solomon R. Guggenheim Museum, New York

Jackson Pollock retrospective, Centre Georges Pompidou, Paris.

1983

February 17–May 23: Exhibition, *Yves Klein, 1928-1962: A*
Retrospective, Centre Georges Pompidou, Musée national d'art
moderne, Paris

1985

July 20–September 1: Exhibition, *Yves Klein*, The Museum of
Modern Art, Seibu Takanawa
September 7–October 6: Exhibition, *Yves Klein*, The Museum
of Modern Art, Shiga
October 12–November 20: Exhibition, *Yves Klein*, Iwaki City
Art Museum, Fukushima

1986

January 2–February 24, 1986: Exhibition, *Yves Klein*, The
Seibu Museum of Art, Tokyo
February 7–March 1: Exhibition, *Yves Klein*,
Fuji Television Gallery, Tokyo
April 6–30: *Yves Klein*, Riva Yares Gallery, Scottsdale, Arizona
April 19–May 31 *Monochrome Paintings and Sponge Reliefs
by Yves Klein*, New York, Sidney Janis Gallery, New York

1989

October 3-28: *Yves Klein: Sponge Reliefs*,
Gagosian Gallery, New York

1990

February 4–April 16: *Yves Klein: Triptychon 1960*,
Kunsthalle Basel, Basel, Switzerland

1995

November 8 1994–January 8: *Yves Klein*, Kunstsammlung
Nordrhein-Westfalen, Dusseldorf
February 9–April 23: *Yves Klein Now: Sixteen views*, Hayward
Gallery, London
May 24–August 29: *Yves Klein*, Museo nacional Centro
de Arte Reina Sofía, Madrid

1997

April 26–August 17: *Yves Klein*, Museet for Samtidskunst, Olso
September 6–November 23: *Yves Klein*, Sara Hildénin
Taidemuseo, Tampere
December 11– March 29, 1998: *Yves Klein*, Museum of
Contemporary Art, Sydney

2000

April 28–September 4: *Yves Klein: La Vie, la vie elle-même qui est
l'art absolu*, Musée d'Art moderne et d'Art contemporain, Nice
September 23–January 10, 2001: *Yves Klein: La Vie, la vie
elle-même qui est l'art absolu*, Museo Pecci, Prato

2004

February 26–April 24: *Yves Klein: Peintures de feu 1961-1962*,
Galerie de France, Paris
September 17–January 9, 2005: *Yves Klein*,
Schirn Kunsthalle Frankfurt

2005

January 31–May 2: *Yves Klein*, Guggenheim Museum Bilbao
October 26–January 14, 2006: *Yves Klein : Fire Paintings*,
Michael Werner, New York

2006

June 23–September 17: *Marie Raymond–Yves Klein*,
Musée des beaux-arts, Carcassonne, France
June 25–September 17: *Marie Raymond–Yves Klein*,
Museum Ludwig, Coblence, Germany
February 27–June: *Yves Klein Hommage-Ausstellung*,
Kestner-Gesellschaft, Hanover, Germany
October 3–February 5, 2007: *Yves Klein: Corps, couleur,
immatériel*, Centre Georges Pompidou, Musée national
d'art moderne, Paris
April 27–February 5, 2007: *Yves Klein dans ses murs*,
La Coupole, Paris

2009

May 16–September 13: *Yves Klein & Rotraut*,
Museo d'Arte & Sculture in Città, Lugano, Switzerland
October 28–January 17, 2010: *Marie Raymond–Yves Klein.
Herencias*, Circulo des bellas artes, Madrid

2010

May 16–September 19: *Yves Klein*, Hirshhorn Museum,
Washington, DC
October 23–February 13, 2011: *Yves Klein*,
Walker Arts Center, Minneapolis

This chronology was compiled by Thomas McEvilley with help from many sources. He was especially aided by Virginie de Caumont's detailed chronology of Klein's life, by the research of Nan Rosenthal, and by materials in the Centre Georges Pompidou. Listings after 1982 were provided by Philipe Siauve of the Yves Klein Archive, Paris.

Notes

I: Living a Contradiction : *pages 17-33*

1. For Klein's connection with Max Heindel's brand of Rosicrucianism, see in this volume "Yves Klein and Rosicrucianism," pp. 193-221 above . The essay was first published in exh. cat. *Yves Klein (1928-1962): A Retrospective* (Houston: Institute for the Arts, and New York: The Arts Publisher, 1982), pp. 238-255. Reprinted as "Yves Klein et les rose-croix," in exh. cat. *Yves Klein* (Paris: Centre Georges Pompidou, 1983), pp. 233-245.

2. One might suppose that the delicacy of Klein's art resided in his balancing of these two limbs—the transcendentalist and the neo-Dada. Sometimes, however, authors choose one or the other as his *true* self, and may thereby miss the edgemanship of his perilous balancing act. Rotraut Klein-Moquay, for example, in her foreword to this volume, focuses on the transcendentalist aspect and chooses not to mention the aspect of neo-Dada reductionism. This choice has dominated much of the French literature on Klein, going back to Pierre Restany's *Yves le monochrome* (Paris: Librairie Hachette, 1974).

3. For more on the Malevichean and Duchampian avant-gardes see Thomas McEvilley. "Mute Prophecies: The Art of Jannis Kounellis." in exh, cat. *Jannis Kounellis* (Chicago: Museum of Contemporary Art, 1986), pp. 15-174, 18 ff. Klein, notably, had little or nothing to do with the third, Matissean, strain.

4. For a fuller discussion of this overlap between Hegel's myth of history and the Theosophical one, see Thomas McEvilley, "The Opposite of Emptiness," *Artforum* 25, no. 7 (March 1987), pp. 84-91. Reprinted in Thomas McEvilley, *The Exile's Return: Toward a Redefinition of Painting for the Post-Modern Era* (New York: Cambridge University Press, 1993), pp. 57-64.

5. See Thomas McEvilley, "Seeking the Primal Through Paint: The Monochrome Icon," in *The Exile's Return*, pp. 9-56.

6. See in this volume "Yves Klein: Conquistador of the Void," pp. 66-191 above. First published as "Yves Klein, Conquistador of the Void" in *Yves Klein (1928-1962): A Retrospective* (op. cit.).

7. For more on the International Klein Bureau see Thomas MeEvilley, *The Impregnation of the Guggenheim Museum*, New York, The Guggenheim Museum, 1982.

II: Messenger of the Age of Space : *pages 35-63*

1. Yves Klein, in *Dimanche: The Newspaper of a Single Day,* p. 2. There is no definitive French edition of Klein's essays. The mss., when I visited them, were in the Klein archive, Musée National d'Art Moderne, Centre Georges Pompidou, Paris. I will refer to published versions whenever possible. Unless otherwise noted, translations from Klein's writings are my own. A facsimile of *The Newspaper of a Single Day* may be consulted in Giuliano Martano, ed., Yves *Klein: il Mistero Ostentato* (Turin, 1970), insert.

2. See, e.g., Clement Greenberg, *Art and Culture* (Boston: Beacon Press, 1967), pp. 12-26.

3. *Art News*, May 1961;*Time,* January 27, 1961; New York *Herald Tribune,* April 16, 1961.

4. *New York Times,* February 5, 1967; New York *World Journal Tribune,* February 5, 1967. The almost worshipful tone adopted by Ronald Hunt in *Artforum* for January 1967 didn't help: the cultic atmosphere was perceived as part of Klein's "vaudeville."

5. Susan Sontag, *Against Interpretation and Other Essays* (New York: Delta Books, 1981), p. 11.

6. In *The Inner and the Outer Space,* exh. cat. (Stockholm: Moderna Museet, 1965), n.p.

7. Typescript in Klein archive, Musée National d'Art Moderne, Centre Georges Pompidou, Paris.

8. Joseph Kosuth, "Art After Philosophy," in Gregory Battcock, ed., *Idea Art: A Critical Anthology* (New York: Dutton, 1973), p. 100.

9. Harold Rosenberg, *The Anxious Object* (New York: MacMillan, 1973), p. 77.

10. Yves Klein, "The Monochrome Adventure," typescript in Klein archive, Musée National d'Art Moderne, Centre Georges Pompidou, Paris. Selections have been published in various exhibition catalogues, including *Yves Klein,* exh. cat. (New York: The Jewish Museum, 1967) (which I quote). Recently an English language edition of Klein's writings has been issued: *Overcoming the Problematics of Art: The Writings of Yves Klein,* trans. Klaus Ottmann (Putnam, Connecticut: Spring Publications, 2007).

11. See, for example, E.H. Gombrich, "Botticelli's Mythologies: A Study in the Neo-Platonic Symbolism of His Circle," in *Symbolic Images: Studies in the Art of the Renaissance* (New York: Dutton, 1972).

12. Pierre Restany, "L'Epoca blu: il secondo minuto della verita," in *Yves Klein*, exh. cat. (Milan: Galleria Apollinaire, 1957).

13. For example, in *The Perfection of Wisdom in Eight Thousand Lines*, trans. Edward Conze (Bolinas, California: Four Seasons Foundation, 1973), pp. 97-98.

14. Klein, "The Monochrome Adventure."

15. Donald Judd, *Complete Writings, 1959-1975* (New York: New York University Press, 1976), p. 68.

16. The sentence appears in several of Klein's writings; for example, Yves Klein, *Le Dépassement de la Problématique de l'Art* (La Louvrière, Belgium: Editions de Montbliard, n.d.), p.3. Hereafter *Dépassement*.

17. Klein, "Discourse on the Occasion of Tinguely's Exhibition in Dusseldorf, January 1959," in *Dépassement*.

18. Max Heindel, *The Rosicrucian Cosmo-conception* (Oceanside, Calif.: The Rosicrucian Society, 1937), p. 247. Hereafter *Cosmo-conception*.

19. Yves Klein, "Attendu que j'ai peint…," in *Yves Klein*, exh. cat. (Paris: Musée des Arts Décoratifs, Paris, 1969), pp. 38, 40; *Dépassement*, p. 2; letter of Klein to Yamazaki, February 15, 1960, Klein archive.

20. The quoted phrases are from Klein's own description of the event in *Dépassement*, pp. 4-13.

21. Klein, *Dépassement*, p. 14.

22. Heindel, *Cosmo-conception*, pp. 305, 311

23. Klein, "Theater of the Void," in *Dimanche: The Newspaper of a Single Day*.

24. Ibid., p.1; *Dépassement*, p. 2.

25. The author has copies of these photographs, but has not published them at the request of Rotraut Klein-Moquay, the artist's widow.

26. This evidence is reviewed in *Yves Klein: A Retrospective*.

27. Klein, *Dépassement*, p.21; Musée des Arts Décoratifs catalogue, p. 22.

28. Greenberg, *Art and Culture*, p. 139.

29. Ibid., p. 6.

30. See, for example, Douglas Davis, *Artculture* (New York: Harper and Row, 1977), pp. 134-138

31. For "indexing" see Timothy Binkley, "Piece: Contra Aesthetics," in Joseph Margolis, ed., *Philosophy Looks at the Arts* (Philadelphia: Temple University Press, 1978).

32. As, for example, Davis puts it, *Artculture*, p. 49.

33. In Martano, *Yves Klein: il Mistero Ostentato*, p. 110.

34. Sextus Empiricus, *Outlines of Pyrrhonism,* 1.202, my translation; for the text see *Sextus Empiricus,* trans. and ed., R. G. Bury, 4 vols. (Cambridge, Mass.: Harvard University Press [Loeb Classical Library], 1933), vol. 1, p. 118.

35. "Truth Becomes Reality," in *Zero* (Cambridge, Mass.: MIT Press, 1973), p. 88.

III: Conquistidor of the Void : *pages 66-191*

1. In *Yves Klein,* catalogue of exhibition at the Jewish Museum, New York City, 1967, pp. 4, 7 (hereafter "Jewish Museum cat.").

2. Ibid., p. 16.

3. In *Yves Klein,* catalogue of exhibition at the Tate Gallery, London, 1974, p. 8.

4. Giuliano Martano, *Yves Klein, Il Mistero Ostentato* (Turin: Martano Editore, 1970), p. 154.

5. Paul Wember, *Yves Klein* (Cologne: Verlag DuMont Schauberg, 1969), p. 45.

6. Jewish Museum cat., p. 11.

7. "Due to the Fact That," in *Yves Klein,* catalogue of exhibition at the Alexandre Iolas Gallery, New York, 1962. Translated by Klein in collaboration with Neil Levine and John Archambault in spring, 1961.

8. Ibid.

9, "Truth Becomes Reality."

10. Roland Barthes, *Mythologies* (New York: Hill and Wang, 1972), p. 142.

11. Hans-Georg Gadamer, *Wahrheit und Methode: Grundzuge einer philosophischen Hermeneutik* (Tübingen: J. C. B. Mohr, 1960), p. 104.

12. References to interviews will be made by the name of the interviewee, in this case Bernadette Allain. Interviews have been conducted by me, by Dominique de Menil, by Benedicte Pesle, and by Virginie de Caumont, as follows: Bernadette Allain, May 22, 1980, Paris. Rotraut Klein-Moquay, June 30, 1977, Paris; May 25, 1979, Houston; March 26, 1981, Paris. Claude Pascal, July 3, 1977, March 26 and May 4, 1981, Paris. Arman, December 29, 1977, New York; May 27, 1979, Houston; January 15, 1981, Paris. Rose Raymond Taramasco Gasperini, June 30, 1980, April 16 and 29, 1981, Nice. Marie Raymond, June 10, 1980, and April 17, 1981, Paris. Fred Klein (by telephone), December 12, 1980, Paris. Pierre Restany, June 28 and December 26, 1980, April 30, 1981, Paris. François Mathey, April 3, 1980, Paris. Jean Tinguely, June 17, 1980, Paris. Claude Parent, July 1, 1980, Paris. Edouard Adam, February 24, 1981, Paris. Karl Flinker, March 7, 1981, Paris. Ed Moses, February 26, 1981, Los Angeles. Iris Clert, March 10, 1981, Paris. Jean Larcade, March 26, 1981, Paris. Tarica, March 20, 1981, Paris. Marcel Boulois, May 2, 1981 Paris. Jean Laffont, May 6, 1981, Paris. George Marci (by telephone), June 14, 1981. Walter Hopps, October 13, 1981, Houston.

13. Bernadette Allain.

14. In *Yves Klein*, catalogue of exhibition at the Palais des Beaux-Arts, Brussels, 1966.

15. Claude Pascal.

16. The essay "Yves Klein and Rosicrucianism," printed in this book, documents this influence in detail. Only broad outlines will be mentioned here.

17. St-John Perse, *Winds*, trans. Hugh Chisholm (New York: Bollingen, 1953), p. 210.

18. Bernadette Allain.

19. The division into animal, vegetable, and mineral realms came from Heindel. Arman recalls that they patterned the event after the story in Homer (*Iliad* V. 185 ff).

20. Arman.

21. *The Poetics of Space*, trans. Maria Jolas (Boston: Beacon, 1969), p. 183.

22. "Discourse on the Occasion of Tinguely's Exhibition in Düsseldorf, January 1959."

23. *Dimanche, the Newspaper of a Single Day*, p.1, Klein's tour de force imitation newspaper that he submitted to the Paris Festival d'Art d'Avant-garde, 1960.

24. "Du vertige au prestige."

25. *Myths, Rites, and Symbols: A Mircea Eliade Reader*, 2 vols., ed, W. C. Beane and W. C. Doty (New York: Harper and Row 1975), 2:354.

26. Robert Savage, on Old Brompton Road.

27. St-John Perse, *Winds*, p. 190.

28. MS V 2288: "Compte rendu de l'exposition en collaboration avec Jean Tinguely chez Iris Clert," Klein archive, Documentation Arts Plastiques Musée National d'Art Moderne, Centre National d'Art et de Culture Georges Pompidou, Paris (hereafter "Klein archive").

29. "Discourse on the Occasion of Tinguely's Exhibition."

30. "Dissolve the body and coagulate the spirit," Nicolas Valois, alchemist. Cited in Stanislas K. De Rola, *Alchemy, the Secret Art* (New York: Bounty, 1973), p. 17.

31. Klein archive.

32. This is the only entry which specifies the year of writing, and it is not consistent with the day-date correlations on all the entries: July 14, for example, was a Friday in 1950, a Saturday in 1951. In other words, either Klein specified the wrong year in the entry of August 5, or the wrong (by one digit) date of the month in all the entries. The latter assumption is almost certainly correct, as an abundance of external evidence shows. The same error occurs in a letter Klein wrote on July 11 but is corrected in his letter of July 21 (see n. 37 below).

33. Klein archive. My translation.

34. Ibid.

35. Klein's relatives generously provided many personal letters from him for photocopying.

36. April 20, 1952.

37. Rough draft of letter, November 1951, Klein archive.

38. The exact departure date is not known but seems to have been either August 22 or 23.

39. A photocopy of the Japanese article was provided by Marie Raymond.

40. Letter to Rose Raymond Gasperini, December 7, 1953.

41. The Kodokan Institute states that "he was confirmed 4th *dan* as of December 12 [?], 1953." Letter to author, October 27, 1980, from Ichiro Abe, International Division, Kodokan Judo Institute, Tokyo.

42. Klein archive.

43. Nan Rosenthal [Piene] was, as far as I know, the first to focus critical attention on this pamphlet and to recognize it as not precisely a fraud but a trick. See "The Blue World of Yves Klein," Ph.D. dissertation, Harvard University, 1976, pp. 81-87. This study pursues, often with interesting results, an analysis of Klein's deliberate ambiguity similar to that of Ronald Hunt in "Yves Klein," *Artforum* (January 1967), pp. 33-37.

44. In *Yves Klein, Paintings, Reliefs, Sculptures* (Belgrade: Museum of Contemporary Arts, 1971), translated from Serbo-Croatian by Goran Milutinovic for the Institute for the Arts, Rice University, Houston, Texas.

45. Edouard Adam.

46. "La Minute de vérite"; the exhibition, which ran from February 21 to March 7, was titled *Yves: Propositions monochromes*.

47. Klein patented his distinctive blue in May 1960, as International Klein Blue. It has sometimes been described as cobalt; visually it is somewhere between ultramarine and cobalt, but closer to the former. The Klein archive contains a typescript of the formula, as follows; Medium fixatif de 1IKB./ 1 kilo 200 Rhodopas (c'est un produit pateux) MA (Rhone poulenc) (Chlorure de Vinyle)/ 2 kilo 200 Alcool Ethylique. 95% Industriel. Denature/ 0 kilo 600 Acetate d'Ethyle./ [total:] 4 kilo 000/ Melanger a froid/ en agitant energiquement/ ne jamais chauffer a feu nu. Danger." Then, in Klein's handwriting: "700 kg Outremer Blue Pur/ ref 1311."

48. So Sheldon Nodelman speaks of Stella's paintings, in *Marden, Novros, Rothko: Painting in the Age of Actuality* (Seattle: University of Washington Press for the Institute for the Arts, Rice University, 1978), p. 13.

49. "The Monochrome Adventure" is a group of Klein's writings which he collected for publication as a book; his death aborted the project. The typescript is in the Klein archive.

50. *Marden, Novros, Rothko*, p. 65.

51. The complete text of "The War" was published in *Dimanche* in 1960.

52. Ibid.

53. *The Journal of Eugène Delacroix*, trans. Walter Pach (New York: Crown, 1948), entry for October 5, 1882.

54. "The War."

55. "The Monochrome Adventure."

56. Ibid.

57. Quoted by Klein in "The War."

58. Ibid.

59. Letter 459; quoted by Klein in "The War."

60. *The Poetics of Reverie*, trans. Daniel Russell (Boston: Beacon, 1969), pp. 72-73,

61. Iris Clert, Francois Mathey, etc.

62. *Iris-Time (L'Artventure)* (Paris: Editions Denoel, 1978), pp. 146-47.

63. *Donald Judd, Complete Writings 1959-1975* (New York: New York University Press, 1978), p. 68.

64. Klein added this text to the photograph in his scrapbook; it may be compared to a speech balloon in a cartoon panel.

65. "Preparation and Presentation of the Exhibition of 28 April, 1958."

66. *Iris-Time*, p. 155. The record is strangely confused on the question of how many visitors entered at a time; Klein says ten, Iris Clert three, Claude Pascal five.

67. Ibid., p. 156.

68. *Le Dépassement de la problématique de l'art* (La Louvière: Editions de Montbliart, 1959); Rotraut Klein-Moquay.

69. The idea appears repeatedly in Klein's writings, for example in the essay "Preparation and Presentation of the Exhibition of 28 April 1958."

70. *Being and Nothingness*, trans. Hazel F. Barnes (New York: Philosophical Library, 1956), pp. 600-603.

71. The Klein archive contains the following books by Bachelard: *L'Eau et les rêves* (Paris: José Corti, 1942); *La Terre et les rêveries de la volonté* (Paris: José Corti, 1948); *La Terre et les rêveries du repos* (Paris; José Corti, 1948); *La Philosophie du non* (Paris: Presses Universitaires de France, 1949); *La Dialectique de la durée* (Paris: Presses Universitaires de France, 1950); *La Formation de l'esprit scientifique* (Paris: Librairie Philosophique J. Vrin, 1957); and *La Poétique de l'espace* (Paris: Presses Universitaires de France, 1958). The Klein archive contained, in July 1977, six copies of the last-named work. Although the archive contained no copy of *La Psychanalyse du feu* (Paris: Gallimard, 1949), or of *L'Air et les songes*

(Paris: José Corti, 1943), it is certain from other evidence that Klein read them.

72. *On Poetic Imagination and Reverie*, trans. C. Gaudin (New York: Library of Liberal Arts, 1971), p. 23.

73. *Myths, Rites, and Symbols: A Mircea Eliade Reader*, I:195.

74. *The Psychoanalysis of Fire*, trans. Alan C. M. Ross (Boston: Beacon, 1964), p. 111.

75. "Due to the Fact That."

76. *Psychoanalysis of Fire*, p. 111.

77. "Truth Becomes Reality."

78. *Dépassement*.

79. *Psychoanalysis of Fire*, p. 112.

80. Ibid., pp. 100-101; see also *Poetics of Space*, p. xxv, and *Poetics of Reverie*, p. 58.

81. "Du vertige au prestige."

82. "The War."

83. *On Poetic Imagination and Reverie*, p. 23.

84. "Les Vrais Createurs," Klein archive.

85. *Psychoanalysis of Fire*, p. 112. Prometheus stole fire from heaven; Empedocles leapt into the mouth of the active volcano Mount Aetna.

86. Klein archive.

87. Ibid.

88. See MSS V 2288 and C 2310, Klein archive: "Compte rendu de l'exposition en collaboration avec Jean Tinguely chez Iris Clert," and Iris Clert's statement, "A la suite d'une série de terribles malentendus." In 1967 Tinguely described Klein as "a beautiful megalomaniac,…the best friend and best provocateur I have ever encountered" (Martano *Mistero*, p. 110).

89. Paris: Librairie Hachette, 1974.

90. *Dépassement*.

91. Jean Tinguely.

92. *Iris-Time*, p. 175.

93. Ibid.

94. "The Void belongs to me": letter to a M. Yamazaki, February 15, 1960, typescript in Klein archive; "The Monochrome Adventure."

95. "The Monochrome Adventure."

96. Ibid.

97. Ibid.

98. *Iris-Time*, p. 185.

99. Peppino Palazzoli, director of the Galleria Apollinaire in Milan, where the Blue Epoch had been inaugurated in 1957.

100. Klein archive.

101. Geber, *The Sum of Perfection*, cited in F. J. Holmyard, *Alchemy* (Baltimore: Penguin 1957), pp. 134, 140.

102. See "Ritual for the Relinquishment of the Immaterial Pictorial Sensibility Zones," quoted in full in Nan Rosenthal's essay in the Rice Museum catalogue.

103. *Iris-Time*, p. 192.

104. *L'Air et les songes*, p.194.

105. Klein's Sorbonne lecture was made into two long-playing records titled *Conferences a la Sorbonne, 3 juin 1959* (Paris: RPM, nd.).

106. *L'Air et les songes*, p. 188.

107. Ibid., p. 191.

108. "Criticism and the Experience of Interiority," in *The Structuralist Controversy*, ed, Richard Macksey and Eugenio Donato (Baltimore: Johns Hopkins University Press, 1972), p. 59.

109. *Inner and Outer Space*, catalogue of exhibition at the Moderna Museet, Stockholm, 1966.

110. "Truth Becomes Reality."

111. The story is told by Werner Spies, who attributes it to Norbert Kricke as eyewitness.

112. *Iris-Time*, p. 175.

113. See Nan Rosenthal's essay in the Rice Museum catalogue.

114. Klein archive.

115. As interviewed by Nan Rosenthal in New York City in 1975; see "The Blue World of Yves Klein," pp. 256-57.

116. Mircea Eliade, *Myths, Dreams, and Mysteries* (New York: Harper, 1967), pp. 104-107.

117. *Poetics of Reverie*, p. 79.

118. See Henry T.. Bowie, *On the Laws of Japanese Painting* (New York: Dover, nd.), pp. 15, 79, 82-83.

119. Frederick Jameson, *The Prison House of Language* (Princeton: Princeton University Press, 1972), pp. 50-51.

120. Wember, *Yves Klein*.

121. M. Caron and S. Hutin, *The Alchemists* (New York: Grove, 1961), p. 147.

122. This piece is described in detail by Pierre Restany in the Rice catalogue.

123. "Truth Becomes Reality."

124. "Due to the Fact That."

125. "Truth Becomes Reality."

126. *The Rosicrucian Cosmo-conception* (Oceanside, California, 1937), p. 397.

127. "Les Fenétres," trans. C. F. MacIntyre, in *Stephane Mallarmé, Selected Poems* (Berkeley: University of California Press, 1965), p. 11.

128. *Writing Degree Zero*, trans. Annette Lavers and Colin Smith (New York: Hill and Wang, 1968), p. 25.

129. On *sprezzatura*, the self-eternalizing posturing of the Renaissance aristocrats, Castiglione cautioned, "Nor must one be more careful of anything than of concealing it, because if it is discovered, this robs a man of all credit." Baldesar Castiglione, *The Book of the Courtier*, trans. Charles S. Singleton (New York: Doubleday, 1959), p. 43.

130. Ellen Moers, *The Dandy: Brummell to Beerbohm* (New York: Viking, 1960), p. 101.

131. Ibid., passim.

132. Maud Sacquard de Belleroche, *Du dandy au playboy* (Paris: Editions Mondiales, 1964), p. 55.

133. Friedrich Wilhelm Joseph von Schelling, *System of Transcendental Idealism*, VI.3, in Albert Hofstadter and Richard Kuhns, eds., *Philosophies of Art and Beauty* (Chicago: University of Chicago Press, 1964) p. 372.

134. In *Yves Klein*, catalogue of exhibition at the Palais des Beaux Arts, Brussels, 1966. And see Restany's 1981 essay in the Rice Museum catalogue, which shows that the myth still lives.

135. *System of Transcendental Idealism*, VI.3, in *Philosophies of Art and Beauty*, p. 373.

136. *The Anatomy of Criticism* (Princeton: Princeton University Press, 1957), pp. 210, 216.

IV: Yves Klein and Rosicrucianism : *pages 195-223*

1. Joseph Kosuth, "Art after Philosophy," in Gregory Battcock, ed., *Idea Art: A Critical Anthology* (New York: Dutton, 1973), p. 168.

2. Hans-Georg Gadamer, *Philosophical Hermeneutics*, trans. and ed. David E. Linge (Berkeley: University of California Press, 1976), pp. 102-103.

3. Michel Foucault, *The Order of Things* (English translation of *Les Mots et les choses*) (New York: Random House, Vintage Books, 1973), p. 9.

4. Paris, 1947. Published in English as *The Rosicrucian Cosmo-conception* (Oceanside, California, 1937), from which all my citations are taken; the two editions are identical except for minor changes in format. Klein's own copy of the *Cosmogonie* (much annotated and dog-eared), as well as many of his Rosicrucian lessons and

related journals, are gathered in the archive of the Musée National d'Art Moderne, Centre Georges Pompidou, Paris. My thanks to Rotraut Klein-Moquay for her permission to study these and other materials in the Klein archive.

It should be noted that the Rosicrucian Society centered in Oceanside is to be distinguished from the Rosicrucian Order or AMORC, which is a separate organization with different literature. (The AMORC is the one which advertises in magazines.)

5. My thanks to Jean de Galzain, director of French students at the Rosicrucian headquarters in Oceanside, California, for kindly opening the Klein file for my inspection on August 6, 1979.

Certain misapprehensions about the Rosicrucians and Klein's relationship with them have entered the record. In general, all authors have underestimated his devotion to this body of doctrine. In his journal for May 8th, 1950, for example, Klein wrote, "Je n'ai plus qu'une chose a faire, *La Cosmogonie* et étude constante de la merveilleuse science que j'ai a ma disposition!" In 1952 he wrote that he was still devoting four hours a day to the study of this book.

In addition there are various specific misapprehensions. Paul Wember, for example, underestimates the duration of Klein's Rosicrucian period (*Yves Klein*, Cologne: Verlag M. DuMont Schauberg, 1969, p. 45). Giuliano Martano confuses the Rosicrucian Society with the AMORC, and wrongly attributes the *Rosicrucian Manual*, an AMORC publication, to Max Heindel (*Yves Klein: II Mistero Ostentato*, Turin: Martano Editore, 1970, p. 48, n. 14) (hereafter "*Mistero*"). Several authors treat the Rosicrucian Society as a continuation of the seventeenth-century Rosicrucian Brotherhood, with which in fact it has no known connection (e.g., *Mistero*, p. 41). The distinction is important, because Heindel, like Blavatsky and other nineteenth-century-type occultists, had received Indian and Tibetan input which seventeenth-century occultists lacked.

6. No definitive French edition of the writings exists; the manuscripts are in the Klein archive. Where possible, I will cite the published selections of these works: in the Rice catalogue; in the catalogue of the exhibition *Yves Klein*, at the Jewish Museum, New York, 1967 (hereafter "Jewish Museum cat."); the catalogue of the exhibition *Yves Klein* at the Union Centrale des Arts Décoratifs, Paris, 1969 (hereafter "Union Centrale cat."); *Le Dépassement de là problématique de l'art* (La Louvière, Belgium: Editions de Montbliart, 1959) (hereafter "*Dépassement*"); and *Mistero*. Translations from *Dépassement*, the Union Centrale cat., and *Mistero* are my own.

7. Terms capitalized with surrounding quotation marks are generic titles of Klein's works ("Cosmogonies"); terms capitalized without quotation marks are those which Klein and Heindel capitalized as religious terms (Space, God, Life, etc.).

8. *Cosmo-conception*, p. 247.

9. Ibid., p. 252.

10. "Due to the Fact That," in *Yves Klein*, catalogue of exhibition at the Alex-

ander Iolas Gallery, New York, 1962. Translated by Klein in collaboration with Neil Levine and John Archambault in spring, 1961.

11. Ibid.

12. "The Monochrome Adventure."

13. "Due to the Fact That."

14. *Cosmo-conception*, p. 189.

15. Ibid., p. 190.

16. Ibid., p. 249.

17. Ibid., pp. 178-79.

18. Ibid., p. 29.

19. *Dépassement*, p. 22.

20. Max Heindel, *Occult Principles of Health and Healing*, 4th ed. (London: L. N. Fowler and Co., 1919), p. 163. Various Eastern traditions have the same doctrine, and they probably lie behind Heindel, as behind Blavatsky. See, e.g., Swami Muktananda, *Play of Consciousness* (San Francisco: Harper and Row, 1978), pp. 141, 146, 177-78, 184, etc., on "the eternal Blue of Consciousness," which "lives within all, pervades the entire universe, and sets it in motion."

21. *Dépassement*, p. 22: "Vide [=] Lumière bleue."

22. *Cosmo-conception*, p. 306.

23. Ibid., p. 315.

24. Ibid., p. 311.

25. Ibid., p. 125.

26. See, e.g., Francis Yates, *The Rosicrucian Enlightenment* (London: Routledge and Kegan Paul, 1972), pp. 48, 57, 97, 119, 129, 213. In Heindel, Eden was the "Lemurian Epoch" of the Earth Period (two Epochs ago), and the next Epoch will recapture the essential feature of the Edenic or Lemurian condition, access to the Desire World (see *Cosmo-conception*, pp. 275-82, 305). In Klein's writings see the Union Centrale cat., p. 12; "Due to the Fact That"; "The Monochrome Adventure"; and "Le Théâtre du vide" in *Dimanche, the Newspaper of a Single Day*, an imitation newspaper that Klein published on November 27, 1960. See also Pierre Restany, *Yves Klein le monochrome* (Paris: Librairie Hachette, 1974), p. 24.

27. *Cosmo-conception*, p. 517.

28. Ibid., p. 305.

29. *Dépassement*, p. 2.

30. *Cosmo-conception*, p. 119.

31. "The War."

32. "Due to the Fact That."

33. "The War."

34. Ibid.

35. Ibid.

36. Ibid.

37. *Dépassement*, p. 19

38. Ibid.

39. Ibid.

40. Preface to 'The Monochrome Adventure," Klein archive.

41. They certainly included D. T. Suzuki's *Studies in Zen Buddhism* and Eugene Herrigel's *Zen and the Art of Archery*, but just as certainly there were others which are not known (interview with Arman, New York City, December 13, 1977).

42. G. C. C. Chang, ed., *The Hundred Thousand Songs of Milarepa* (New Hyde Park, New York: University Books, 1962), p. 102.

43. *Dimanche*, p. 1.

44. "Due to the Fact That."

45. Chang, ed., *Songs of Milarepa*, pp. 128, 146–47.

46. See, e.g., Chogyam Trungpa, "Space Therapy," *The Middle Way, the Journal of the Buddhist Society of London* 50.3 (November 1975), pp. 107-11.

47. Herbert V. Guenther and Chogyam Trungpa, *The Dawn of Tantra* (Berkeley and London: Shambala, 1975), p. 27.

48. John Curtis Gowan, *Development of the Psychedelic Individual* (Buffalo: Creative Education Foundation, 1974), p. 55.

49. Jewish Museum cat., p. 22.

50. *Dépassement*, p. 1.

51. Ibid., p. 2.

52. Ibid., p. 20.

53. In fact, the earliest true monochromes are seventeenth-, eighteenth-, and nineteenth-century Tantric depictions of Pure Consciousness or the Unmanifest Absolute as an empty monochromatic ground. See, e.g., A. Mookerjee, *Tantra Asana* (New York: G. Wittenborn, 1971), p. 97, and *Tantra Art* (New Delhi, New York, Paris: Kumar Gallery, 1966), p. 95.

54. *Dépassement*, p. 19.

55. "The Monochrome Adventure."

56. Ibid.

57. "The War."

58. Union Centrale cat., p. 21.

59. Interview with Rotraut Klein-Moquay, June 30, 1977, Paris.

60. *Cosmo-conception*, p. 253. For other traditional interpretations of these colors

see Wember, *Yves Klein*, pp. 21-24.

61. The chapter "Le Ciel bleu" in *L'Air et les songes* (Paris: José Corti, 1950).

62. "The Monochrome Adventure."

63. *Dépassement*, p. 5.

64. "The Monochrome Adventure."

65. MS 12174, Klein archive: fragments of an interview of Klein by Pierre Restany.

66. Ibid.

67. Typescript carbon, Klein archive: "Remarques sur quelques oeuvres exposés chez Colette Allendy."

68. *Cosmo-conception*, p. 53.

69. Ibid., p. 55.

70. "The Monochrome Adventure."

71. *Dépassement*, p.4.

72. "The Monochrome Adventure."

73. Ibid.

74. *Dépassement*, p. 6.

75. The Monochrome Adventure." This essentially alchemical view of art, which makes both the producing and the beholding of art works into a kind of yoga, has a parallel in the tradition of Taoist painting, where it is understood that, if the artist's mind is established in the non-ego of *wu-wei* ("actionless action"), then the *ch'i*, or universal vital energy, flows through his brush and is crystallized onto the surface of the paper, from whence it may be regained by a viewer also in the state of *wu-wei*. Like Klein, the Taoist painters worshipped space: "Space of any sort was regarded as filled with meaning since it was filled with Tao" (Mai-mai Sze, *Tao of Painting* (New York: Bollingen, 1956), p. 171). The Taoists' emphasis on the "unhewn block" is again similar to Klein's rejection of Form in favor of Prime Matter, as is the Taoist penchant for *i-hua* or "one-painting," "painting-the-oneness." (See Mai-mai Sze, *Tao of Painting*, p. 88 et passim, and Philip Rawson and Laszlo Legeza, *Tao* [New York: Crown Publishers, 1973], pp. 19-20.) It is quite possible that Klein encountered something of this view in the Zen painting tradition of Japan, but the evidence indicates that his own system had already been formed, by long study of Heindel, before his visit to Japan.

76. *Cosmo-conception*, pp. 248-49.

77. *Dépassement*. p: 24.

78. "The Monochrome Adventure." This statement, along with many writings on Klein, implies that *l'époque pneumatique*, the age of immaterial art, succeeded and replaced *l'époque bleue*; this seems not to be the case, however. The exhibition *Le Vide*, for which the term *époque pneumatique* was coined, involved many Blue Epoch motifs, and as late as 1960-62 Klein was making "Anthropometries of

the Blue Epoch." It should be noted that Klein himself provided the term *époque bleue*, whereas Pierre Restany, who was not totally privy to Klein's Rosicrucianism, supplied the term *époque pneumatique*.

79. "The Monochrome Adventure."

80. Ibid.

81. "Due to the Fact That."

82. *Cosmo-conception*, p. 423.

83. Ibid., p. 118.

84. Ibid., p. 427.

85. Richard Wollheim, in *Minimal Art*, ed. Gregory Battcock (New York: Dutton, 1968), p. 392.

86. Interviews with Claude Pascal, July 3, 1977, Paris, and Arman, December 13, 1977, New York.

87. Interview with Rotraut Klein-Moquay, June 30, 1977, Paris.

88. *Cosmo-conception*, pp. 488-89.

89. Ibid., p. 41.

90. Ibid., pp. 118-19.

91. *Dépassement*, p. 4.

92. In fact, it seems possible that Klein had performed this "specialization" of the Prime Matter for each of his monochromes, too, as is suggested by his statement that of the visually identical blue monochromes exhibited in 1957 each "revealed an entirely different essence;…none resembled another" ("The Monochrome Adventure"). This would seem to be the basis of Klein's idea of selling physically identical paintings for different prices.

93. MS 12174, Klein archive: fragments of an interview of Klein by Pierre Restany.

94. Restany, *Yves Klein le monochrome*, p. 61.

95. Interview with Rotraut Klein-Moquay. June 30, 1977, Paris,

96. *Cosmo-conception*, pp. 62, 64.

97. *Dépassement*. p. 13.

98. *Cosmo-conception*, p. 186.

99. "Due to the Fact That."

100. Interview with Rotraut Klein-Moquay, June 30, 1977, Paris.

101. This has often been misreported; the Jewish Museum catalogue, for example, says, "Single C Major note is played for ten minutes" (p. 37; and cf. p. 24). A glance at the music itself would show the D-major triad.

102. So the Jewish Museum catalogue translates this passage from "The Monochrome Adventure" (p. 32). But the typescript in the Klein archive reads:

> elle etait le résultat de toutes mes recherches passionées d'alors. Judo (1946), cosmogonie des roses-croix (1947) (interpretation Max Heindel, Ocean-side, Californie), jazz, je jouais du piano et révais d'avoir un grand orchestre.

Note the punctuation: no quotation marks around "judo"; comma after the parenthesis; "jazz" outside the parenthesis. The syntax is confusing. Most likely the catalogue that begins the new paragraph is meant to explicate the phrase "toute mes recherches passionees d'alors." I suggest: "it [the monochrome] was the result of all my passionate researches at that time, to wit, judo (which I was practicing in 1946), the *Cosmogonie des Rose-Croix* (which I was studying in 1947) (the interpretation [of everything] of Max Heindel of Oceanside, California), and jazz; I used to play the piano and dream," etc. The disadvantage of this reading is that I have to insert a stop after "jazz." If the first translation is preferred, then the Monotone Symphony was originally to be entitled Judo and is identified as an interpretation of Heindel's *Cosmogonie*. If the second, then judo and Heindel's *Cosmogonie* are both asserted as sources for the monochrome idea, and the passage then modulates into the Heindel-and-jazz background of the *Monotone Symphony*.

103. *Cosmo-conception*, p. 119.

104. Ibid., p. 123.

105. Ibid., pp. 369-70.

106. Ibid., p. 127.

107. Ibid., p. 123.

108. Ibid., p. 438. It should be noted, however, that Klein showed virtually no interest in the earth element, which represented the age of bondage to matter and thus was in effect the enemy of his cause. In some passages he refers specifically to "the three elements, air, water, and fire"; occasionally, when four are implied, they seem to be air, water, fire, and light. See, e.g., "L'Eau et le feu" and "Avec les trois éléments classiques, feu, air, et eau," typescripts, Klein archive. The Planetary Reliefs, though they relate to the earth element, are redeemed by their reference to outer space.

109. Ibid., p. 234.

110. "Due to the Fact That."

111. Following the numeration of Paul Wember, *Yves Klein*.

112. *Cosmo-conception*, pp. 250-52.

113. Ibid., pp. 258 ff.

114. Ibid., p. 180.

115. Muneshige Narazaki, *Hokusai* (Tokyo: Kodansha International, 1968), p. 16.

116. See e.g., Henry P. Bowie, *On the Laws of Japanese Painting* (New York: Dover, nd.), pp. 20-26.

117. Restany, *Yves Klein le monochrome*, pp. 146-47.

118. *Dimanche*, p. 1.

119. "Due to the Fact That."

120. See, e.g., Chang Chung-yuan, *Original Teachings of Ch'an Buddhism* (New York: Vintage, 1971), p. 43 et passim.

121. See, e.g., *Mistero*.

122. Both Klein's Sorbonne lecture (recorded on two long-playing records titled *Conférences à la Sorbonne, 3 juin 1959* [Paris: RPM, nd.]) and a manuscript note in the Klein archive give this date.

123. *The Poetics of Space* (New York: Orion, 1964), p. 206.

124. Interview with Arman, May 27, 1979, Houston.

125. *Cosmo-conception*, pp. 250-51; see also pp. 400, 521, 528-29. It is interesting to note that Klein's one meeting with Bachelard was "a disaster " (Rotraut Klein-Moquay): Bachelard regarded him as "a crazy man" (Arman), and did not in the least accept him as a companion in the realm of ideas.

126. "Discourse on the Occasion of Tinguely's Exhibition in Düsseldorf, January 1959."

CREDITS AND ACKNOWLEDGMENTS

Essays in this volume were initially published in somewhat different form as follows: "Living a Contradiction" as "Living a Contradiction: Yves Klein and the Art of the 1960s and 70s" in the exhibition catalogue *Tinguely's Favorites: Yves Klein*, published by Museum Jean Tinguely, Basel, Switzerland, 2000; "Yves Klein: Mesenger of the Age of Space" in *Artforum* 20, no. 5, January 1982; "Yves Klein: Conquistador of the Void," "Yves Klein and Rosicrucianism," and "Chronology" in the exhibition catalogue *Yves Klein (1928-1962): A Retrospective*, published by Institute for the Arts, Rice University, Houston, in association with The Arts Publisher, Inc., New York, 1982, copyright © 1982 by Thomas McEvilley.

PHOTOGRAPHIC CREDITS

The publisher and author gratefully acknowledge the following permissions to reproduce photographs in this book: All photographs are provided courtesy of the Yves Klein Archive, ADAGP, Paris. Photographs of Yves Klein and his works are © The Estate of Yves Klein. Photographs on pages 1, 49, 56, 64-5, 104, 118, 146, 154, 176-7, 182, and 192-3 are by Shunk-Kender, © Roy Lichtenstein Foundation. Photographs on pages 44 and 164 are by Pierre Joly and Véra Cardot. Photograph on page 224 is by Charles Wilp, Düsseldorf.